Greenhill Books

THE BODYGUARD MANUAL

By the same author

The Counter-Insurgency Manual
The Hostage Rescue Manual
Greenhill Military Manual:
Combat Shotguns
GI Series:
America's Commandos
Special Operations Forces of the Cold War

THE
BODYGUARD
MANUAL

PROTECTION TECHNIQUES OF THE PROFESSIONALS

Leroy Thompson

GREENHILL BOOKS, LONDON
STACKPOLE BOOKS, PENNSYLVANIA

Greenhill Books

Dedication

For my wife Margie, my favourite VIP.

The Bodyguard Manual: Protection Techniques of the Professionals
first published 2003 by Greenhill Books, Lionel Leventhal Limited, Park House,
1 Russell Gardens, London NW11 9NN
www.greenhillbooks.com
and
Stackpole Books, 5067 Ritter Road, Mechanicsburg, PA 17055, USA

The right of Leroy Thompson to be identified as the author of this work has been asserted
by him in accordance with the Copyright, Designs and Patents Act 1988.

British Library Cataloguing in Publication Data
Thompson, Leroy
The bodyguard manual
1. Bodyguards
I. Title
363.2'89
ISBN 1-85367-529-6

Library of Congress Cataloging-in-Publication Data available

Designed by Ian Penberthy

Printed in Great Britain by
Biddles Limited

Contents

Introduction 6

Chapter 1: General Precepts of VIP Protection 8

Chapter 2: Threat Assessment and Level of Protection 15

Chapter 3: Hardening the VIP Lifestyle 23

Chapter 4: Advancing a VIP Visit 27

Chapter 5: Area Security Procedures 36

Chapter 6: Appearances and Social Engagements 57

Chapter 7: Foot Escort Techniques 71

Chapter 8: Vehicle and Motorcade Security 89

Chapter 9: Travel on Planes, Ships and Trains 114

Chapter 10: Explosive Ordnance Recce 138

Chapter 11: Weapons and Tactics 148

Chapter 12: Conclusions 171

Appendix
• Threat Assessment Protectee Questionnaire 175
• City File 177
• Airline Check-list 179
• Airport Check-list 180
• Route Check-list 181
• Hotel Check-list 182
• Restaurant Survey 184
• VIP Appearance Site Survey 185
• Daily Operations Order 187

Recommended Reading 190

Index 191

Introduction

Once, while working on a protection detail for a member of a Third World royal family, I had a conversation with a couple of bodyguards, old friends, who were working on the team of another dignitary who was attending the same meeting as my charge. One of them, who spent much of his free time reading, posed the question as to whether we were the modern equivalent of the Praetorian Guard of ancient Rome. Since none of us was actually a citizen of either of the countries our principals represented, I countered that for the analogy to hold true, actually we were closer to the Varangian Guard of ancient Byzantium, which was recruited from Vikings, Russians, Normans and Britons, among others. I also suggested the premise that whereas the Praetorian Guard had assumed the role of king maker during the later Roman Empire, in theory, we were apolitical in our approach to protecting our clients, being more like 'king keepers' than makers. Strictly speaking, however, this was not true, since each of us, I'm sure, would have refused to work for certain world leaders.

Nevertheless, that conversation does raise an important point about those in VIP protection. It is a job, or, more accurately for many, a career, even in some cases when guarding certain charismatic leaders, a calling. The good bodyguard really should remain apolitical. Regardless of whether the US Secret Service agent votes Republican or Democrat, he or she must still be willing to stand between the principal and a bullet. Ideology may influence how bodyguards live their lives and may affect their rules of engagement or threat assessment, but, if they're good at their job, it doesn't affect their performance all that much.

US Secret Service agents always found that their KGB equivalents were among the most competent and most reliable of the foreign protective personnel with whom they worked. Some basic techniques varied, but members of each service were highly trained and were dedicated to protecting their clients. In fact, during the attempted coup against Gorbachev in August 1991, his KGB bodyguards showed their dedication and loyalty by holding firm around their principal, even when KGB Alpha Teams (special forces) were poised to capture him. They may have been good Communists and certainly were good KGB agents, otherwise they would not have received such an important assignment, but most of all, they were Gorbachev's protective team, which meant that to get him, even fellow KGB agents would have to go through them.

I've been asked if I would take a bullet for someone for whom I was working. By choice, no, I would not take a bullet. That's one reason I wear a ballistic vest; however, I would place myself between a threat and the person who had given me their trust. VIP protection training incorporates so many drills requiring the bodyguard to move between a protectee and a threat that it is an instinctive action. The professional bodyguard attempts to anticipate threats to the principal and avoid them, but if the threat cannot be avoided and turns up with a gun in its hand a few feet away, the bodyguard's reflexes and skill with his or her own weapon may dictate the need to move between that threat and the principal. The good bodyguard, however, does not want to stand and fight. No matter how accurate the bodyguard's own shot may be, the attacker might still get off a shot that could harm the protectee. Whenever possible, the good bodyguard will help the principal run away so that he or she can sign the bodyguard's paycheck another day!

Professional bodyguards are not large thugs whose principal function is to bash a path through groupies for a rock star. My British friends term such quasi-bodyguards 'minders' and view them as a separate breed from professional bodyguards. Most of the protective personnel I've known have been well educated and well read, have presented an excellent appearance and moved well in the social situations in which their job has placed them. World leaders, members of royalty and corporate CEOs who can afford well-paid and well-trained protective teams do not want to surround themselves with thugs who will demean them by their presence. My police and military backgrounds have certainly helped me gain employment in VIP protection, but my university education hasn't hurt either! Well-dressed, professional bodyguards who exude an air of competence not only act as a deterrent to attack, but also can enhance the status of their employer.

For a better understanding of how the professional bodyguard thinks and acts, read on.

Leroy Thompson
Manchester, Missouri

CHAPTER 1

GENERAL PRECEPTS OF VIP PROTECTION

In this book, the various aspects of a protective effort will be analysed in some detail. Much of the process of running a protective effort consists of attention to detail and preventative planning, factors that are not as flamboyant as car chases or shoot-outs, but which are intended to preclude the need for evasive driving or engaging in a gunfight with assassins or kidnappers. Good VIP drivers are highly trained in all aspects of offensive and defensive driving, and, indeed, can save their principal with such skills. Members of effective protection teams are also well trained in the use of their weapons and will have fired thousands of rounds during training for the occasion when they must shoot to defend their principal and themselves. However, those in the business of close protection will want to avoid problems whenever possible. Much of this book will be devoted to methods that will allow bodyguards to keep their principal away from any trouble. Tactics will also be presented for those situations when trouble cannot be avoided.

Although the precepts introduced here will be covered in detail in subsequent chapters, it is important to establish the basic tenets that set the parameters within which protective teams normally operate:

1 Be constantly alert, no matter how mundane the task.
Because many tasks in VIP protection are performed again and again, it is very easy to let the routine lull one into sloppiness. Rotating bodyguards among different assignments, varying shifts, carrying out surprise inspections, and allowing time for realistic and interesting training can all help keep team members sharp.

2 Never leave the principal unguarded while you are on duty.
I am sure I am not the only bodyguard who ever urinated into an ashtray or plant pot in a hotel corridor because I could not leave my post. Generally, a good team leader will have planned for relief of a bodyguard assigned to secure an area, but if a team is small or overstretched, one may have to stay on post even when nature calls! Bodyguards must also remain constantly alert to distractions designed to pull them away from their task. Whether it be a flirtatious individual, a drunk who apparently has wandered on to the wrong floor or smoke coming from a stairwell, the bodyguard's primary responsibility is to prevent unauthorised access to the principal.

3 Be ready to place yourself between the principal and the threat.
Bodyguards must train to place themselves between the principal and a potential threat. As a result, they may suffer injury or even death from a thrown object, a blow, a knife or a bullet. In such circumstances, wearing a proper ballistic vest can improve a bodyguard's chances of survival immeasurably. However, placing the body in the line of fire may be done for reasons other than simply stopping a bullet. Body cover also obscures an attacker's aim, making it difficult to target the principal. The effective use of body cover, for example, can make it very difficult for a sniper to identify or get a good shot at the principal. Employing members of a protective team who can make identification of the principal more difficult is highly desirable (*ie* If the principal is a black female, then have at least one black female on the protective team so that a sniper may hesitate in deciding upon the target.).

4 **Do not let yourself be distracted from your main mission – to protect the principal.**

Members of the protective team must remain focused on protecting the principal. This may mean ignoring verbal abuse or running away from an attack. Threatening individuals should only be engaged with hand-to-hand combat techniques or gunfire if that is necessary to stop an attack or buy time for the evacuation of the principal. Training members of protective teams in martial-arts techniques that allow an opponent to be disabled quickly so that the bodyguard can continue to cover the principal is most desirable. The bodyguard must also remain aware of the fact that an attack may really be a distraction to draw team members away from the principal, thus exposing a weakness that another assailant will be able to exploit.

5 **Do your homework: be aware of likely threats to the principal.**

Bodyguards must be familiar with the techniques of threat assessment and should stay abreast of information on terrorist groups or criminals who may target the principal. Good bodyguards also study abnormal psychology and may even observe mental patients to develop a feel for mannerisms that could indicate a deranged individual. In addition, the bodyguard must be aware of threats that may arise because of the principal's religion, political affiliation or social status. Bodyguards must even be aware that a bee could be as dangerous as an assassin to a principal with an allergy to bee stings.

6 **Be alert to anyone or anything that appears suspicious.**

Paranoia is not necessarily a bad thing for those in the close-protection business. The good bodyguard learns to watch constantly for anomalies: the individual who appears out of place, the vehicle parked where a vehicle should not be parked, the tell-tale signs of tampering that might indicate the placing of an explosive device. When bodyguards are trained, drills to enhance observation skills are often incorporated.

7 **Discourage your principal from establishing a routine that will make him or her an easy target.**

Again and again, when terrorist assassinations and kidnappings are studied, it becomes obvious that the terrorists had observed the movements of the target and knew where he or she would be at a certain time. Whenever possible, routes should be varied. Do not leave for the office at exactly the same time every day. If the principal jogs in the morning, vary the place and time. I even advise principals not to use a specific parking spot at their place of business, particularly one identified by name or title. If an office building or hotel has several entrances, use each of them at different times. It is also important to restrict the circulation of any schedules of meetings. Varying routine will not only make it harder for an opponent to plan an ambush, but also ensure that the protective team maintains a high level of alertness.

8 **Maintain a low-profile: keep your weapons, etc, out of sight and remain unobtrusive.**

Bodyguards should be as unobtrusive as possible. Not only does this help the principal and those dealing with the principal to remain comfortable, but also it attracts less attention to the principal. Similarly, the bodyguard does not want to attract too much attention, as this allows a potential assailant to identify whom to eliminate prior to an attack on the principal.

AUTHOR'S NOTE

While attending a VIP protection course in Toronto, I was able to observe a perfect example of the effects of an obvious protective effort. I was acting as the principal, while those on the course were escorting me to the airport to catch my flight back to the USA. Eventually, the presence of a group of men in suits obviously escorting a 'VIP' began to attract attention. Soon, airport workers were finding excuses to pass by in an attempt to figure out the identity of the 'celebrity'.

The protective team should attempt to dress in a manner that will allow them to blend in to their surroundings as much as possible. Casual clothing should be chosen if guarding a principal on the beach, while formal attire should be worn for formal occasions.

One exception to this rule may occur in some Third World countries, where an obvious display of firepower may discourage an attack. In such circumstances, the VIP motorcade might be escorted by gun jeeps, and bodyguards may openly display assault rifles or submachine-guns.

9 Do everything possible to restrict access to information about the principal to those with a need to know.

The protective team should work closely with the principal's administrative assistant or aide to restrict access to information about travel plans, appointments, visits to theatres or sporting events and similar sensitive data. Reservations can be made under the name of an aide or bodyguard. Care must be taken to ensure that computer and communications security are maintained so that the principal's daily schedule is not compromised. In the case of business figures not normally in the public eye, I recommend limiting the availability of photographs. If a photo is published in company brochures, choose one that is outdated or does not really look like the principal. This will make it harder for a kidnapper or assassin who does not actually know the principal to identify him or her.

10 Remember, caution is always necessary: for the bodyguard, a problem avoided is much better than a problem solved; confrontations may be macho, but they're counter-productive to the principal's image and safety.

Close-protection professionals avoid confrontations whenever possible. A gunfight in which all the attackers are killed, but the principal is wounded is less desirable than one in which the attackers escape, but the principal is unhurt. Likewise, if one of the close-protection team stops to thrash an obnoxious member of a crowd, that bodyguard is no longer available as an

element of the escort formation, and also may well draw attention and negative publicity to the client. By all means, fight or shoot if it is the only way to counter a threat, but try to keep your options open and to anticipate threats, taking another route, using another entrance or employing deception to move the principal without confrontation.

11 Pay attention to detail: it's easy to become so wrapped up in worrying about a terrorist group launching a mass attack that you forget to arrange the most secure table in a restaurant.

A close-protection team may train for years in counter-ambush tactics, yet never have to deal with such an attack. However, they may have to put out a fire at the principal's residence or administer CPR while rushing a member of the principal's family to hospital. Be prepared for a wide variety of contingencies, not just those involving an attack on the principal.

12 Learn to watch the hands of anyone near the principal; eyes can be important, too, but hands are the best indicators of hostile intent.

The ability to watch everyone near the principal is gained partially through experience and partially through drill. Good training for VIP protection teams includes work in crowds, which include individuals who take the roles of assassins as well as innocent well-wishers or mildly hostile hecklers. Some Russian VIP protection teams have carried the desire to observe hands to the extreme by pulling them from the pockets of onlookers to make sure they are empty. It is important to remember that anything shielding the hands can also conceal a weapon. A jacket draped across a hand and arm, a folded newspaper, a plaster cast or bandages, a camera, a package – all should cause members of a protective team to be particularly alert.

13 At the first sign of trouble, if possible, get your principal out of there.

The team leader, particularly, should always be aware of alternate routes and escape routes when carrying out escort assignments on foot. Members of the protective team should know the location of points along the route that offer cover from gunfire or explosive fragments. That way, if an attack is launched and immediate evacuation from the area is not possible, a defensible position may be reached quickly. Likewise, the VIP driver should know alternate routes and escape routes anywhere along the passage of a motorcade or commuter journey. Routes to the nearest hospital with a good accident and emergency department, and to the nearest safe haven should also be known. If, when moving on foot, the team leader decides to evacuate the

EXAMPLE

Two assassination attempts, one successful and one unsuccessful, offer some excellent insights into protective techniques.

On 9 February 1998, Eduard Shevardnadze, president of the Republic of Georgia, survived an attack on his motorcade launched by eighteen terrorists who fired sixteen rockets. Shevardnadze had survived a previous assassination attempt in 1995, when he had been trapped in his burning limo. As a result, he was given an armoured Mercedes by the United States, and training was provided for his protective team. In fact, on the night of the 1998 assassination attempt, an advisor from the CIA was riding in the motorcade.

The terrorists, who reportedly were supported by members of a Russian Federal Security Service Alpha Team, had foreknowledge of the route and set their ambush in a park through which the motorcade had to pass. Despite the fact that the attackers managed to launch so many rockets, three of which hit Shevardnadze's vehicle, the president survived the attack virtually uninjured due to the efforts of his protective team.

One of the escort vehicles was positioned to the side of the presidential limo, thus making it difficult for the attackers to get a clear shot. The motorcade was also moving quickly and kept driving through the ambush, thus reducing time in the killing zone.

The armoured limo was so well designed and the driver so well trained that despite the rocket hits, which had set the engine on fire, the driver managed to keep going for 150 yards to clear the killing zone. Once clear, an evacuation-under-fire drill was carried out to transfer the president to an escort vehicle. Although two bodyguards were killed in the ambush, the president survived thanks to the excellent training of his protective team.

On the other hand, the assassination of Ahmed Shah Massoud, leader of Afghanistan's Northern Alliance, was carried out successfully on 9 September 2001, possibly to eliminate him as a threat to the Taliban and Al-Qaeda just prior to the attacks on the World Trade Center in New York two days later.

Two assassins posed as Belgian journalists, originally from Morocco, who wished to interview Massoud, although in fact they were Arab members of Al-Qaeda. Their success can be attributed to lax security. Although Massoud was surrounded by a large number of armed men, they were not trained in VIP protection. As a result, the supposed journalists managed to get near him carrying a video camera filled with explosives, which they detonated.

Had Massoud been protected by trained personnel, the bodyguards would not have let the 'journalists' near him until they and their equipment had been searched thoroughly for explosives. More care would also have been taken in checking their credentials prior to granting an interview.

This attack illustrates the point that it is very difficult to defend against suicide bombers, but particularly difficult if trained VIP-protection personnel are not employed.

principal, he or she must have an evacuation plan – whether to move to the VIP vehicle or have the vehicle come to the principal, or head for the nearest good cover, the location of which must be known, as must any point within a building where the principal may be secured.

14 **Be aware of any medical conditions suffered by the principal and members of the principal's family, of how to contact his or her doctor, of the location of the nearest hospital and of how to administer any special medications.**
The protective team should assemble a medical file on the principal, the principal's family, staff members and the protective team itself. This file should include information that will speed treatment in a casualty department, including blood type, medical history and allergies. Members of the team should all have received basic first-aid and CPR training, while it is useful for at least one team member to have been a military medic or a paramedic. Because of fear of AIDS and hepatitis, many teams now travel with screened blood for the principal and other members of the party.

15 **Normally, precede the principal through doors into buildings, lifts, toilets, etc.**
It is quite common for the untrained bodyguard to defer to the principal as a matter of respect and allow him or her to pass through a door first. This, of course, exposes the principal to any danger lurking on the other side of the door. If a lone bodyguard is on duty, he or she will often take a quick look around the door, then escort the principal through. If, however, a full protective team is on duty, the two leading members of the box will pass through the door first, while the team leader shepherds the VIP through and the remaining members of the team secure the rear.

(handwritten margin note:) Yes / you precede / principal / through / door

16 **Be particularly alert whenever in the presence of unknown individuals, especially in lifts (when possible try to ensure that a lift contains only the principal, members of his or her staff and bodyguards), corridors, stairwells, etc.**

Strangers and confined areas should put bodyguards on special alert.
The protective team will avoid this situation whenever possible, but if an occasion should arise when strangers can get close to the VIP, the team will tighten the protective box so that one or more bodyguards will be between any unknown individual and the principal. In subsequent chapters, special techniques will be discussed for providing cover for the principal in theatres, on aircraft and in other places where strangers may be encountered.

17 **Whenever possible, make travel reservations, hotel reservations, restaurant reservations, etc, in a name other than the principal's.**
It should be obvious that the fewer people who know where or when a VIP will appear, the harder it will be for an assassination or kidnap team to plan an attack. Careful travel planning should also avoid situations where the principal has to stand around in public. First-class travel arrangements and express check-ins and check-outs should be used whenever possible.

18 **Work with local police, hotel security personnel, airport police and others in authority to make travel as smooth as possible.**
The better the contacts a protective team can maintain with local police, customs, immigration and security officials, the easier their job will be. Avoid arrogance and be polite to everyone with whom you deal. If working with hotel personnel, tip them well – *both on arrival and departure* – to ensure that they warn you of anything suspicious and help watch your back. In countries where it is acceptable to pay gratuities to government officials, take care of those who take care of you. Where gratuities or gifts are not allowed, make sure that you thank them profusely and have the principal send a letter of thanks. If the principal is a widely recognised individual, have him pose for photographs with the various police officials and send them prints, which he should sign with thanks. If police officials who have helped you

visit your area at some later date, try to give them VIP treatment. You will be repaid the next time you are in their jurisdiction.

In many parts of the world, retired police officials can be hired as consultants to liaise with their former colleagues, and employing them to help with the details of your visit may be advisable. In some areas, you may even be able to hire off-duty police officers to augment your team. You will need to evaluate the level of their training before deciding how to employ them best, but they should provide good liaison with local police. Good contacts can also overcome any difficulties raised by the protective team being armed. In many cases, authorisation to carry firearms may be obtained under the auspices of a local security company.

19 **Remember that the majority of terrorist incidents occur when the principal is in a vehicle. Plan accordingly.**
It is extremely important to pay great attention to vehicle security. A hardened VIP vehicle is very desirable, while a driver trained at a good security driving school – such as the Scotti Driving School – is an absolute necessity. The vehicle must be kept secure at all times to avoid the possibility of explosives being planted. Members of the protective team need to practise such techniques as debussing under fire, transferring the principal from a disabled vehicle and using trail or lead vehicles to provide cover while the VIP vehicle is evacuated.

20 **Try to prevent the principal's vehicles from attracting attention.**
A stretched limousine is guaranteed to be noticed. A sturdy saloon or sport utility vehicle, which can be hardened and set up as a VIP vehicle without being a magnet for attention is a much better choice. The best package of features for a VIP vehicle will be discussed in detail in a later chapter, but most of these features will not be apparent to the casual observer. The best VIP vehicle will withstand an attack, have the power

and survivability to be driven away from an ambush, yet appear to be a standard large saloon or sport utility vehicle.

21 **Make contingency plans (*ie* escape routes, routes to a hospital, emergency phone numbers, etc).**
A critical aspect of carrying out the advance work for a VIP visit is assembling information about possible routes, including alternates that may be used in an emergency. It is important that the VIP driver and the team leader spend time studying these alternate routes so that they are aware of any construction work, rush-hour traffic or other situations that may affect their use. Each team member should also carry a list of important telephone numbers and be aware of evacuation plans in case one or more team members are incapacitated, necessitating a change in command.

22 **Remember that your job is not only to protect the principal's life, but also his or her privacy, image and self-esteem.**
Principals must trust those who protect them and be confident that they will not repeat anything overheard. The bodyguard must also be aware that steering a VIP clear of a muddy puddle can prevent his or her embarrassment. Bodyguards must take care that they do not gossip, nor make fun of those they protect, as eventually such behaviour will influence their relationship with the principal, and such actions or comments are likely to be picked up by the Press or others.

23 **Display a professional demeanour and your principal will be much more likely to listen to your advice.**
Bodyguards must dress well, have a polite, but firm, demeanor, be prepared for contingencies, and be confident in their training and abilities so that they can project confidence in a crisis. They must not drink, take drugs or make advances to members of the principal's household. When on duty, they should be clean, neat and alert. In simple terms, bodyguards must project an image

that gives the principal confidence and deters any potential threats.

24 **Remember that although you must be ready to give your life for your principal, it's better to make the attacker give his or hers. Wear your ballistic vest; practise with your individual weapons until you can score hits under trying circumstances; anticipate threats; be ready for the few minutes out of untold hours when you face a lethal threat.**

Although those employed in VIP protection drill at placing their bodies between the principal and any threat, extensive training and alertness can reduce the likelihood that they will actually have to take a bullet.

25 **Even though you must do your job, respect the principal's privacy.**

Bodyguards must remain close enough to the principal to be readily available to counter a threat at any time of day or night. However, the principal will need time alone with family, friends and business associates. Members of the protective team must learn to balance their responsibilities with the principal's need for space. With experience, bodyguards learn to be unobtrusive and available without hovering.

CHAPTER 2

THREAT ASSESSMENT AND LEVEL OF PROTECTION

Assessing the threat faced by a principal allows those charged with ensuring his or her safety to determine the level of protection required and to make judgements about the likelihood of imminent danger. A threat assessment or analysis must be constantly updated, based upon factors related to the principal's lifestyle, business or government position and travel plans.

LEVEL OF THREAT

Most protective teams use some type of system to categorise the level of threat at any given time. Whether referred to by colour, number, letter or code-name, usually three to five threat levels will be recognised. For example, Threat Level One might indicate that an attack by committed assassins is anticipated; Threat Level Two might suggest that there is substantial danger of an attack by terrorists, assassins or kidnappers; Threat Level Three might mean that because of the principal's position there is always a possibility of an assassination or kidnap attempt; and Threat Level Four might signify that the principal's lower profile – perhaps because of retirement from government service – has reduced the danger of an attack, but precautions must still be taken.

One aspect of threat assessment is determining the level of risk at any given time. For example, a trip to Switzerland would not normally be considered as risky as a visit to Egypt; however, if the principal plans to ski while in Switzerland, this would increase the risk of injury. Risk level will be changed by virtually anything the principal does; hence, the protective team will have to make constant adjustments to their assessment of threat.

RISK OR THREAT?

Although the terms 'risk' and 'threat' may at times seem to be used almost interchangeably, there are subtle differences between them, which are important for an understanding of this chapter. I should also note that some close-protection professionals include assessment of risks with assessment of threats without differentiating between them. When a differentiation is made, however, normally 'threat' refers to the broader elements affecting the principal, such as countries to be visited, political situations in those countries, or the principal's political or business position. 'Risk' usually applies to elements over which the principal has a certain level of control, such as his activities, social contacts or pronouncements.

Generally, the protective team attempts either to eliminate or to avoid risks whenever possible. An assessment of risk/threat allows the team to determine which elements cannot be avoided and to make plans to counter them.

BALANCING PROTECTION WITH LIFESTYLE

One of the things a careful threat assessment will do is help establish how much of a trade-off a principal will have to make between protection and lifestyle. Generally, the higher the threat level, the more the principal's lifestyle will be compromised. Threat assessment will also help determine which risks can be eliminated, which can be lowered and which will remain constant. Some of these risks will be inherent to the principal, and some to a specific place or event. For example, the risks associated with being the scion of a very wealthy and powerful family are inherent in the person; however, risks that occur when the principal travels to a place controlled by his family's political or business rivals is inherent in that place.

CATEGORIES OF THREAT

When determining threats, not all will be specifically physical threats against the principal. Some close-protection specialists break threats into four main categories:

1 Against the principal's safety.

2 Against the principal's family's safety.

3 Against the principal's psychological well-being.

4 Against the principal's privacy.

Some threats will overlap and fall into more than one category. For example, phone calls threatening the kidnapping of the principal's child would come into categories 2, 3 and 4.

BREAKING DOWN THREAT ASSESSMENT

A simple way to break down the process of threat assessment is to divide the potential areas of threat or risk. First are the threats against the principal because of his own characteristics:

- wealth or social status;
- celebrity or public exposure;
- political views;
- symbolic status;
- travel to certain areas.

Second are the threats based on the principal's position:

- as a symbol of a government, company or philosophy;
- as an authority figure;
- because of political views;
- because of religious views;
- as a public figure with high-profile media exposure;
- because of foreign travel;

- as a representative of a political party or religious group undergoing internal power struggles.

Note that there is a degree of overlap between the two lists.

EXAMPLE

Prior to his assassination, Malcolm X held high symbolic status as a militant black leader and as the visible symbol of the Black Muslim movement. Travel to certain areas of the southern United States would certainly have increased the threat he faced from white supremacists. Nevertheless, Malcolm X was assassinated because of a power struggle within the Black Muslim movement.

TYPES OF THREAT

Threats are often broken down by how they manifest themselves in attacks on the principal and might include:

- verbal assault;
- thrown objects;
- impact weapons (ie clubs);
- edged weapons;
- concealed firearms;
- attack on vehicle/motorcade;
- explosives;
- sniper fire;
- biological or chemical agents;
- kidnapping.

POTENTIAL ATTACKERS

Another aspect of carrying out a threat assessment is determining from whom the threat may come:

- the deranged;
- those with a mental fixation (stalkers);
- disgruntled office or job seekers;
- those pursuing a personal vendetta or seeking revenge;
- criminals;
- terrorists;
- professional assassins;
- foreign intelligence agencies or special forces;
- kidnappers seeking financial gain or intent on taking the principal hostage.

Note that the assessment must be ongoing and constantly updated. For example, a stalker who has been convicted and sent to prison or a mental hospital would move down the threat scale, while the same stalker, if released from incarceration, would move up the scale.

HEALTH RISKS

Threat assessment must take into consideration potential risks to the principal's health:

- heart trouble;
- allergies;
- diabetes;
- previous injuries (*ie* a knee injury that would make the principal more likely to fall).

AUTHOR'S NOTE

A humorous comment on the risk of heart attack faced by US Vice President Dick Cheney appeared as an editorial cartoon, which showed a pizza delivery man at the door of the Vice-Presidential Office while Secret Service agents hurled themselves between Cheney and the threat of cholesterol! Nevertheless, this cartoon did highlight the fact that Cheney's protective detail had to remain constantly aware of his history of heart problems.

THE PRINCIPAL'S REPUTATION

The protective team must also consider possible threats to the principal's reputation. Such threats may include:

- sexual – extra-marital/prostitutes/homosexual;
- contact with criminals or gamblers;
- drunkenness;
- tendency to make comments that would cause problems if quoted in the media.

DANGEROUS ACTIVITIES

Consideration must be given as well to leisure activities that carry a high level of risk. Among these are:

- hunting;
- skiing;
- horse riding;
- flying a private aircraft;
- skydiving;
- boating;
- scuba diving;
- white-water rafting;
- mountain climbing;
- motorcycle riding.

OTHER DANGERS
Consideration must be given to any other dangers that the principal may encounter in a residence, hotel, place of work or other venue, or while travelling:

- fire;
- electrical shock;
- drowning;
- building safety (*ie* stairways, lifts, etc);
- car accidents;
- travel in light aircraft.

SECURITY SURVEY

It is important that as part of a threat assessment, members of the protective team carry out a careful survey of the potential dangers to safety or health at the principal's residence, office and other locations where he or she spends a substantial amount of time. Normally I combine a full security survey (see Chapter 4) in conjunction with an initial threat assessment.

In fact, while assessing threats to the principal, the protective team will normally produce a comprehensive profile of the principal. For this process to be most effective, the principal must trust the head of security/protection enough to be candid with him or her. The head of protection must take the time to explain to the principal why information of a personal nature is necessary to allow an effective assessment of possible threats to be made. Interviews with family members are also important to determine whether they are aware of any specific threats or if aspects of their lifestyle increase risks.

Among the types of information about the principal that can prove useful are:

- relatives, political or business associates, friends, lovers and known enemies;
- birthplace, current residence, place of work, places frequently visited;
- personality quirks (is the principal abrasive, controversial, prone to make enemies?);
- controversial religious, racial or political views;
- aspects of past, such as military service (if so, during a war?) or political office;
- aspects of lifestyle, such as affairs, alcohol use or taking risks.

See Appendix for an example of a questionnaire to be used when interviewing the principal, assistants and family members.

TRAVELLING OVERSEAS

Many aspects of threat assessment relate specifically to trips overseas. The protective team will evaluate the political situation, including stability of the government, socio-economic status, level of crime, level of terrorist or insurgent activity, and perception of the home country of the principal in the country or countries to be visited. If there are active terrorist groups or criminals who carry out kidnappings, the protective team will look closely at the type of person such groups have targeted in the past to determine if the principal fits their target profile. The protection team will also look at the methods used by groups active in the countries to be visited. Do they use bombs, snipers, ambushes?

LEVEL OF PROTECTION

Once a threat level has been determined, the necessary level of protection can be decided. However, many factors other than threat influence this. Although they may face a substantial risk, some principals are not willing to compromise their lifestyle as much as would be necessary to ensure maximum protection. Some political leaders are not willing to accept a level of protection that would isolate them from the population. Moreover, apart from the highest government leaders, few will be able to afford the expense of a comprehensive protection effort.

MAXIMUM EFFORT

The highest level of protection would probably be that enjoyed by the leader of a major power. As many as 75–100 personnel, or even more, might be assigned to protect the principal and family members. This might be broken down into two or three teams of four bodyguards per shift, who form the protective box around the principal, as well as a shift commander. In addition, there would be personnel manning a command post, VIP drivers, counter-snipers, advance personnel, electronic security specialists, intelligence/threat assessment officers, static security personnel at the VIP residence and, perhaps, office, a head of security and an assistant head of security, and various other support personnel. Such an effort might well cost £3.5 million ($5 million) or more per year.

A more feasible level of protection for an extremely wealthy and influential industrialist, or a lower-echelon government official in a country facing a terrorist threat, might be based on 15–20 personnel. Most protective teams like to operate with five members around the principal – a four-man box and the team leader. In addition, it is necessary to have two trained drivers with vehicles – one to transport the VIP and family or staff as well as the protective team leader, and another to transport the rest of the protective team. Additional personnel will be needed to provide static security at the VIP residence and to carry out advance work. If the principal has 24-hour-a-day coverage, enough personnel to cover multiple shifts will be necessary. Generally, once the principal is in the residence, two or three bodyguards can cover the night shift. When the VIP is travelling, protective personnel will often have to work 12-hour or longer shifts to provide full coverage. Bear in mind, too, that to run an effort of this size will still cost well over £650,000 ($1 million) per year.

SMALL TEAMS

With even smaller protective teams of up to five bodyguards, there are substantial difficulties in running a comprehensive effort. Support personnel are not available, and the principal presents a softer target. Less firepower is available, too, if an assault is launched. On the other hand, some principals who could afford a larger detail actually like a smaller team. They have more personal contact with, and confidence in, their protective team. Time is also much more flexible for travel and scheduling. Members of small teams normally keep a travel bag and their passport readily available for quick moves. The smaller team can

also be more innovative and frequently finds creative solutions to problems that would be handled by specialists on a larger team.

AUTHOR'S NOTE

Sometimes the problems encountered by smaller teams are difficult to anticipate. A friend of mine, for example, was assigned as the lone Secret Service agent protecting Tricia Nixon when her father was campaigning for his second term as president. Travelling with a small bag containing a couple of changes in clothing and some spare ammunition, often he moved with his charge to a new venue several times per day. He was finally assigned a second agent to assist him, as the hire cars they were using were constantly being towed away because he could not leave Miss Nixon long enough to park the car and simply had to leave it at their destination, despite any parking restrictions. Although a simple problem for two agents to deal with, it was impossible for one.

FUNCTION OF TEAM MEMBERS

No matter how large the team, a variety of tasks must be performed to provide a principal with effective protection. To illustrate these tasks, it will probably be easier to show the breakdown of a larger team by functions, then explain how these functions are absorbed by members of a smaller team.

SENIOR PERSONNEL

Someone must be in charge. On a large detail, there will be a head of security with subordinates in charge of each shift. One member of the close-protection team will have responsibility for commanding that team. On major protective movements or visits, frequently the head of security will move with the close-protection team while the second-in-command will be in charge of the command post. The command post is the clearing house for information and the central communications point for a protective team. Normally, when the VIP is moving or visiting a site, at least two members of the protective team will man the CP – the second-in-command and a communications specialist. On large teams, there may also be an intelligence/risk analyst assigned to constantly update the close-protection team. Generally, when the principal is at his residence or in a hotel, embassy or other venue for the night, one man handles the command post. In hotels, however, in addition to the team member assigned to the CP, standby personnel, who have not been assigned a post, may relax in the command post between periods at fixed posts and to be available to respond to contingencies.

CLOSE-PROTECTION TEAMS

The actual close-protection teams are normally based on multiples of four, since many teams find the four-man box, supplemented by the team leader, the most flexible escort formation. Some teams actually have two four-man teams on a shift so that one can form up around the vehicle as it arrives or departs, while still leaving a full team embussed and ready to move. This extra team helps the advance party evaluate the situation as the principal arrives and provides additional security as he or she moves from the vehicle to a building. Likewise, this team covers the principal's departure.

Some teams also employ extra personnel to act as 'outriders', who move ahead of and/or to the sides of the close-protection team to give early warning of threats and possibly to engage them while the close-protection team evacuates the principal. These additional team members may also be used to cover a doorway, stairway or other possible route of attack until the principal has passed. Whenever, possible, however, coverage of problem areas is assigned to fixed-post personnel from the local police. Even teams that normally function with just the basic four-man box plus team leader may have one extra man

who trails the close-protection team to watch for problems from the rear. Other teams may detail a couple of members dressed in 'civilian clothes' to move through the crowd, watching for problems.

I should note that not everyone working in VIP protection uses exactly the same terms. Although I employ the designation 'close-protection team' when referring to those who actually move with the principal, forming body cover around him or her, other terms describing this function may be encountered – 'personal escort section' for example.

FAMILY PROTECTION UNIT

Because of the danger that being in the spotlight brings to those surrounding some VIPs, many details will include a smaller protective team for the principal's spouse and children. Such teams may consist of only one or two personnel, whose primary concern is to prevent kidnapping, but they still act as a drain on personnel and money.

COVERT PROTECTION

There are definite advantages, too, if a couple of trained close-protection specialists are not readily identifiable as members of the protective team. If a member of the team is usually identified as an aide, administrative assistant or secretary, this bodyguard may be allowed to accompany the principal into meetings or other situations where the protective team would not normally be allowed. In some cases, a trained female protection specialist can stay close to the principal in this way, while outsiders assume that all the bodyguards have been left behind.

VIP DRIVER

Protective teams must also provide for transportation. If there is only one bodyguard, he or she may function as a bodyguard/driver, having received training in offensive/defensive driving as well as close-protection skills. It is far more desirable, however, for the driver to concentrate on that function. In fact, it is best for the driver to stay with the VIP vehicle to be able to quickly respond if an evacuation is necessary, and to prevent tampering with the vehicle. Even a relatively small protective team will need at least two drivers, one for the VIP car and one for the tail car. Many teams employ a lead car and a tail car in addition to the VIP car, thus necessitating three drivers. Large teams may require more drivers to cover evening and weekend shifts as well as day shifts. Large teams may also have their own mechanic to maintain and check the vehicles. On small teams, the driver is responsible for these duties, although he may take the vehicle away for actual maintenance.

SPECIALISTS

Large teams may have specialised personnel who form part of the protective effort. The US Secret Service, for example, has a CAT (counter-assault team) unit assigned to the president and vice-president as well as other officials in special circumstances. This unit is more heavily armed than the rest of the protective team and trained in paramilitary tactics. They will come into action if an attack is launched by heavily armed terrorists. The CAT unit can normally be identified in a presidential motorcade by their black Chevrolet Suburban, which is designed to allow them to observe in all directions and to bring their weapons into action very quickly. In Great Britain, the Special Air Service sometimes performs the function of a CAT unit by providing heavily armed and highly trained support to the close-protection teams from the Metropolitan Police. In some Third World countries, the equivalent unit will be a very overtly armed portion of the presidential guard, often deploying gun jeeps or other armed vehicles as part of a motorcade. On small teams, a couple of assault rifles and/or sniping rifles may be carried in the VIP or escort vehicle to allow a response to more heavily armed terrorists, but the personnel are not available to form a specialised team.

Another specialised portion of some large teams is a counter-sniper unit. Specifically trained to take up positions from which they can search for snipers during a VIP appearance, counter-sniper specialists are expected to

acquire and engage a target very quickly. They may also warn of any suspicious individuals or movements they spot, allowing an entry team to make checks prior to the VIP arrival. Once again, small teams cannot deploy a specialised counter-sniper team, but may carry one or more tactical rifles so that a team member or two can be detached for this mission.

An important part of the protective effort is providing permanent security at any VIP residence. Generally, this is the entry-level job on the protective team. Those charged with security at a residence will walk perimeters, secure entrances and monitor intrusion-detection systems. In some cases, they will patrol with trained security dogs. When the VIP is not in residence, a security team, even if reduced in size, must remain on duty to prevent intrusions and possible planting of explosive devices or electronic eavesdropping devices. Those charged with securing the residence will normally receive specialised training in electronic security and will consult with the head of security on updating security systems.

When the principal is actually at his residence, at least some members of the close-protection detail will be assigned to augment the residence security team, although in many cases members of the close-protection team have responsibilities inside the residence, while the residence security team has responsibilities outside. Even if only two or three personnel are assigned to residence security on each shift, this adds another 10–12 to the strength and payroll.

On large teams, there will be other specialised members as well. Among those who might be encountered are magnetometer operators, training specialists, intelligence officers, administrative officers and technical security specialists. Large teams will also have personnel assigned to act as advance parties for out-of-town or out-of-country visits, as well as appearances at local venues. Even on large teams, advance parties will generally be selected from members of the protective team, particularly those who have language skills when foreign visits are anticipated. However, those selected to do advance work must exhibit good attention to detail to be effective.

SMALL-TEAM MULTI-TASKING

In small teams – let's say one with a total of a dozen personnel – individual members will have to carry out two or more functions to provide effective protection. The team leader and second-in-command will usually handle all administrative details as well as intelligence and threat assessment. One or two team members – perhaps with military backgrounds – who are skilled with rifles will be designated to deploy assault or sniping rifles if there are indications that they will be needed. A technically-competent team member will be in charge of technical security, while whichever team member is available will handle the magnetometer if a portal model is deployed or if handheld metal detectors are used. Personnel with specialised expertise will be in charge of training in their fields (ie the best martial artist will take charge of keeping the team sharp in hand-to-hand combat, while a skilled marksman will set up handgun and submachine-gun training sessions).

THE VALUE OF THREAT ASSESSMENT

The key point to remember about threat assessment is that it is an ongoing process, which allows the protective team to allocate its assets most effectively. With small teams, particularly, threat assessment may be used to determine when it will be necessary to augment the permanent protective team with additional personnel, particularly individuals who are indigenous to a country that will be visited. The necessity to ensure that even a small protective team covers all of the major assignments necessary to carry out a truly professional protective effort also dictates that versatility and diverse skills are important prerequisites for the good bodyguard.

Obviously, even the best protective team cannot anticipate every threat, nor prepare for every contingency. However, the combination of a good threat assessment with a well-organised and well-trained protective team can substantially reduce the principal's vulnerability, making him or her a 'hard target' that will prove less appealing to the potential assassin or kidnapper.

CHAPTER 3

HARDENING THE VIP LIFESTYLE

Once the protective team has drawn its conclusions about the threat level faced by its principal, the head of the protective effort must meet with the principal and explain the implications to his or her lifestyle and the family's lifestyle if a protective effort commensurate with the threat is implemented. The VIP must also be made aware of the need to take a certain amount of responsibility for his or her own security, both in working with the protective team and in being alert at all times. This requirement for alertness will be magnified if the principal does not have full-time protective personnel who are on duty at all times. On the positive side, I also assure the principal that the very act of taking security precautions is a great deterrent that will often discourage potential attackers.

The first step in implementing tighter security is making the principal and principal's family, friends, business associates and staff aware of the need for security and the need to limit access to information about the principal and family. Any information about the VIP's business or personal life should be released on a need-to-know basis. The principal should keep as low a profile as possible, although his or her profession will dictate to what extent this is viable. A politician, for example, will require more public exposure than most businessmen.

RESTRICTING INFORMATION

Information that might help an attacker learn more about the principal should be closely guarded. For example, at the office, it is better not to have the principal's name on his or her office door, nor on a reserved parking space. Using numbers, although less 'prestigious', is far safer. Telephone numbers should not be listed, neither should addresses. If possible, avoid issuing recent photos, which make it easy to identify the principal. However, if a current photo is needed, do not shoot it in front of the principal's home or business, or in an easily identifiable location. Do not allow publication of the school attended by the principal's children. Distribution of the principal's schedule, including both business and social events, should be restricted on a need-to-know basis. One important move when attempting to limit access to critical information is to make household staff aware of what is thrown out with the rubbish. Use a shredder for virtually any paperwork related to the principal, even junk mail if it bears the address.

INTERVIEWS

Give careful consideration to how much information is provided during interviews. Once data about the principal or family appears in print, it might aid an attacker, either immediately or years in the future. It is also a good idea for protective personnel to run a security check on any interviewer before granting a meeting with the principal.

RESIDENCE

Although the principal's residence may be a showplace, it's better for it not to appear in *Country Life* or similar publications. Access to the residence should not be too easy either. A well-fenced or walled location on a dead-end street would make a good choice. Additional residence security precautions will be discussed in detail in Chapter 5.

VARY ROUTINE

Avoiding routine is very important in thwarting assassination and kidnap attempts. Routes to and from the office should be varied. If the principal or spouse jogs or exercises at a gym, alter the times and locations as much as possible. The principal should try not to eat at the same restaurant every day, or visit the same hairdresser at the same time and day of every month. Changing routine is an excellent pro-active security procedure that is relatively easy to implement.

PRINCIPAL'S CHILDREN

It is essential for the principal and/or spouse to talk to any children seriously about security – for themselves and in respect of strangers seeking information about their parents. As soon as they are old enough, teach children to make emergency phone calls. As part of this training, also instruct them not to talk to strangers who might call, nor provide any information about themselves or their parents. Children should also receive the normal warnings about getting into cars with strangers, talking with strangers, walking alone, etc. They should be told to report any approaches by strangers to their parents, teachers or bodyguards.

CHOOSING A SCHOOL
Some private schools are more attuned to security than others; it is best to choose one for the VIP children that has put security procedures into effect.

WATCHING FOR SURVEILLANCE

The principal's family and staff must be made aware of the need to watch for surveillance.

Members of the protective team can brief them on the types of surveillance they might encounter at the residence, on the road or at the office. Any of the following should be viewed with suspicion:

- service vehicles;
- private vehicles;
- parked enclosed vans;
- individuals (mother and child, man walking a dog, etc);
- utility company employees;
- canvassers or religious missionaries;
- anyone else who seems to be hanging around and is not recognised as a resident or worker in the neighbourhood.

As a matter of routine, the licence number of any suspicious vehicle should be recorded and passed on to those in the protective team.

VEHICLE PRECAUTIONS

Many of the most basic precautions must be taken when the principal or family members are driving by themselves. In addition to watching for surveillance, several other simple steps can make travelling in cars substantially safer. Note that most of these precautions apply to situations in which the principal or family member is not being transported by members of the protective team. Protective operations involving vehicles will be discussed in Chapter 8.

CHANGING VEHICLE
One simple precaution is to vary the vehicle driven. If the family owns three or four cars, a certain amount of variation is relatively easy to achieve. If the principal's company has a fleet of vehicles, it will be even easier for him to change frequently. Whether driving or walking, the principal and family members should each carry a mobile phone at all times. In the case of small children, the nanny should have a mobile phone. Numbers for the police, the head of the protective

team, etc, should be programmed into the phone for speed dialing.

VEHICLE EQUIPMENT

Each vehicle used by the VIP family should be equipped with a tracking system, which will make it easy to locate if hijacked. Note here that the principal will have to arrange for the head of the protective team to have the access code for the tracking system, otherwise the monitoring agency will not release information. It is also advisable to leave a schedule with a reliable member of the staff so that someone will be aware if the principal or a family member does not arrive somewhere on time.

All vehicles used by members of the VIP family should be fitted with alarms that not only protect against entry to the passenger compartment, but also the engine compartment and boot. If the vehicle has to be left with a mechanic or parking attendant, only the ignition/door key should be left with it. Remove house or any other keys.

ACTIONS WHILE DRIVING

When actually driving, it is important that the principal or family member avoids going on to 'automatic pilot' and ignoring the surroundings. He or she should stay alert for vulnerable points along a route (ie traffic lights, traffic jams, road construction or, in some countries, even assassins on motorbikes). It is important to know the location of police stations along the routes to and from the office, the children's school, etc.

The VIP residence should have remote-control garage doors so that it is not necessary to get out of the vehicle to open a door. Note, however, that, as with house keys, the garage door opener should be removed if the vehicle is left with an attendant or for servicing.

A CRUCIAL REQUIREMENT

In the case of a family with a full-time and comprehensive protective team, most of these driving precautions will be handled by trained drivers or protection specialists. However, for those families who only have one or two bodyguards and often one or more members of the family without full-time coverage, such awareness can be absolutely crucial.

SECURING THE RESIDENCE

Special care must be taken around the VIP residence, particularly if there is not a full-time security force with members on duty twenty-four hours a day. Normally, the protective force will be augmented by electronic security systems; however, such systems may also grant a degree of security when no bodyguards are present to monitor them and react to an identified threat. Among the systems that may be installed are closed-circuit television (CCTV), motion detectors, access controls and security lighting. The pros and cons of various electronic security systems will be discussed in Chapter 5. For now, it is important to note that such systems play a vital role in making the VIP residence and office more secure. Another aspect of electronic security is protection against eavesdropping. Therefore, both home and office should be swept periodically for surveillance devices – 'bugs'. It is also worthwhile having a good computer security expert install protective programs on any computers in the VIP residence and office.

DOOR AND WINDOW SECURITY

When there is no bodyguard on duty, members of the VIP's family or staff should be very circumspect about answering doors. As an aid to security, friends and relatives should advise in advance of visits so that the staff or security personnel can be alerted to expect them. Some method of seeing who is at the door without exposing oneself is absolutely critical.

Another precaution is to take care when entering a darkened room at night. Before turning on any lights, make sure the curtains are drawn to avoid presenting a shot to a sniper. During the day, curtains that allow in light, but restrict the view from outside, are desirable as well.

SECURITY AT NIGHT

When retiring for the night, keep a mobile phone handy in case regular telephone lines are cut. It is also advisable as a precaution against kidnapping to put children in upstairs bedrooms. In fact, the best system when security personnel are on duty is to have all family bedrooms above the first level so that an intruder would have to pass through the bodyguards on duty to reach family members.

SAFE ROOM

If possible, the VIP residence should have at least one 'safe room', which is designed to withstand gunfire and which can be locked securely from inside. This room should have its own communications system so that a call for help can be transmitted. Those VIPs who are familiar with weapons may keep a firearm in the safe room. This room is meant to be a final bastion, to which the VIP and family can retreat if intruders have managed to enter the house. If a security team is on duty, this offers a final defence in case the security team is 'taken out'. It also helps protect the family from gunfire if a fire fight takes place.

OTHER LIFESTYLE ADJUSTMENTS

The VIP will have to adjust his or her lifestyle in other ways. At the office, for example, the principal should learn to clear his or her desk every afternoon so that nothing critical is left out for cleaning staff to peruse. The principal's administrative assistant, secretary and other staff should follow the same practice.

When making hotel, restaurant or other reservations, it is advisable to make several, then cancel all but one at the last minute. Also, use the name of an aide or someone who will not be easily associated with the VIP.

DURESS CODE

The VIP and family members should have a duress code for use during phone calls so that it is immediately apparent if they are being forced to make a call. Staff should also be given a duress code – but not the same as that used by the VIP family – for the same reason.

MEETINGS

Care must also be taken in arranging meetings. Sneaking off to a private meeting in a remote location without a protective team is an invitation to kidnappers or assassins. Some principals have to be particularly careful about their tendency to sneak off for sexual encounters, which may have been arranged to entice them to a place where they will be vulnerable to attack.

TRAVEL CONSIDERATIONS

Precautions are necessary when travelling as well. Luggage carried on trips should have the business rather than home address on any tags. The principal should avoid public transport if at all possible. If it is necessary to take a taxi, a licensed cab should be chosen, as opposed to a 'gypsy cab'. In any foreign country, it is important to know how to operate public telephones and to carry the correct change for their use. It is also essential to know the numbers for police, the hotel and emergency medical assistance.

It should be borne in mind, too, that in virtually every major city there are areas that, although safe during business hours, are very dangerous after dark. Great care should be taken about where the principal goes at night. In general, he or she should avoid walking alone, even near home.

Giving the principal a thorough briefing on basic precautions and adjustments to lifestyle can often serve a dual purpose. First, it makes the principal aware of the need to be alert to his or her surroundings and of the need to ensure that any family and staff are as well. Second, it can drive home the point that the principal is vulnerable to the extent that he or she will raise the level of protection, so that bodyguards are available to increase both physical and mental security for both principal and family.

CHAPTER 4

ADVANCING A VIP VISIT

To properly understand the function of those who carry out advances for a VIP visit, it is necessary to clarify some terms. Those charged with 'advancing' a visit have a wide variety of responsibilities, many of which will be discussed in the following pages. Advances are not only carried out at venues around the world that a principal will visit, but also in his or her home city. As a result, I'm going to use two designations to help clarify functions. Henceforth, I will refer to those assigned to visit sites days or weeks ahead of a VIP junket as an advance team (AT), even though this 'team' may consist of only one member of the protective personnel and the site may be close to the principal's home. Those assigned to move ahead of the actual close-protection team to make sure no problems will be encountered along the route or at the venue will be designated the security advance party (SAP).

ANTICIPATE POTENTIAL PROBLEMS

One of the greatest talents that can be possessed by members of advance teams or security advance parties is the ability to anticipate potential problems. Those who advance a visit are trained in this skill and how to deal with problems prior to the principal's arrival. A great boon for those who carry out advances was the invention of the lap-top computer. Now, the reams of maps, diagrams, itineraries, check-lists and other data that are generated by an advance team may be easily organised and quickly duplicated on the computer. Of course,

this necessitates constant awareness of computer security to prevent relevant information from falling into the wrong hands.

THE ITINERARY

One of the first steps in advancing a visit or appearance is obtaining an itinerary. Consequently, it is important to have a good relationship with the aide who schedules travel and/or appearances so that even during the planning stages, the head of the protection team sees a preliminary itinerary. If the head of protective security has gained the principal's confidence, he or she may be asked for input on the itinerary, based on security concerns and the current threat level in the area to be visited. As a result, one of the first steps is to update the threat assessment based on travel plans.

UPDATING THE THREAT ASSESSMENT

For the threat assessment to be most current, some information will have to come from the actual advance team on the ground; however, there are other sources, not least the news media. Those working in close protection should monitor international and local TV news, and read news magazines and newspapers. There are also international services that will actually prepare an up-to-date threat analysis for any part of the globe. Although these can provide valuable information, they should not be relied upon in lieu of a threat assessment carried out by the protective team itself. For a small team that is already overstretched with its duties, however, subscribing to such a service can ease the burden of keeping current on threats around the world.

The US State Department also maintains a website (www.state.gov) where current information about threat levels in different countries is assembled. This site is quite useful, not only for information on terrorist and criminal activity, but also details of notable medical problems in specific countries.

THE VALUE OF CONTACTS
An invaluable resource is 'humint' (human intelligence) from contacts developed by members of the protective team on previous travels. Individuals working in law enforcement, private security, journalism or other professions likely to have a 'finger on the pulse' of their country can be invaluable, and can often supply timely information through a telephone call or an e-mail. Such sources can also be of immense help on the ground during an actual advance and VIP visit.

CITY AND COUNTRY FILES
Yet another valuable aid in carrying out preliminary work on an advance is a good file based on previous visits to cities or venues. A well organised city file can save many hours during the preparation work for an advance and also reduce the time an advance team will actually have to be on the ground. Such a file can be even more invaluable if a principal decides to visit a venue at the last minute, in which case the information already on file may be the only advance work available. I try to keep a preliminary advance file on every major city I visit, updating it on each visit or with information from friends who have recently escorted a principal there (see Appendix).

I have also found it useful to create a file on each country, which includes useful information on the geography, climate, politics, religion and culture. Not only does this aid the advance work, but it is also useful for briefing members of the protective team and/or the principal's party to help them avoid faux pas. For example, in my file

on operations in Japan or elsewhere with Japanese businessmen, I note that it is considered insulting to show the soles of one's shoes to a Japanese; hence, crossing one's legs in such a way that would present the bottom of the shoe should be avoided. I also note that bowing is an art, with great importance being attached to who bows the lowest; therefore, normally I recommend that members of the VIP party and protective team do not attempt to bow to their counterparts unless they are very cognisant of Japanese customs and nuances.

PAPERWORK

Many of the preliminary steps in advancing a visit will consist of dealing with paperwork. Laws regarding the carrying of weapons and required permits must be checked. Making sure that every team member and member of the principal's party has a valid passport and determining what visas are required are absolute necessities. Finding out if any special medical precautions are necessary, including vaccinations, carrying screened blood or arranging special medications can all be handled as part of the preliminary portion of the advance.

RESERVATIONS

Flight reservations can be made once it has been decided whether to travel with a commercial airline or in a chartered aircraft. Often, the principal will want to stay in a particular hotel. If so, reservations can be made and the principal's favourite suite, penthouse, etc, arranged. If the principal does not have a preferred hotel, the head of security/protection can choose, based on the principal's known tastes combined with security considerations. Normally, in the preliminary stages, the head of the protective effort will be required to submit a budget based on the number of protective personnel to be deployed.

AIRPORT SURVEY

Getting the principal into and out of airports quickly and safely is always an important consideration when travelling. As a result, a significant amount of advance work will concentrate on the airports to be visited. Basic information should be on file for the home airport and any airports visited frequently. For example, I keep a file in my computer on each major world airport, which includes such useful information as the distance from the city centre. However, although the length of the journey from the city centre will not change – unless a new airport is built – the travel time will differ, depending on construction work, traffic, time of day and other variables. Consequently, the advance team should travel the route to the hotel or other venue at approximately the time the principal will be making the drive to obtain a good idea of the travel time. Additionally, If the principal is to be transported by helicopter from the airport to a venue, the security of the heliport and the flying time should be evaluated by the advance team.

Normally, the evaluation of the airline and airport can be expedited by using check-lists (see Appendix), as will many other aspects of the advance. Diagrams showing the concourses and other major features of large airports are generally available. One of these should be used and coded with numbers and/or letters to coincide with notes in the advance check-list. Then VIP lounges, airport police, airport medical services, toilets, etc, can be quickly located. The advance team should also identify the fastest route to each applicable boarding area and walk that route. As part of the airport survey, it is useful to note the alertness of the security personnel operating metal detectors and working at check-points.

AIR MARSHALS

In the USA, advance work concerning air travel and airports can be made even more efficient if the team has a good contact among the FAA air marshals. Since they constantly monitor the safety of flights and airports, they can often pass useful information to a protective team. The air marshals also rate airports around the world for security, and these ratings can be an invaluable resource. In return, trained security personnel may be able to give their air marshal contact useful information from time to time.

EXAMPLE

A good example of the type of useful information that can be gleaned from an air marshal contact occurred a few years ago, when a friend of mine in FAA security and his partner stopped by to visit while I was waiting for an international flight at the airport where they were based. My friend noted the type of aircraft on which I was flying and mentioned that if there should be a fire to head for the emergency exits rapidly, as testing had shown this type of aircraft tended to burn relatively quickly. Needless to say, that point went into my computer for future reference.

CHARTERED AIRCRAFT

The pros and cons of using chartered aircraft will be discussed in a later chapter on VIP travel; however, if a chartered aircraft is being used, special consideration must be given to the advance work concerning the air carrier. The names of the pilots and their qualifications should be noted, as should the type of aircraft, its number of flying hours and the attention paid to scheduled maintenance. The aircraft's range is important if the flight will be a long one. It is useful, as well, to know how flexible the carrier will be with regard to arrival and departure times, and how completely the company can accommodate the principal's schedule. It will have to be determined from which airport the carrier flies and at which airport or airports at the destination it will be allowed to land.

THE ADVANCE TEAM

For visits to other cities or other countries, the advance team can be as small as one person, but for the best results, it should include at least one member of the protective team and one VIP driver. This will not only allow the coverage of different specialities, but it will also permit the advance team to split up to evaluate routes and venues most efficiently. If the personnel are available and the principal will be visiting several cities, it is often best to have two or more advance teams, which can leap-frog each other. The team that advances one city can wait for the arrival of the principal and the protective team, then use the knowledge they have gained of the city to function as the security advance party. This arrives at each venue ahead of the principal and gives the 'all clear' for the close-protection team to bring in the principal. Meanwhile, another team will be acting as the advance team for the next city to be visited. Once a visit is complete, the team that was in charge of advance work for that city can move on to another venue on the itinerary. This is a very efficient system, but it is manpower intensive and normally only viable with a large protective force.

SURVEYING ROUTES

Route surveys are important both for security and efficiency in getting the principal from place to place quickly. Not only should the advance-team driver survey primary routes from the airport to the hotel or venue, but also possible alternate routes. Notes should be kept on road construction, potential traffic bottlenecks and dangerous neighbourhoods. Once again, in the USA or other countries where such services as On Star are available, a vehicle monitoring system can often vector a driver around traffic jams or road construction work. Also in the United States,

the computer program Road Atlas, USA has a Global Positioning System (GPS) link, which will actually superimpose one's movement on a map on the computer screen. This is a great aid for route planning and generating maps for the protective team, since the locations of hospitals, etc, can be added to the maps, as can potential block points.

Each route survey should include information on the nearest hospital with an accident and emergency department at each point along the route and also the nearest 'safe haven', whether it be a police station, an embassy, a military base or a secured residence. Radio checks must be carried out as well, to determine whether any 'dead spots' exist along the route. The VIP driver or the bodyguard carrying out the advance should examine routes for potential ambush points and note any areas that would seem to offer particular danger. Once again, a good check-list, will allow this aspect of the advance work to be completed expediently (see Appendix).

EVALUATE HOTELS

Once routes have been checked, or simultaneously if a driver is carrying out that part of the advance work, hotels and other venues can be visited. When evaluating hotels, it is advisable to have at least two or three acceptable choices, although the principal may have a strong preference for only one.

Some protective teams like to make reservations at more than one hotel and only confirm the establishment they will actually use at the last minute. Some hotels are especially conducive to VIP visits, having one or more floors

AUTHOR'S NOTE

The Sultan of Brunei has been known to purchase hotels he likes to make sure their standards remain high!

designed with security in mind, with controlled access, electronic security systems and other amenities to make the bodyguard's job easier.

SUITE AND FLOOR

When selecting a suite for the VIP, the advance team will need to consider the optimum floor. Normally, the fifth, sixth and seventh floors make a sound choice, as they are high enough to prevent objects thrown from the street from entering the room, yet low enough to allow relatively easy evacuation in case of fire; even in very large cities, fire-engine ladders cannot usually reach above the seventh or eighth floor. The advance team will also want to select a suite that allows them to take the rooms on each side for the protective team and across the corridor for the command post.

EXITS

The advance team will pay particular attention to the number of exits from the hotel, noting which offer the greatest degree of privacy.

If there is a relatively private exit that allows the principal to be picked up by a limo, that is even better. In some cases, underground garages allow transfer directly from a lift. Speaking of lifts, the advance team will pay particular attention to the hotel lifts to determine their capacity, travel time between floors, privacy, etc. If suites are available with private lifts, these are preferable.

AUTHOR'S NOTE

I once guarded a principal in Amsterdam who liked to visit the Red Light District, so we chose a hotel with a small exit that allowed quick access to 'window shopping' Dutch style.

DINING

The advance team will also look closely at the restaurant facilities and room-service menus in the hotel. Normally, a restaurant in the hotel is desirable, since it will preclude the need for travel to another venue for meals. Even when the VIP is dining at events or outside restaurants, the hotel restaurants and, especially, the room-service menu are important, as often these will offer the only opportunities for those on the protective team to obtain meals. A fitness centre in the hotel is also valuable for members of the protective team, who must grab chances to stay in shape whenever they are presented.

HOTEL SURROUNDINGS

The advance team will pay particular attention to the area around the hotel. In some cities, even the most luxurious hotels are located in areas where crime is relatively high. Therefore, secure parking is of the utmost importance. In many cases, there will be a few prime parking spaces right in front of the hotel, which are under the purview of the doorman. A substantial gratuity will usually assure one of these spaces as well as encourage the doormen to keep a close eye on the vehicle to ensure that no one tampers with it. By the way, I advise passing out gratuities during the advance to let hotel staff know that their co-operation during the actual visit will be well appreciated.

HOTEL SECURITY DIRECTOR

Good relations should be established with the hotel security director during an advance, and discussions should take place about the function his security personnel will have in any protective effort. Generally, their responsibility is for the hotel as a whole, but they make an excellent adjunct because they know the hotel well and can normally recognise who does and does not belong. The head of security may also be able to let the advance team know if any other dignitaries will be staying at the same time who may attract attention and may also have a protective team. In addition, he will know of any events scheduled at the hotel that will attract undue attention or large numbers of visitors during the principal's visit.

SAFETY SURVEY

The advance team will want to carry out a safety survey of the hotel during their initial visit. The presence of fire extinguishers and fire hoses should be noted, as should evacuation routes. The team can verify that smoke detectors are operational and also that there are no obvious fire hazards, such as exposed wiring.

AUTHOR'S NOTE

On one advance to New York, we were planning a one-night stay at a very well-known hotel near JFK Airport, prior to catching the morning Concorde flight. However, we found that the building's wiring was in such atrocious shape that we opted for a hotel farther away from the airport.

In many cases, if a minor safety problem is noted, a comment to the security director or assistant manager will normally ensure that it is fixed quickly.

CHECK OUTSIDE

The advance team will want to inspect any balconies to see if they allow access to the room from a point not controlled by the protective team. Nearby buildings should also be evaluated to determine if they offer a shooting position for a sniper or a perch for *paparazzi*. In many cities, too, one side of a hotel will be much less subject to street or construction noise than another. If the choice of the quietest location does not compromise security in other ways, this should also be considered.

HOTEL STAFF AND GUESTS

In addition to an advance check-list (see Appendix), the advance team will need to assemble hotel plans, restaurant and room-service menus, radio frequencies that may be used, the locations of vendors of any equipment or material that will be acquired locally and, if possible, a photo file of hotel personnel who will have access to the floor where the principal will stay.

If possible, discussions should be held with the hotel security head to determine whether security checks have been carried out on hotel personnel,

and to arrange for staff who have been with the hotel for some time and who have proved themselves to be assigned to the principal's floor. Once again, gratuities can help assure co-operation from staff.

If your principal has enough political clout, it may be possible to obtain a list of hotel guests who will be staying on the same floor, and perhaps the floors above and below, so that they may be vetted as well. However, this may not be possible. If the VIP party with staff and protective team is large enough, it may be advisable to reserve an entire corridor to be sure of those located in rooms near the principal.

RESTAURANTS

Once the hotel has been checked out, other venues to be visited by the principal should be evaluated. In the case of restaurants, if the principal is familiar with the city, he or she may have one or two favourite establishments that will have been advanced already. In this case, it may only be necessary to make a quick update of the data on file. In many cases, though, it will be necessary to carry out a full advance of a restaurant.

When a restaurant is being evaluated, the advance team or, if the restaurant is a relatively last-minute choice, the security advance party will be concerned with the following questions:

1 Is secure parking available?

2 Are there private dining areas?

3 Will it be possible to position the principal away from windows looking on to the street?

4 Can the VIP party be placed in a corner or private room where other patrons will not need to approach them?

5 Can arrangements be made for the protective team to occupy tables around the VIP party?

6 Can the VIP be quickly evacuated from the restaurant if necessary?

ACCESS

Special attention must be paid to the ease of entering and leaving the restaurant. In many cases, restaurants where access is somewhat difficult have the advantage of being easy to secure. However, they may not lend themselves to rapid evacuation of the principal.

EXAMPLE

A good example of a restaurant that is easily secured, but difficult to evacuate is The Pearl, generally conceded to be the best restaurant in Reykjavik, Iceland. One or two men would have no trouble in guarding access to this revolving restaurant, located atop the city's fresh-water tanks, but it would be very difficult to get out quickly in an emergency.

Fortunately, many top-notch restaurants make privacy part of their service, which simplifies the job of the protective team.

DINING

Most chefs will not like the idea of a bodyguard being posted to watch them work. As a result, those who fear poisoning will arrange for one member of the protective team or VIP party to order for everyone so that the waiter does not know in advance who will receive which meal.

Frequently, the protective team will not dine at the restaurant, but if they will be dining, advance arrangements should be made for them to be served quickly so that they can stay at least one course ahead of the VIP party and be ready to leave quickly.

ENSURING CO-OPERATION

A substantial gratuity to the manager or head waiter when carrying out the advance check will help ensure co-operation during the actual visit. As with other aspects of an advance, a check-list will prove a great time saver (see Appendix).

EXAMPLE

Sometimes a survey of a restaurant or other venue will suggest that there are pros and cons to its use, which will affect a visit. For example, when I was advancing a visit to St Petersburg, one restaurant under consideration for a high-level business meeting was a faux hunting lodge on the outskirts of the city. It was very private because of its location, and approaching traffic could be monitored easily. On the other hand, assassinations and kidnappings in Russia may well be carried out by heavily armed Russian criminals, and this venue lent itself to an ambush or assault. Complicating matters, on the night I visited the restaurant, one of the private dining rooms appeared to be hosting a group that had the strong appearance of being Russian organised-crime figures. Since they had a substantial number of security men posted, I did get a chance to see how the locals 'secured' the location. On balance, although I liked the restaurant, I felt that there were too many question marks attached to it, so I vetoed it.

OTHER VENUES

A VIP visit will probably entail visits to other sites. The principal may attend a sporting event, theatrical performance or building dedication. He or she may be in town for a speaking engagement, political rally or business meeting. Whatever the reasons for these appearances, an advance survey will need to be carried out. In the case of sporting events or entertainment, the advance team will be particularly concerned with the security of seating arrangements, the block booking of seats around the principal for entourage and security personnel, quickest methods of entry and exit, and the location of a private area where the principal can escape the crowds during the intermission or other breaks. Where speaking engagements are involved, the advance team will evaluate the location of the speaking platform to determine what security concerns there may be.

OUTDOOR ENGAGEMENTS

If the principal will be speaking outside, or otherwise appearing in the open, the advance team will look very closely at the positioning of the speaking platform, VIP grandstand, etc, and the survey will be extended to cover nearby buildings that could conceal a sniper. Frequently, simply moving a platform slightly will interpose a building or terrain to prevent a possible sniper shot. If a counter-sniper team is to be deployed, the advance team will also determine the best point for it to dominate any potential sniping positions. For more details, see the site survey check-list in the Appendix.

RECEIVING LINE

In any type of appearance where the principal will be greeting large numbers of people, the advance team will need to determine the best site for a receiving line and also whether it is practical to set up portal magnetometers, through which the crowd must pass.

CHECK FOR EXPLOSIVES

For any type of visit, if the principal is a potential assassination target, arrangements should be made during the advance for explosives sniffer dogs to clear the venue. At this point, the advance team may well liaise with local police or military bomb-disposal personnel.

IDENTIFICATION PROCEDURES

As part of an advance, arrangements will often be made for identification procedures to be in place during the VIP visit. The specifics of ID badges will be discussed later, but decisions about who will need such badges should be made during the advance. Distribution of the ID badges, however, should be delayed to as close to the VIP visit as possible to reduce the possibility of one being lost, stolen or copied.

GAINING CO-OPERATION

The advance team will also want to emphasise to those representing any sites to be visited that confidentiality regarding specific details of the VIP appearance is very important. Good advance team members can make those with whom they deal feel important and 'part of the team', thus gaining co-operation and confidentiality.

OTHER CONSIDERATIONS

Parking, and routes into and out of the venue will be surveyed and timed. Members of the advance team will also note points where fixed-post security, either local police or private security guards, should be stationed. In addition, the advance team will look for the best places to locate a command post and a safe room in case the principal has to be evacuated within the site. Among other items of interest are the availability of emergency lighting in case of power failure, location of fire extinguishers and hoses, presence of clutter blocking any doors, sanitary condition of any food preparation areas if a banquet is being held, location of toilets, especially private ones, and myriad other small details that could affect the principal's comfort or safety.

MAXIMISING DATA

It is a given that the advance team will be unlikely to obtain all of the information or make all of the contacts that they would desire. For example, it is unlikely that any but a national dignitary protection team – such as the US Secret Service – will be able to obtain complete guest lists and employee lists for events, sites or hotels, then run a security check on everyone on the list. Even so, an advance team should attempt to secure such lists if possible.

In some cases, subterfuge may work. For example, a guest list may be requested 'so that the principal can study it to be sure he greets everyone of note'. Similarly, an employee list may be sought so that 'the principal can be sure everyone who helped make his visit a success receives thanks'. Whatever means are used to obtain such lists, even a small team can take a look for any known threats and perhaps check out anyone who seems to be a potential danger.

Members of the advance team should accumulate as much information as possible, including maps, diagrams, schedules and anything that may help them prepare their advance survey. Each evening, in their hotel or on their flight, the members of the advance team can sift data and incorporate it into materials that will be used for planning the visit, and for briefing the protective team and, eventually, the principal.

SECURITY ADVANCE PARTY

As has been mentioned already, in some cases, the advance team will function as the security advance party once the principal arrives in the city they have advanced. If this is the case, they will move ahead of the principal, along the route he or she will take, so that they can alert the VIP motorcade to any traffic difficulties, accidents or potential security problems.

At each site to be visited, the security advance party will arrive sufficiently early to make a quick check that preparations are in order for the principal's arrival and that security has not been breached. Normally, at least one member of the

SAP will wait on the kerb to let the protective team know that all is secure for the visit. The SAP will also have maintained radio contact with the head of the protective team and/or the command post to advise of their progress ahead of the principal.

It should be noted that the security advance party will carry out its mission while keeping as low a profile as possible so that it does not telegraph the impending arrival of the VIP.

ATTENTION TO DETAIL

The successful completion of an advance for a VIP visit requires personnel who pay attention to detail, since there are myriad details to consider. Many protective teams, however, like to rotate the assignment so that each member of the team gains experience in this task. By varying the routine in this way, personnel will remain sharp and become more versatile through having performed a variety of functions. It is important, though, that anyone chosen to carry out the advance be utterly reliable, highly organised and very diplomatic. The last skill is particularly important, since members of the advance team must be willing to assert themselves to achieve their goals, yet must be able to work with the diverse people who will contribute to a VIP visit. Any team member who does not have these characteristics should not be assigned to an advance team.

A substantial contribution to the success of VIP travel is made by those who advance the visit. A good advance team and security advance party can help implement a dictum that holds particularly true in VIP protection – a problem anticipated and avoided is much better than a problem solved!

CHAPTER 5

AREA SECURITY PROCEDURES

Whenever the principal remains in one location, the protective team has to undertake measures to prevent an attacker from taking advantage of the fact that the target is at a known point. When putting area security procedures into effect, the protective team wants to maximise protection while minimising disruption of the principal's lifestyle. In many cases, because cost is a factor in determining the extent of a protective effort, it will be necessary to strike a balance between a maximum effort involving extensive electronic security assets and a massive allocation of manpower, and the best protection possible within the principal's budget.

DEFENCE IN DEPTH

Since not only the principal, but also his or her family, will use their residence as a safe haven, substantial precautions must be taken in protecting the principal's home. The type of area security plan put into effect will vary substantially, however, depending on whether the principal lives in an urban penthouse or town house, a suburban estate, or a country house or farm. That said, certain basic precepts do apply. The security team will try to establish a defence in depth, which will give them early warning of an intrusion and allow time to react.

Normally, residence security systems are designed to perform four basic functions:

1 Deter an intruder because of obvious hardened approaches and surveillance systems.

2 Prevent an attack by stopping intruders at the perimeter.

3 Give early warning of an attempted intrusion.

4 Slow an intruder to allow a response from security personnel.

PERIMETER BARRIERS

The first actual tier of physical security will normally be a wall or fence around the VIP residence. Even in the case of town houses, it is usually possible to incorporate some type of barrier between the street and the actual house, although not always. When this is not possible, hardening windows and doors becomes even more critical than usual, an aspect of security that will be discussed later. Obviously, where a large country estate or farm is concerned, it would be very difficult to incorporate a security barrier around the entire property. There may, of course, be fences to keep in livestock, but not normal security fencing. The best method in dealing with a very large property is to establish a small walled or fenced area within it.

TYPES OF BARRIER
When enclosing an area, there are advantages to both masonry walls and chain-link or wrought-iron fences. Walls grant privacy and prevent outsiders from seeing into the property. They also make it more difficult for security personnel to see out; however, closed-circuit television (CCTV) cameras located strategically can alleviate this problem. If a chain-link or wrought-iron fence is used, security lighting facing outward can blind anyone attempting to see into the property at night and also help expose anyone lurking near the fence.

Whether a fence or a wall is chosen, it should be sufficiently high that it cannot be scaled easily.

Generally, eight feet is considered the minimum desirable height, although some security professionals opt for an even greater height. Whether a fence or wall, the barrier should also be topped with razor wire, overhanging steel spikes or some other deterrent to climbing. Y-topped arms or a top guard with a forty-five-degree overhang generally work best. Razor wire or other types of barbed wire can be attached to these to make climbing extremely difficult. Note, however, that tests have shown that even the best barriers will only slow down a determined, trained intruder. That's why perimeter barriers must be supplemented with lighting, intrusion-detection systems, dogs and armed patrols.

AUTHOR'S NOTE

One situation that I have encountered when hardening security at a property is local planning rules that regulate the type of wall or fence. On the property where we were working, visible chain-link fencing and razor wire were not allowed. The property was already enclosed by a six-foot brick wall, so we decided that the most effective way of dealing with the situation was to add spikes to the top of the wall, then build a chain-link fence, eight feet high and topped with razor wire, eight feet inside the wall. Security lighting was installed to illuminate the fence and wall, the latter being painted white on the inside to silhouette any intruder.

I should note that the property concerned was large enough that losing an eight-foot strip of ground around the perimeter was not considered an issue. Moreover, the principal had already survived more than one assassination attempt and was attuned to stringent security precautions.

At one point, we considered spreading sand between the two fences so that any intruder's footprints would be visible, but instead opted for grass. We also patrolled periodically between the two fences with guard dogs.

ELECTRONIC INTRUSION DETECTORS

Intrusion-detection systems of various types should be combined with perimeter barriers. I've already mentioned CCTV. Very compact CCTV cameras are now available in sturdy weatherproof casings, which may be located at critical points around the outside and inside of any perimeter wall or fence. To preclude the need for constant monitoring, these cameras may be combined with a system that actually detects motion, often through a change in the pattern of light and dark on the screen, to alert security personnel monitoring the cameras. Since a large property may well need dozens of cameras, a system that will switch immediately to any camera where motion has been detected will be invaluable.

I also recommend that the CCTV system be combined with a recorder so that the image of anyone showing up on the CCTV can be pulled for further analysis and identification.

MOVEMENT DETECTORS

In addition to CCTV, the electronic security perimeter may include seismic detectors attached to fences to warn of anyone trying to climb them. The sensitivity level of these detectors can be adjusted so that small birds or the action of wind will not set them off.

Seismic or weight sensors can be buried in the ground at critical points to detect movement in that area. Again, sensitivity can be adjusted to prevent small animals from setting off alarms. Infra-red or other detection systems may also be placed inside fences or walls to alert security personnel to anyone who has penetrated the barrier.

Those designing an intrusion-detection system have a wide range of sensing methods from which to choose, including:

- breaking an electrical circuit;
- breaking a light or microwave beam;

- detecting sound;
- detecting vibration;
- detecting motion;
- detecting a change in an electric or a magnetic field;
- CCTV.

Normally, a combination of these systems will prove ideal for each specific area to be protected. Any entrances that allow access through the outer barrier may be wired with alarm systems as well to ensure continuity of protection.

MONITORING THE SYSTEM

To utilise an extensive detection system effectively, at least one member of the security team on each shift should be assigned to the screens and monitors in the command post. Actually, to help keep the person monitoring the security systems alert, and to give those who carry out mobile security around a property a chance to come in from the weather, I like to rotate this job so that the person assigned to the central monitoring station only has to do a two-hour shift.

KEEP ABREAST OF DEVELOPMENTS

I should also note at this point that unless a protective team is large enough to have one or more full-time electronic security specialists, those engaged in VIP protection will not normally have the time to stay completely cognisant of the latest advances in intruder detection systems. Nevertheless, they should certainly attempt to keep abreast of the basics of new systems so that they have an idea of what will be most effective when hardening a property. For example, reading the publications of the American Society for Industrial Security or similar professional journals will normally give those in VIP protection a good basic knowledge of innovations. It is important, however, to cultivate contacts who specialise in electronic security and who can be brought in to advise on the technical specifications and installation of intruder detection systems.

GATES

In addition to walls or fences and intruder detection systems, the perimeter around a property will require one or more gates designed with security in mind. I used to believe that a property needed at least two gates, to provide an emergency escape route should an attempt to breach the main gate be under way; however, I have concluded since that one secure gate is better, as two gates double the security problems, especially because it is best if a gate-house is manned around the clock. Indeed, if an attempt is made to breach the gate, the security team should receive enough warning to take the principal and family to the most secure location in the residence and to prepare a warm reception for any attackers.

THE GATE-HOUSE

As already stated, it is best if there is a gate-house, which should have tinted windows so that anyone approaching the gate cannot determine the number or location of security personnel within the structure. Normally, the security staff assigned to the gate will have a list of any expected visitors and will check each vehicle arriving – whether guests, service personnel, mail or other callers – against this list. Only when the gate security team is satisfied that a caller has a valid reason for entry will they be admitted. Normally, no vehicle should be allowed to enter without being assigned a member of the security team to accompany it. If roving security patrols are on the property, one of them can be summoned to escort those admitted to the residence. Service personnel, delivery-men, etc, may then be handed over to security personnel at the residence.

REMOTE OPENING

The gate should be as sturdy as possible to resist ramming, yet still allow opening remotely. In addition to the ability to open and close the gate from the gate-house, there should be controls in the command post in case a situation arises where the gate-house is unmanned for a time or for other contingencies. CCTV monitors for those cameras covering the gate and area around it should be located in the gate-house.

CRASH BARRIER

As a back-up to the gate in case someone does attempt to drive through it, a crash barrier that can be lowered remotely may also be installed inside the gate. Alternatively, a decorative concrete planter, which blocks the road and must be driven around very slowly, may be positioned just inside the gate to slow or stop a crash vehicle. Even more effective are tyre-slashing spikes, which can be raised and lowered from the gate-house. If such spikes are left in the raised position whenever the gate is closed, they will prove an excellent deterrent to a vehicle attempting to crash through the gate. If a more subtle approach is desired, the driveway can be constructed so that there is a very sharp bend immediately after the gate, thus slowing any vehicle that makes it through.

ARMED RESPONSE

Some security teams in very high-threat circumstances deploy a sniper with a .50-calibre sniping rifle or, in some circumstances, a belt-fed machine-gun to disable any vehicle that attempts to crash through a gate. Certainly, the gate guard or guards should have access to an assault rifle of .308 calibre loaded with armour-piercing/tracer bullets to stop a vehicle that attempts to ram the gate.

PREPARATION OF GARDENS

Within the barriers and intrusion-detection systems around the perimeter of a hardened property, security is often supplemented by mobile patrols, often with dogs, and CCTV cameras. Most principals will not want their property denuded of trees, shrubbery, flowers and other flora for security purposes; hence, a certain amount of co-operation with the gardener will usually be necessary when implementing security procedures. It is particularly important to ensure that the gardener is aware of the location of underground cables and other components of the security system that might be cut or disrupted by his activities.

DEAD GROUND

Between the perimeter and the residence, at least some areas should be laid out as dead ground, with an expanse of open lawn, which any intruder who made it past the perimeter systems would have to cross. These areas may be lit or covered by infra-red or other low-light television cameras. Security concerns usually dictate, also, that any shrubbery is cleared from close proximity to the residence. However, where a property is located in a heavily populated area, it may be necessary to use shrubbery to hide some of the security measures. In this case, shrubs with thorns, which themselves act as an intrusion deterrent, should be considered.

SECURITY LIGHTING

Many security systems also incorporate lighting that illuminates the sides of the residence so that anyone attempting surreptitious entry will be silhouetted against the walls, which are often painted in light colours to make concealment in shadows more difficult.

There are three possible methods of handling security lighting around the house:

1 Lights can be on at all times during the hours of darkness to identify any intruder.

2 Lights can be off, but controlled by motion

sensors that will switch the lights on if any movement is detected near the house.

3 A combination may be used whereby some lights around the house are on all night, while others are linked to motion detectors and will only come on if an intruder enters the area they cover.

Note that security lighting and other security systems should have all wiring underground so that it cannot be cut easily. Fuse or switch boxes should also be of sturdy construction and locked to prevent tampering. A back-up generator, which comes on automatically during a power failure, is also highly desirable.

WATERSIDE PROPERTIES

If the property fronts on to a lake or the sea, additional security concerns arise. It may be necessary to put lighting beneath the water near the house to pick out any swimmers approaching, although in many cases lights that illuminate the water and the points of possible egress from above will suffice. Intrusion-detection devices will also have to be placed at the point where a swimmer would leave the water as well. In very high-security situations, additional personnel assigned to boat patrols might be necessary.

MOBILE PATROLS

Depending on the manpower available, there may be roving foot patrols with dogs, a mobile patrol in a vehicle that constantly cruises the estate, frequently stopping to check wooded areas, or a combination of the two. I've generally found the best system is to have one or more foot patrols with dogs, backed up by a mobile response team in a vehicle, which can assist the foot patrols, the gate guards or be dispatched wherever needed. The mobile team can also augment the security force on duty inside the residence.

URBAN CONSIDERATIONS

When guarding the perimeter and approaches to an urban property, a protective team will have much greater difficulty in preparing a defence in depth. However, some type of fencing or wall should still be incorporated, as should a sturdy gate. Intrusion-detection systems may also be installed, although if the residence is located on a busy street, many types will be difficult to employ due to the close proximity of traffic.

THE IDEAL PROPERTY

If the security team has any input in the purchase of an urban property, one on a dead-end street – preferably at the end – which will limit passing traffic is desirable, not only because of the effect heavy traffic may have on electronic security systems, but also because it will simplify the task of monitoring those who approach the residence.

GUARDS AND PATROLS

Since urban residences will often back on to an alley, which allows passers-by to approach very close to the house, some type of fixed guard post or roving patrol may be necessary. Actually, on country properties and in some urban areas, bicycle patrols have proved quite effective, as they allow the security team to move quickly and very quietly around the area they patrol.

PREPARATION OF THE RESIDENCE

The construction of the residence is of prime importance where security is concerned. Brick or stone construction makes it more difficult to shoot into a building and provides good resistance to blast. Doors should be very sturdy; in fact, steel-core doors are most desirable. They should be kept locked at all times – day and night. Windows should be fitted with bullet- and blast-resistant glass. Certainly in an urban property located near the street, and possibly even in a country residence in the middle of a large estate, windows and doors should be barred. Decorative ornate bars are available that actually will enhance the look of the residence, while making entry much more difficult. Basement windows, garage windows and others that provide access to areas of the residence that are often deserted must be barred.

ELECTRONIC SYSTEMS

Windows and doors will be wired for intrusion alarms, and, most probably, there will be additional interior intrusion-detection systems, including CCTV. However, during the day, when the principal, family, guests, staff and security personnel will be moving about, many interior systems will be turned off.

CURTAINS

Also during the day, windows should be shielded by curtains that admit light, but do not allow an outsider to see into the rooms. Heavier curtains, which do not allow the silhouette of anyone inside to be seen, should be provided for use at night.

ACCOMMODATION

Although the number of floors in a VIP residence will vary, a general rule of thumb is that the ground floor is not used for sleeping quarters, and that only on-duty security personnel will occupy that floor at night. Normally, guest rooms will be on the second floor, while the principal and family will have their quarters on the third floor. Staff will be on the top floor or, in some cases, in an adjacent building. I have also seen some country estates where a coach house has been used as the command post for the security team and, perhaps, sleeping quarters for off-duty, but standby, protective personnel.

ENTRY TO VIP SUITE

Access to the VIP family suite should be very restricted, with only trusted personal staff being allowed to enter. Frequently, if the layout of the residence allows it, a bodyguard will be stationed at the entrance to the VIP suite whenever the family is present. Normally, too, when guests are at the residence, unless instructed otherwise by the principal, they will not have access to all parts of the house, particularly the VIP family suite.

SAFE ROOM

Within the VIP suite, there will often be a 'safe room', which offers a refuge should the residence come under attack. It should be relatively small, have no windows, and feature bullet- and blast-resistant walls. The safe room should contain a phone, first-aid materials and, if the principal is trained in the use of firearms, a weapon.

Many safe rooms are actually constructed in bathrooms, since water and sanitary facilities will already be in place. Some safe rooms can also be sealed against gas, being provided with their own oxygen supply.

The theory behind the safe room is that it offers a retreat for the principal and family in the event of a concerted attack and, in a worse-case scenario, provides a refuge until reinforcements can arrive should the security team be overwhelmed.

COMMUNICATIONS

Within the residence, all phones should be programmed so that police, fire and ambulance services are on speed dial. Telephones should be positioned so that they are not directly in front of windows. Additionally, in case phone lines are cut, the principal and family members should have mobile phones, as should members of the protective team. At critical points throughout the residence, telephones on direct lines to the command post should be located. There may also be 'panic buttons' hidden around the residence.

When activated, these will alert the security team, either silently or with a loud alarm, of a problem in a specific part of the residence.

DAY-TO-DAY CONCERNS

Various administrative details relating to day-to-day activities at the residence should be evaluated by the protection team, and the staff should be briefed on correct procedures. For example, they should be instructed to watch for strangers and suspicious activity around the residence, and immediately to alert a member of the protective team if anything is spotted. A system for receiving mail and packages should be implemented so that first they go through the command post for security screening before being delivered to the principal or family. Staff should also be instructed to be careful about what is thrown out as rubbish. All papers relating to the principal's schedule, business, leisure activities or any other aspects of his or her lifestyle should be shredded.

ELECTRONIC SECURITY CHECKS

As part of information security, electronic countermeasures specialists should be brought in periodically, unless the team is large enough to have its own expert. During such sweeps, checks should be made for 'bugs' in telephones and fax machines, for listening devices planted around the residence, for possible eavesdropping from outside the residence and for computer security. A good electronic countermeasures specialist will also advise on steps to update secure phones, fax machines, computers, etc. Mobile phones, although very handy, cannot be considered secure. As a result, the principal and family members should be aware that anything they say on a mobile phone may be intercepted.

As with many other aspects of security, electronic countermeasures is a speciality that requires constant training to keep up with developments in the field. Consequently, I recommend that a protective team develop contacts with such specialists in areas where their principal spends substantial amounts of time.

To give an idea of how complex an electronic security check can be, one service that I've used normally carries out an 18-part technical countermeasures survey. Among the checks made during this survey are:

- a free air radio frequency analysis;
- a test for audio emissions through doors, walls, ceilings, etc;
- a physical examination of all telephone cables to look for tie-in connections or taps;
- the location of all possible listening posts near sensitive areas and searching them for recording devices, etc;
- an evaluation of the probability of an infra-red light or laser carrier for an audio pick-up;
- a test of all electrical outlets in sensitive areas for eavesdropping devices, as well as numerous other steps, including a thorough examination of walls, light fixtures, furniture and virtually everything in the sensitive areas.

Where communications security is concerned, members of protective teams should also consider the following:

- baby monitor transmissions can normally be picked up outside a residence and used for eavesdropping;
- pager messages can be intercepted – the use of a digital PCS phone with built-in pager is more secure, but not totally so;
- other encrypted mobile phone and/or pager systems are available;
- computer communications can be encrypted using PGP (Pretty Good Privacy);
- devices such as MicroSpy can be attached to

computers to 'steal' everything that is typed into them;

- residences with cable television will often still have an unused aerial on the roof. This should be removed, as it can be utilised by anyone attempting to eavesdrop on the residence;
- plan to counter 'phone phreakers', the telephone equivalent of computer 'hackers';
- 'bug' detectors offer various levels of sophistication and require different amounts of training. Normally, transmitter detectors are easiest to learn to use;
- default passwords should be changed on all voice-mail systems, answering machines, etc;
- faxes may be intercepted;
- Motorola offers 'secure' mobile phones, but even these are not totally secure.

FIRE DRILL

The security team, the principal and family, and the household staff should all be familiar with procedures in case of fire. Evacuation plans should be practised, and members of the security team should be familiar with the location of fire extinguishers and hoses. The importance of fire prevention and contingency planning cannot be overemphasised. A substantial number of those working in VIP protection have saved a principal and/or family from fire, since they are on duty 24 hours a day and are trained to watch for anything out of the ordinary.

PERMANENT SECURITY STAFF

Even if the principal is not present at the residence, it is important to maintain at least a skeleton security staff at all times. Many protective teams have a full-time staff assigned permanently to the residence. When the principal is at home, this staff is augmented by members of the close-protection team, who take on the duties necessitated by the higher threat level when the principal is in residence. Any leave time owed to personnel on the residence security staff should be scheduled during periods when the principal is not present, but normally I would recommend that at least two or three personnel remain on duty during each shift at a country estate, and one or two at a house in town. Generally, there will also be some household staff and/or caretakers permanently assigned to a residence, who can provide eyes and ears to back up the security team when the principal is not at home.

OTHER RESIDENCES

Many additional problems arise if the principal is staying at the residence of a friend, or political or business associate. In some cases, this could be even more secure than the principal's home – if, for example, it is an embassy or military installation that has extensive security precautions in effect. More likely, however, will be a stay at a private home. One of the first questions the protective team will want answered is what type of security is in effect at the residence where their principal will be staying. If the owner has his or her own protective team, some of the perimeter security duties will fall to them. However, it must be borne in mind that the primary concern of that team will be their own employer. Most likely, however, they will be willing to work with a protective team accompanying a visitor.

Usually, a well-trained team can evaluate the skills of another by observing their demeanour, dress and methods of operation. The world of close protection is small enough, too, that I can usually call an aquaintance who will know the head of a protective team with which I might be working and get a quick evaluation of his competence.

Assuming that a resident team is in place, has already run security checks on the staff and has established contacts with the local police, the prime concern of a visiting team will be to check the quarters assigned to their principal and family, and to decide how they can provide security specifically for them. It will also be important to determine where members of the protective team will stay.

PORTABLE SECURITY SYSTEMS

If there are no resident security staff, perimeter and close security will have to be handled by the protective team travelling with the principal. Portable intrusion-detection systems are available and may be quickly installed during such visits. For example, very compact systems exist that may be carried in a briefcase, yet incorporate a combination of magnetic, infra-red and pressure detectors, as well as a panic button for the principal. The briefcase may also contain a monitor, or the information can be fed to a lap-top computer. All of the sensors/detectors are wireless and may be placed around the VIP suite in minutes.

A similar system exists for use outdoors around a temporary residence and utilises passive motion detection sensors. Again, signals can be sent to a briefcase monitor, to a lap-top computer or to pagers worn by members of the protective team. Very compact CCTV cameras are available as well, and can be monitored through a lap-top computer or a dedicated compact monitor.

As electronic equipment continues to become more compact, it is safe to assume that portable intrusion-detection systems will follow suit, a real boon for those in VIP protection.

PERMANENT SECURITY

If the principal will visit the same residence frequently, as in the case of a relative or close friend, it might be worthwhile to work with the owner of the property to install alarms, lighting, and CCTV on a permanent basis. In general, too, any perimeter security effort will need to keep a relatively low profile so as not to draw attention to the owner of the residence or the visiting principal.

HOTELS

Another situation in which a protective team will have to provide extensive area security is when a principal is travelling and stays at a hotel. Normally, unless the visit is a result of a last-minute decision or the team is so short-handed that a proper advance could not be made, the advance team should have arranged for most special needs and selected the best rooms possible based on security considerations. Note that the best rooms from a security standpoint may not be the best rooms in the hotel, and this may be a matter for discussion with the principal, especially since many of those who can afford a protective team have extensive travel experience, and have favourite hotels and preferred suites in many cities.

On the positive side, many of the world's most luxurious hotels have a great deal of experience in catering for clients who travel with security teams. As a result, normally they will be able to anticipate many of the requirements of a protective team and have their own security personnel who will be used to working with bodyguards. This makes the job of the protective team much easier.

CCTV

Many top hotels also have a VIP floor or even a special security floor, where access is limited and security hardware – such as CCTV in the corridors – is already in place. Note that most hotels with a professional security staff retain tapes from the CCTV system for a period of time. As a result, if there is any suspicion that the principal is being stalked or watched, a member of the protective team can examine those tapes for evidence.

A large number of hotels now have time-lapse VCRs, which allow the exact time a person enters a specific area to be identified. This can be invaluable if it is suspected that attempts have been made to tamper with vehicles or rooms, since anyone entering the relevant area at the appropriate time can be identified.

LOGICAL CHOICE

Some establishments even have what is, in effect, a super luxury hotel within a hotel, where security is much tighter. Some of the 'high roller' accommodation in Las Vegas, for example, is much easier to secure than the general hotel. As a rule, if such a VIP facility is available, it will be the logical choice for housing a principal.

SECURING THE LOBBY

By their very nature, hotels do not lend themselves to a secure 'outer perimeter', as there will be constant traffic through the lobbies. Depending on the size of the protective team, different approaches are taken to security in the lobby. Many teams will not station any personnel in the lobby until just before the principal passes through. Frequently, offering substantial gratuities to the head porter and concierge will give them an incentive to act as an early warning of anything in the lobby that might be of interest to the protective team. In fact, I advise that the head of the protective team tips key hotel employees upon arrival as a gesture of good faith and tips them again upon leaving. This will ensure that staff not only act as part of the 'intelligence net' for the protective team, but also that they give good service and help out with matters that may arise – for example, suits belonging to members of the protective team needing quick repairs, or extending room-service hours so that members of the team who had to miss dinner can be served.

Another approach to lobby security is to post a member of the protective team to watch for anyone entering who appears to be a potential problem. In my experience, however, this is usually a waste of manpower. That said, I have found that on a lot of hotel protective jobs, off-duty personnel like to relax in the lobby, where they can watch the world go by. Even though they're off duty, any personnel in the lobby will still note anything suspicious and contact the command post.

PRIVATE LIFTS

A further option in regards to the lobby arises if the VIP is in a penthouse or another suite served by a private lift. In this case, it is often advisable to post a team member at the lift, and sometimes it is a good idea to dress this bodyguard as a member of the hotel staff to blend in. The downside is that the individual is more likely to be approached by hotel patrons if he or she appears to work for the hotel. Note, however, that this precaution is not so necessary as in the past, since many private lifts may now be locked out on the floor where the suite or penthouse is located, and will only be sent after it has been ascertained who has summoned the lift.

KEY CARDS

In many better hotels, lifts and stairway doors will only allow access to areas for which the key card being used is authorised. Since situations may arise where members of the protective team may have to quickly access other floors during an evacuation or while taking an evasive route, if such cards are in use, it is advisable to request master cards that grant wider access.

VIP ACCOMMODATION

Location of the VIP room or suite is important in providing security. In choosing the floor, consideration must be given to fire safety as well as privacy. Rooms should be high enough that objects thrown from the street cannot reach them. Thus, somewhere above the third floor is normally most desirable. Too high, however, and evacuation in case of fire becomes difficult. Also, the higher the suite is located, the more stops a lift will have to make and the longer it will take, unless a private lift is available. Therefore, somewhere between the fourth and seventh floors will normally be the best choice, unless a penthouse with a private lift is available. The penthouse becomes particularly appealing if the hotel has a helipad on the roof, and the principal has access to a helicopter. Evacuation in case of fire remains a problem from a penthouse, although a helicopter on standby could be used for evacuation as well as other transport.

EVACUATION ROUTES

Once the location of the VIP suite has been determined, it is important to check the evacuation routes in case of fire. Since the corridor might be filled with smoke during an evacuation, it is advisable to count the doorways between the VIP suite and the stairwell so that the route may be followed by feel if obscured by smoke. In a few cases, I have even crawled or walked the route with my eyes closed after the door count to double-check that I can find the stairwell by touch. It is also advisable to keep in the command post enough compact smoke hoods, which will allow breathing during an evacuation, for the principal, the protective team and the VIP party. All fire extinguishers should be checked for full charge and to determine the types of fire they are designed to quench. Fire hoses should be checked to ensure that they're in good condition and that the water is turned on.

AVOID BEING OVERLOOKED

When considering room location, the advance team should have noted rooms that are overlooked by another building or wing of the hotel, and these should be avoided, as they compromise the principal's security and privacy. If the principal is travelling with a large personal staff as well as the protective team, an entire corridor may be booked. This is not usually the case, however. Instead, it is more likely that the VIP party will book a portion of a corridor. In this case, try to obtain a section that has a dead end so that there will be no traffic past the room.

ADJOINING ROOMS

Normally, the VIP suite should not be next to a stairway or lift. If a doorway is at the end of the corridor, try to put staff or bodyguards in the rooms right next to the door, and the principal in a room between staff and bodyguards. If the principal has a suite, which is often the case, there may be a substantial gap between the doors to rooms on the floor. When selecting the VIP suite/room, make sure it does not have a balcony that adjoins the balcony of any other room, nor doors between the room and others.

COMMAND POST

If possible, the protective team should use the room across the corridor from the principal as a command post as well as occupying the rooms on each side. If necessary, however, sleeping arrangements for the staff can be made on another floor, but the location of the command post across the corridor is very important. In some cases, if this is also a suite, it will act as the command post and the sleeping quarters for off-duty members of the protective team.

OTHER GUESTS AND STAFF

The protective team will need to know who else is on the floor. One of the first tasks the team leader will carry out is to meet with the hotel's head of security to determine if there are any potential security risks among guests or staff. For example, there may be staff members who are entirely reliable in their normal day-to-day duties, but due to ethnic, religious or political background may hold particular animosity towards a specific dignitary or a dignitary perceived to represent a certain belief or system.

HOTEL SECURITY

The head of security can also brief the protective team on his own security arrangements, including patrols of the hotel, how to identify his personnel and whether or not they are armed. Often, however, giving a good tip to the hotel cleaning staff will gain even more information about those on the same floor. By the way, the advance team should have found out if it is acceptable to offer hotel security personnel gratuities. If it is not, check if a personal gift from the principal – such as gift certificates to a good restaurant or a watch – is acceptable.

ENTRANCES

Another important consideration is the hotel entrances that will be used. Entrances that are not overlooked by other buildings are most desirable; those with covered pick-up areas even more so, although these also tend to be the most heavily used entrances and, thus, attract the most attention. If the hotel has an underground garage, it may be possible to take the principal directly from the lift to the vehicle. Many luxury hotels also have a few parking places directly in front, and often a good tip to the doorman can assure parking there for a VIP vehicle if no other secure parking is available. To avoid the need to check the vehicle for tampering or explosive devices, however, it will be necessary to have secure parking somewhere or to have someone assigned to guard the vehicle constantly.

Often there will be a dozen or more entrances to a good-sized hotel, and it is important to check each of them in case an alternate way in or out is needed. The closer the VIP vehicle can be parked to an entrance, the better, so particular attention should be paid to those that allow ease of loading and unloading.

SECURING THE VIP SUITE

A variety of other considerations are important to ensure that a protective effort in a hotel runs smoothly. All rooms occupied by the VIP and his party, as well as the protective team, should be swept for explosive devices and electronic eavesdropping devices ('bugs') before the VIP moves in. The bomb search may be carried out under contract by an explosives sniffer dog.

Once the VIP suite has been declared 'sterile', it should be secured and no one other than the VIP, family and staff allowed to enter it, unless accompanied by a member of the security team. This, of course, means that at least one member of the protective team will have to remain at the hotel at all times. Since the command post will be across the hall, if at all possible, this bodyguard may also have to man the CP, locking it for the few minutes it takes to supervise the cleaning of the VIP suite.

If a trusted member of the VIP's staff can stay at the hotel to assist in the supervision task, that is acceptable as well. For example, if the principal has a personal servant such as a valet, he can help supervise anyone entering the VIP suite to make sure there is no tampering.

INTRUSION DETECTION

If the hotel does not already have intrusion-detection equipment installed – as might be the case on a specific VIP floor – it will be advisable to deploy portable intrusion-detection systems of the type already discussed. Many establishments will have CCTV installed, but whether hotel security will approve the connection of cameras applicable to a principal's security to the CP is questionable. This may, in fact, be more difficult than simply deploying portable CCTV equipment.

LUGGAGE

Luggage should be kept under the supervision of the protective team upon arrival and departure. One member of the team can accompany porters to ensure that nothing is tampered with and that luggage is placed in the correct rooms. In the VIP's rooms, the bodyguard accompanying the porters can also make sure that curtains are closed so that there is no direct line of sight into the room. This will be particularly important at night if there are buildings nearby that would allow a view – or a shot – into the room.

TELEPHONE CALLS

Some protective teams like to have all telephone calls routed through the command post so that the team can determine if they are valid. This procedure will depend upon the principal's wishes, but it is a good one to prevent unwanted calls. In some countries, particularly in the Third World, it may be advisable to equip the command post with at least one portable satellite phone as well.

ROOM SERVICE
Certainly, all room-service orders, whether for the principal, staff members or protective team, should be delivered to the command post. Not only does this allow the protective team to control access by waiters, but also it prevents anyone in the kitchen from establishing which food or drink is going specifically to the principal.

SENSITIVE INFORMATION

The principal, staff members and protective team should be careful not to leave any sensitive paperwork lying around where hotel staff might see it. Anything valuable can be left at the command post if it is manned 24 hours a day, which should be the case if at all possible.

COMMAND-POST LOG
To ensure the efficient functioning of the CP, a 24-hour log should be kept, detailing telephone calls,

valuables left, requests from the principal, visitors, 'intelligence' from staff members, any alerts or anything else that might be useful to the protective staff. Normally, as each new shift comes on duty, they will stop by the command post for a quick briefing about what has transpired on the preceding shift.

HOSPITALS

Other situations that may arise when the principal is living away from home may be handled by varying the hotel procedures to fit the temporary residence. For example, if the principal has to spend time in a hospital, security may be handled as if it were a stay in a low-key hotel. Many hospitals have private wings or VIP floors. The more private the hospital, the better, although many of the best specialist hospitals are relatively large. Certainly, the principal should have a private room, preferably at the end of a corridor. At the very least, a room across the corridor should be taken to provide a command post. Hospital administration and security will usually support this to keep the protective effort as low-profile as possible.

SECURING THE VIP ROOM
By installing portable CCTV to cover approaches to the principal's room, a photo file of hospital personnel approved to care for the principal may be checked quickly to clear anyone approaching the room. Normally, two bodyguards will be posted outside the principal's room, one of whom will accompany anyone entering to administer to the principal. Members of the protective team with emergency medical training should be assigned this duty whenever possible.

WORKING WITH HOSPITAL STAFF
Doctors like to exert their authority, so it must be established that the security team will stay out of the doctors' way as much as possible, but without compromising their job. The principal's

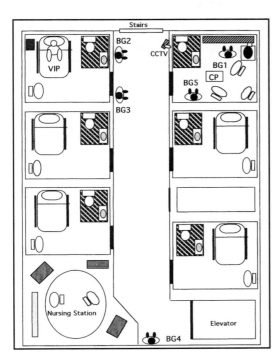

Fig. 5.1 When using five bodyguards to secure a hospital room, two (BG2 and BG3) should remain on duty outside the VIP's room. The command post (CP) will be manned by BG1, who will monitor the CCTV camera and communications. BG4 occupies the nursing station and also watches the lifts. BG5 is a rover who moves about the floor, checks the stairs and relieves any other BG who needs a break.

personal physician can help establish procedures with medical staff. The protective team should also work closely with hospital security, and, as with a hotel, leave much of the security away from the principal's corridor to them.

ADDITIONAL DEPLOYMENTS

In addition to covering the principal's room, it may be advisable to station a member of the protective team to watch the nursing station that monitors his condition, and another to keep an eye on the lifts and/or stairs leading to the floor. If the nursing station is located near the lift, one bodyguard can cover both (see fig. 5.1 for an illustration of a possible deployment of a five-man team to cover a principal in hospital).

VIP CHILD PROTECTION

Another variation on hotel procedures might arise if a protective team is assigned to a VIP child attending a university. This is actually a relatively standard assignment. The US Secret Service has had to protect children of Presidents Clinton and Bush at universities, as well as some other children in the past. Chelsea Clinton's Secret Service detail at Stanford, for example, was reported to be twenty-six agents. Hundreds, even thousands, of other VIP children around the world have pursued their education while under the protection of bodyguards.

KEEP A LOW PROFILE

One of the basic precepts that should be followed is that the protective team should allow the child the most normal growing and educational experience possible while maintaining security. As a result, there may be times when the team will have to run a looser effort than would be the case under other circumstances. The VIP child attending university will want to attend cultural or sporting events, go on dates and just hang out with friends.

SELECTION OF BODYGUARDS

Because of the special circumstances surrounding the provision of protection on a university campus, bodyguards selected for the team should, if possible, appear young enough to pass for upper-level university students or perhaps graduate students. Older members of the team might be able to pass for faculty members if they cultivate the 'academic' look. Bodyguards with a university background are most desirable, as they

AUTHOR'S NOTE

As I write this, one of President Bush's daughters has just got into trouble for attempting to buy alcohol while under age, using a fake ID card. A common college-student peccadillo, but in the case of a presidential daughter, this has drawn a great deal of publicity. Even so, the Secret Service, which must maintain the trust of their charge, handled the situation correctly. Their job was not to stop her drinking, but to prevent her from coming to harm. Consequently, they would have stepped in had she chosen to drive after imbibing, or if someone in a club had appeared to be a threat. Otherwise, the protective team should stay in the background.

will be able to blend in better on a campus. If the VIP child is female, at least some members of the protective team should be female as well, to allow coverage within the halls of residence.

CHOOSING A UNIVERSITY

When choosing the university, the smaller the better, as it will prove easier for members of the protective team to learn who belongs on the campus. If a larger university is chosen, avoid one in a major city. One factor among many that weighs against universities in large cities is that they are frequently located in high-crime areas, thus adding more threats to those the protective team must normally deal with.

If the VIP child is from outside the USA, Great Britain, etc, and belongs to a family involved in governing their country, it will be important to make sure that the university chosen does not have a substantial number of radical students from that country.

LEARN THE ENVIRONMENT

A university campus is normally a relatively self-contained environment, where the student will spend much of his or her time. As a result, the protective team will be able to learn the

environment quite well and determine the fastest route to the university medical centre or the response time of the local police. Good liaison will be necessary between the protective team and the campus security personnel.

AVOID ROUTINE

The nature of college life also will dictate a certain routine on the part of the student. Lectures will occur on a set schedule, use of a university dining hall will fall within set hours, etc. As a result, the protective team must work to ensure that a potential kidnapper or assassin cannot take advantage of this routine. Routes to classes, for example, can be varied, and meals can be taken at different times. Many universities allow students to dine anywhere on campus rather than in one set dining hall. If this is the case, the protective team can encourage – but not demand – their principal to vary dining hours and location.

COMMAND POST

Within the halls of residence, at a minimum, the room across the corridor from the principal's room should be occupied as a command post. In a building that is co-ed by floor, the command post may be staffed by either sex, but where buildings are allocated to a particular sex, the command post will have to be staffed by male or female personnel accordingly. Since it is normally more difficult to recruit a substantial number of well trained female bodyguards, female members of the team will have to be utilised to best effect if the principal is female.

PANIC BUTTON

Since the principal will be alone during classes, although bodyguards will be outside, and on many social occasions, he or she should be equipped with a panic button so that members of the protective team can be summoned immediately if required. The principal should also carry a mobile phone that has the number of the team leader's mobile phone programmed in to allow speed dialing, once again to summon assistance instantly.

OTHER CONSIDERATIONS

Weapons should be kept as inconspicuous as possible. If weapons heavier than handguns are carried, a book bag, musical instrument case or art portfolio will not look out of place on a university campus. In moving ahead of the principal around campus and providing protection, at least a couple of team members on bicycles may prove advantageous, as this will grant mobility that will not be inhibited by the non-vehicular design of many campuses.

Normally, members of the protective team will make a quick check of areas that the principal will be using (ie library, swimming pool, classrooms, etc), then stay as near as possible in case they are needed. If the campus security force will issue members of the protective team with pass keys, this will make movement of the principal in and out of buildings easier, as less-busy entrances may be used.

FREEDOM WITH SAFETY

A good college protective effort should allow a VIP child the freedom to enjoy his or her youth and education, yet provide the necessary safety to complete that education and graduate. For the well trained protective team, though, all it requires is some adjustment to basic precepts and a substantial amount of common sense.

Whether guarding a principal in a residence, a hotel, a hospital or a college, the protective team's job is to be as unobtrusive as possible so that the principal can lead the most normal life possible – but also to allow him or her to keep living that life!

WORKPLACE SECURITY

Many principals will spend almost as much time at their office as at home; thus, good security at the principal's workplace is extremely important.

In fact, there is normally a greater threat while travelling from the VIP residence to the office than when actually at the office. As a result, at least some principals have their residence located within the same compound as their business or office complex. Despite the advantages of such an arrangement, however, most principals, and even more spouses, want their home located in an exclusive residential neighbourhood rather than in an industrial or commercial area.

POTENTIAL THREATS

Although attacks on VIPs at the office have occurred, such events are relatively rare. Letter, parcel and car bombs have all been used, either targeting the business in general or one of its executives. Remember, however, that even the headquarters of OPEC was occupied by terrorists and hostages taken, so the protective team must plan to deal with myriad potential threats while the principal is at the workplace.

COMBATING CAR BOMBS

If a building has been designed with security in mind, it will have features that will increase survivability in the event of a car bombing. For example, although underground parking is convenient, it may allow placement of a car bomb that could bring down the building. Limited underground parking for upper-echelon staff may be viable if a guard is constantly on duty to check every vehicle entering. In general, however, parking beneath the building should be prevented.

Visitor parking facilities should be relatively far away from the building and, if possible, at the base of a terrace that will direct an explosion upward. Buildings designed for security may also be surrounded by landscaping that, while attractive, prevents a suicide bomber from actually driving into a building. Steps, ponds, trees, heavy sculpture and massive planters may all be combined to prevent a vehicle from reaching the building.

More overt controls, such as tyre shredders or crash barriers, which may be lowered for admittance, may also be used, but may alarm business associates, unless, of course, the office is located in a country where such precautions are considered a matter of course. Bear in mind that in some Latin American countries, a motorcade – including gun jeeps – to escort children to school is considered a normal precaution, so tyre shredders at the office will be rather mundane!

THE BUILDING

The location of a building can also be a consideration in security planning. For example, if an office is part of a manufacturing plant sited in a high-crime neighbourhood, the threat level rises. It is preferable, too, for the office building not to be overlooked by other buildings that offer shooting positions for a sniper. A covered drop-off point, which allows the principal's limo to pull up to the door, can help neutralise buildings that overlook entrances.

Secure parking is also important for the principal's vehicle and vehicles used by the protective team; a parking area with a full-time guard is the minimum level of acceptable security. The VIP parking area should not be marked to attract attention to it, but the guard should be able to see it from his post and should be instructed to watch for any attempts at tampering with the vehicles. A good Christmas bonus each year can help ensure that he takes this task seriously.

OTHER OCCUPANTS
From the point of view of VIP security, it is best if the principal's company owns or leases the entire building, as it grants maximum control. If this is not the case, then at least an entire floor or wing of the building should be dedicated to the principal's business activities. It is important, as well, to check the other occupants of the building.

Generally, unless the principal is CEO of a government contractor that needs to be close to its customer, it is not advisable to occupy a building that contains government offices, which might attract a terrorist attack. Likewise, a building occupied by the Israeli or Turkish consulate, or other diplomatic or business entity more likely to draw an attack should be avoided.

MULTI-TIERED DEFENCE

As with residence security, the basis for office security is defence in depth. The first line will be handled as part of the overall building and employee safety and security procedures. These should include a limited number of entry points, which are covered by CCTV, an ID tag system and key cards to allow control of lifts or to open doors. Security/reception personnel in the lobbies are also highly desirable.

If the entire building does not use a system whereby employees may only enter areas for which they are authorised by swiping a card through a scanner, such a system should be in effect to control access to the VIP office floor or wing.

CHECKING THE MAIL
Because explosive devices pose a substantial threat, employees should be trained to recognise suspicious packages, and a system for dealing with them should be put in place. Either for the entire building or the VIP area alone, an isolated mail room should be used to check all mail before it is delivered. It is possible to make such a room relatively blast resistant by adding ballistic mesh and incorporating a skylight, which will vent a blast upwards. In fact, atriums within office buildings can be useful for diverting blasts as well as being decorative.

VIP OFFICES

If at all possible, the VIP floor should have its own lift and stairway, which do not serve other floors.

Note, too, that the VIP floor should be relatively high in the building. Lift and stairway doors should be openable only with a key card, and should be located so that they are covered by CCTV. The entrance to the VIP office area should be hardened, and it is very desirable to incorporate a double door system, which channels visitors to a secure waiting area before they are admitted. A receptionist or security guard will have to pass them into the actual office area after verifying that they have a valid reason for visiting. Normally, they will be issued with a temporary ID and will be escorted to their destination.

THE VIP OFFICE SUITE

The design of the VIP office suite itself should also incorporate certain concessions to security. There should be at least four rooms: the actual office, a VIP washroom (which doubles as a safe room), the reception room/secretary's office and the command post, which adjoins the secretary's office. Any visitors to the principal should pass through the secretary's office and then be admitted to the inner office.

In addition to the door into the VIP office from the secretary's office, an optimum design of VIP office would incorporate another door opening on to a private corridor to allow entrance or exit without passing through the public areas of the office complex. Preferably, this corridor will lead to a private lift or stairs descending directly to the VIP parking place or a secure pick-up area. This door should be kept locked and, preferably, guarded by a member of the protective team.

It is also desirable to have a door that allows direct access from the command post/security room to the VIP office. In some cases, a two-way mirror can be built into this door to allow observation of any meetings that raise security concerns (see fig. 5.2 for a typical VIP office site layout).

ARRANGEMENT OF THE VIP OFFICE

The layout of the VIP office can also be undertaken with security in mind. I have found

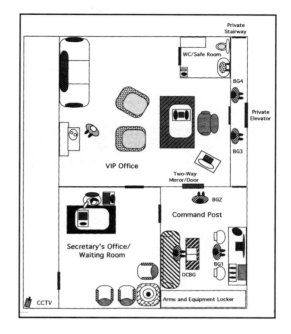

Fig. 5.2 *In this plan, the CCTV camera allows BG1, who is monitoring communications, to give early warning of anyone approaching the VIP office suite. When visitors enter the secretary's office, they must wait for the secretary to buzz them into the VIP office. Note that visitors have to pass the door of the command post to enter the VIP office. BG2 can watch anyone in the VIP office through a two-way mirror set into a door, allowing rapid response if needed. The OCBG checks the log of the day's activities or prepares other paperwork. BG3 and BG4 are positioned to cover the private corridor outside the VIP office. However, one of them, as well as one of the BGs in the CP, can be detached for other duties as needed, or can cover for team members using the toilet or eating a meal.*

that most VIPs agree readily to some of the suggestions for arranging their office, since most of them also help develop it into a 'power office'. For example, a large, relatively high desk and a chair that seats the principal quite high not only give the VIP an aura of authority, but also make it difficult for someone to reach across the desk to harm him or her. Chairs for visitors should be quite comfortable and deep, thus making it more difficult to leap up quickly and attack. Other furniture can also be arranged to make a physical attack on the principal difficult.

TERMINATION OF STAFF EMPLOYMENT

Although, in general, the CEO is only likely to fire the highest ranking staff, if this is necessary, members of the protective team should be on alert and nearby in case of a confrontation. One of the protective team should escort anyone whose employment has been terminated from the building after confiscating any security passes, key cards or ID badges. Then, all computer access or key-pad codes should be changed immediately.

If other members of the management team have to fire anyone, the principal can decide whether they should be escorted from the building by a member of the close-protection team or by corporate security, but someone on the protective team should make sure that the procedures to collect their access cards, keys and codes are carried out.

COMMAND POST

The command post should not only be able to monitor security within the actual VIP suite, but also the entire VIP office complex. Consequently, CCTV, alarms, fire sensors and other such devices should all be connected to monitors in the CP. If the building has an electronic security centre, as many do, the command post should be linked to this centre and be able to receive the feed from CCTV cameras throughout the building.

The command post may also incorporate an armoury containing heavy weapons, such as assault rifles, and heavy ballistic vests. Emergency medical kit and other contingency equipment, as well as communications gear, may be kept in the CP.

DAILY CHECK
Each morning, the member of the protective team assigned to the command post should check with the building security personnel to confirm that nothing of note has happened overnight and also to alert them that the CP is staffed in case they have any information to pass on.

LOCATION OF VIP OFFICE

Within the actual office complex, the VIP office suite should be located as far as possible from the public entrance to the area. There are sound arguments for locating the VIP office suite in the centre of the building, since an office without windows reduces the chance of a rifle grenade or rocket being fired, of audio or visual surveillance, or of a sniper shot. In practice, however, most principals will want an office with a window. If this is the case, blast- and bullet-resistant windows should be installed. It may also be advisable to install Mylar coverings on any other windows in the building to limit glass fragmentation in case of an explosion.

The VIP office suite should be linked to other offices by a corridor, with higher-echelon aides or assistants being assigned those offices closest to the principal; additional doors, which may only be opened with programmed access cards, may be desirable as well. This restricts access to the area of the VIP suite to senior personnel and escorted visitors. Other staff members needing to visit the principal can be escorted through doors that normally would remain locked to them.

ELECTRONIC SECURITY

Corridors approaching the VIP suite should be covered by CCTV cameras, monitored by a bodyguard in the command post. Doors should be alarmed, and the secretary and principal should have panic buttons at their desks to summon help. When a high level of threat is perceived, a portal metal detector and an X-ray machine for checking packages can be installed at the point where visitors enter the office complex.

> More information on the correct use of magnetometers (metal detectors) will be given in Chapter 6.

FIRE PRECAUTIONS

Members of the protective team should make sure that smoke detectors and fire extinguishers are in good working order. The type of smoke hoods discussed for use in hotels should also be kept in the command post in case of an emergency.

EMERGENCY DRILLS

Comprehensive plans for dealing with fire, bomb threats and actual explosions should be in effect and should be practised – if not for the entire building, then for the principal's staff.

EVACUATION
The protective team should have carefully planned evacuation in case of explosion, fire or attack, and have covered all possible routes many times so that every team member is familiar with them. During each shift, one member of the team should walk evacuation routes to check for doors that

may be blocked and other potential problems.

Evacuation routes should have emergency lighting installed in case of a power cut, but each protective team member should also carry a compact torch, such as the Sire Fire Tactical Light, at all times.

The location of, and route to, the nearest hospital with an accident and emergency department should be determined, and each team member should be aware of the drill for getting the principal to the hospital quickly.

SECURITY OF INFORMATION

The protective team should also work with the principal's chief of building security, or independently, to make sure information is secure. Thus, all employees should operate a clean-desk policy so that nothing sensitive is left on a desk overnight. Safes should be used for sensitive material, but the combination must not be written on the side of the safe, or beneath a blotter – both all too common occurrences. Paper shredders should be available and used before throwing away any papers of importance. Computers should incorporate 'firewalls', passwords and other security precautions. Computer and electronic eavesdropping specialists should be brought in periodically to sweep the offices.

The principal's secretary and administrative assistant especially should be briefed on the importance of keeping travel plans, appearances, addresses and similar data under close control.

MONITOR WORKMEN AND CLEANERS

It is important that any workmen entering the VIP office suite are escorted at all times by a member of the security staff. This does not have to be one of the close-protection team if corporate security or uniformed security guards are available. Also, if cleaning personnel have not been thoroughly vetted, they must be monitored while in the VIP office suite. A reliable member of the night security staff should be assigned to check that the VIP suite is secure after it has been cleaned. A member of the protective team will normally arrive early each morning to make a sweep of the VIP office suite before the start of business.

WORK WITH OFFICE STAFF

As with any other area security assignment, protecting an office must be a compromise between allowing the principal and colleagues to work – remember this is how your boss earns the money to pay you! – while keeping them secure. In simplest terms, the protective team must do their job without interfering with everyone else doing theirs. Common sense and good planning will usually permit this co-existence to progress relatively smoothly.

AVOID OFFICE POLITICS

Care must be taken in dealing with office staff, as the members of the close-protection team have direct access to the principal, often a highly desirable situation in the corporate environment. As a result, the bodyguard must remain friendly

AUTHOR'S NOTE

My experience has been that once those who work closely with the principal become used to the protective team, they accept them quite readily. On one job, when I was assigned to the principal at his corporate offices, I was occasionally asked to attend meetings related to some of the company's defence products to give an opinion based on my military experience. The principal and his associates had the attitude that as long as I was there anyway and already a known quantity, they might as well pick my brain.

with members of the staff, but avoid becoming involved in office politics.

The principal's personal secretary and/or administrative assistant and principal aide are especially important, as they will often work with the protective team when planning VIP appearances or travel. The head of the protective team also needs to work with the person who prepares company press releases to ensure that nothing that could compromise security is divulged.

In this chapter, I have discussed area security as it relates to places where the principal will be working or staying for a substantial amount of time. There are other situations that require area security procedures when the principal will only be spending a matter of hours, or even minutes, at a specific location. These procedures will be discussed in Chapter 6.

APPEARANCES AND SOCIAL ENGAGEMENTS

Providing security for a principal at a residence, office or even a hotel involves a certain degree of permanence, but a protective team will have to deal with much shorter-term area assignments as well when their charge has a speaking engagement, attends a banquet, dines at a restaurant, visits a casino, attends the theatre or opera, or appears at a sporting event. In each case, the team will be concerned with getting the principal in and out quickly, having a sound emergency evacuation plan, limiting the principal's vulnerability, maintaining privacy, and anticipating problems and limiting or eliminating their potential to disrupt the principal's itinerary.

Unlike more permanent area security assignments, few high-tech intrusion-detection systems will be in place for most appearances, although at major political engagements and some speaking engagements of a political nature, magnetometers may be in place. In the main, however, the primary intrusion-detection systems will remain the eyes and ears of the protective team.

RESTAURANTS

If possible, the protective team should be able to advise on, or even veto, the choice of a restaurant. Normally, such power of veto would only be exercised in cases where security concerns were quite extensive. For example, a favourite restaurant of the principal would be opposed if it had been shown to have numerous health-code violations during recent inspections, a fact an advance team might have ascertained.

As a rule, the leader of the protective team would oppose a restaurant that was located in the middle of a pedestrian-only mall, which required a lengthy walk to reach it. In certain cases, ethnic restaurants might be opposed if their clientele was known to include those opposed politically or religiously to the principal. In general, however, restaurants likely to be chosen by the principal will be of high quality and will not engender opposition from the protective team.

PRELIMINARIES

Among the preliminaries to a VIP restaurant visit, the team leader should determine proper attire so that the protection team can blend in relatively well. Reservations should be made in the name of the team leader or a fictitious name, but normally the principal's name may not be used. An exception this rule may occur with extremely trendy restaurants, where only those with a 'name' can get in. If the principal insists on going to such a restaurant and using his or her own name, the team will have to cope, but as a rule, anonymity is preferable.

AUTHOR'S NOTE

Special situations may weigh in favour of a restaurant, even if it does cause security concerns. For example, a friend of mine headed the protective team for a very wealthy businessman who still liked to visit a tiny café in his old neighbourhood, even though the area had declined and the establishment usually attracted a rough clientele. However, that same clientele recognised that anyone with bodyguards makes a hard target, and gave the principal and his team a wide berth.

TABLE SELECTION

The security advance party will generally arrive a few minutes ahead of the VIP party and will give the restaurant a quick recce. Often, it is advisable to have the SAP tip the manager or head waiter to speed seating. If an advance team has already visited the restaurant, they will have advised on the best location for seating the VIP party; if not, the SAP will arrange the best table. In many cases, if the VIP party is quite large, a private dining room may be reserved; otherwise, a table away from windows facing the street or doors, and also not on a direct path to the bar or toilet should be chosen. If the only acceptable table is by a window that does not face the street, consideration should be given to posting a member of the protective team outside the window. This situation may arise in restaurants that have a patio or garden area, in which case one of the protective team may occupy a table outside near the window.

In a private dining room, the principal may ask the protective team to dine as well. In this case, if there are several tables, they will take one near the entrance to the room that allows them to view the principal. In some restaurants, the principal's party will be at a private table, but members of the protective team will need to be nearby. In this situation, they should take a table or two tables that will allow them to intercept anyone approaching the VIP table (see fig. 6.1).

PREPARING FOR DEPARTURE

Wherever the protective personnel are positioned, the team leader should arrange for the principal to give a signal a few minutes before he or she is ready to depart so that the vehicle can be summoned and the team can be ready to move. If the protective team is dining, they should have tipped their waiter to keep them at least one course ahead of the principal. They should also have paid for their meal as soon as it was delivered so that they are ready to leave immediately if necessary.

In many cases, the principal will also have arranged for the team leader to pay for the VIP

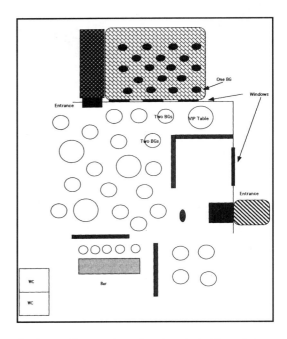

Fig. 6.1. *In this restaurant plan, the principal is seated well away from the entrance and from heavily travelled areas. Note also that an alcove has been chosen for greater privacy. Since the VIP table is near a window on to a patio, one bodyguard (BG) is seated at a table near that window to observe anyone approaching. The remaining members of the close-protection team occupy tables that can control access to the VIP table. Note also that the door on to the patio offers a quick evacuation route if needed.*

party's meals as well. Some principals will give their order, along with the orders for the rest of the VIP party, to the head of the protective team, who will give a waiter one order for all to be served, thus keeping confidential the meal intended for the principal. Although this sounds like a good security technique, in practice it is time consuming and chaotic. Not only that, but most principals like the banter with waiters at a top restaurant as they select their meal and wine.

This does leave some chance of poisoning, but the odds are small at a good restaurant.

DROP-OFF/PICK-UP POINT
The advance team will have advised on the best evacuation routes from the restaurant, and the best point to drop off and pick up the principal. As a rule, a side or car-park entrance will be better than one located on a busy street. The SAP will double-check that the planned drop-off point is unobstructed and will call in the principal's vehicle over the radio.

While the principal is in the restaurant, the vehicle should not be parked in front, but should be driven to an unobtrusive spot, either in the car park or nearby. The driver should remain with the car, monitoring the communications link in case an immediate evacuation is necessary.

KEEP A LOW PROFILE
Restaurant visits normally go much more smoothly when the principal is not a 'celebrity'. If the protective team works at keeping the meal low-profile, and the principal and his guests are not immediately recognisable, the party can usually move in and out of the restaurant with virtually no fanfare and little attention from other diners.

Bear in mind, too, that the more expensive the restaurant, the less likely that other diners will cause problems. As a rule, restaurants with a dress code will normally have a calmer and quieter atmosphere due to the psychological factor of 'best clothes, best behaviour'.

Remember, also, on restaurant assignments that it is important to be available to protect the principal, but not to hover – waiters do that – and not to be obtrusive. Bodyguards who are so omnipresent that they cause a waiter to spill the entrée on the principal are not likely to get a bonus!

THEATRE VISITS

Another type of short-term area protection assignment occurs when the principal attends a

EXAMPLE
Just before I began writing this section on theatre visits, I mentioned it to my friend Tim Mullin, who often helps me in training protective teams. His advice was, 'Advise them not to attend a performance of *Our American Cousin*!' Of course, his reference was to one of the most famous of all assassinations, that of Abraham Lincoln. And, indeed, Lincoln's theatre visit can act as a tutorial on what not to do when protecting a principal.

In the aftermath of the Civil War, the threat level for Lincoln was quite high. John Wilkes Booth had made no secret of his views either and should have been on a 'watch list'. Adding to the high threat level was the fact that Lincoln only had one bodyguard, who left his post to have a drink. Even the lock on the door to Lincoln's box was not working properly, thus allowing Booth to step right in.

The lessons should be obvious:
1 Know the threat level and individual potential threats.
2 Carry out good advance work and choose the most secure seating possible.
3 Provide a protective team commensurate with the threat level.

performance at the theatre or opera; some principals also like to visit the cinema. If attending a premiere of a film, the protective operation will follow the same lines as at a theatre or opera house. If, however, the principal and family suddenly decide to 'take in a film', the extemporaneous nature of the visit will often allow them to slip in and out with only a couple of bodyguards and the minimum of fuss.

BASIC GUIDELINES
I've actually worked on a substantial number of protective details escorting principals to the theatre and opera, and I have developed some basic guidelines that normally make this type of protective assignment easier.

SEATING – BOXES

A primary consideration is choice of seating for the principal, his party and members of the protective team. Normally, a box is the most easily secured; however, there are some special considerations in protecting a principal seated in a box. For example, a box often makes the principal more conspicuous than good seats on the floor of a theatre or opera house. However, the fact that boxes often have private staircases or lifts, as well as restricted-access toilets and lounges/bars weighs in their favour.

If the VIP party is seated in a box, the protective team should attempt to secure the box above the VIP party's – if there is one – and the box on each side. Positioning protective personnel in these boxes not only prevents anyone else from getting too close to the principal, or dropping objects from above, but also allows a good view of anyone in the crowd who might point a weapon towards the principal. Some teams also like to take the box directly opposite the principal's, but I have not normally found this necessary.

When the principal is seated in a box, at least two bodyguards should be assigned to secure the approach to it. Depending on the layout of the access corridor, one can be at the door and the other at the stairway/lift, or both can be at the door.

SEATING – THEATRE FLOOR

If for some reason, the VIP party is seated on the floor of the theatre or opera house, members of the protective team should be in the seats directly behind the principal to protect his or her back and observe anyone approaching. Other members of the team may be positioned on each side of the VIP party, or in front. I also like to place at least one bodyguard farther back in an aisle seat to watch the backs of the bodyguards and warn of any approaches from the rear (see fig. 6.2). The VIP party should not be seated under a balcony where objects can easily be dropped upon them.

EMERGENCY EVACUATION

If possible, it is best to choose seats that offer relatively quick access to an exit for evacuation in

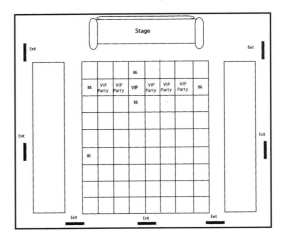

Fig. 6.2. *In this illustration, the assumption is that the VIP theatre party is large enough to fill an entire row. If it is necessary to sit in stalls, taking the entire row is very desirable to prevent other patrons from climbing over the principal. If the party is not large enough, some seats may be purchased and left empty, with BGs on the ends to prevent anyone from occupying those seats. Note that BGs are positioned in front of and behind the VIP. Others are at each end of the row. A fifth BG is seated farther back, on the aisle, to observe anyone approaching the VIP row. Note also that this seating arrangement allows quick access to two exits located at the front of the theatre.*

case of fire or attack. The advance team should have carried out a survey of all possible exits as an aid to evacuation planning.

Consulting in advance with the theatre management to determine the procedure in case of a bomb threat is a good idea, particularly when attending performances in London, where most theatres do have such contingency plans. Other cities, such as Paris, where terrorist bombings have become endemic, would also make a check on bomb threat procedures advisable.

DROP-OFF/PICK-UP POINT

It is important to determine the best point for the

limo to drop off and pick up the principal. Often, just before or after a performance, there will be such heavy pedestrian traffic that it is very difficult to get close. On the other hand, I prefer to bring the VIP party into the theatre just before the lights go down so that they attract the least possible attention for the least possible time.

If the protective effort is an official operation, the police directing traffic will often arrange for the limo to pull up quite close to the theatre and will clear a path for it to leave. Otherwise, it may be advisable to use an exit on a side street, where the limo can be parked close by. The advance team should have visited the theatre on the night of a performance to evaluate the traffic flow.

If the theatre is particularly congested at the end of a performance, it may prove advisable to wait ten or fifteen minutes until the crowd has thinned before escorting the VIP party out. In this case, it may be possible to take advantage of some type of VIP lounge where drinks can be served while the principal's party waits.

Speaking of drinks, since most theatre lounges/bars become very crowded during intermissions, one of the bodyguards should place drink orders for the VIP party prior to the intermission and pick them up in advance.

BE VIGILANT

Although a protective team has to be ever vigilant, my theory about people in dress attire causing fewer problems normally runs true at the opera and theatre. However, these are crowded venues where an assassin who has been stalking your charge might feel the time was right for an attack.

One final warning: don't become too interested in the performance. Your primary job is to watch the audience; remember, however, that John Wilkes Booth was an actor!

BOOKING TICKETS

Whether booking for the theatre, a sporting event or any other performance, the same policy as

AUTHOR'S NOTE

When I worked in Vienna, we found that boxes for the opera were in such demand and held by so many influential people that, at some performances, two or more protective teams were on duty guarding different principals in the box area. In this situation, if possible, some co-ordination should take place between protective teams, perhaps in respect of the coverage of certain staircases or lifts; however, it must be remembered that each protective team will give their own principal the highest priority – justifiably so.

To take this situation a step further, I consulted on protection at an Olympics, where it was assumed that at some high-visibility events, dignitaries with protective teams – official and private – would amount to a dozen or more. In this case, ID pins or tags for armed security personnel (discussed later in this chapter) became essential. Since there were going to be so many armed bodyguards at some events, however, I determined that during an attack, the best tactic would be to get the principal to the ground and covered, as probably there would be gunfire – friendly and unfriendly – coming from all points of the compass.

applies to restaurants should be followed. Reserve tickets in the name of someone other than the principal. If, however, the principal maintains a box at the opera, theatre, etc, make sure no details are given about who will be using it for a specific performance.

SPORTING EVENTS

When attending sporting events, some of the same precepts that apply to a detail at the theatre or opera are relevant. However, the wider open spaces of an athletics arena, the high state of emotions that often accompany such events, and the distance between a vehicle drop-off point and the seating all offer special problems.

VIP ACCOMMODATION

Although many principals who are sports enthusiasts enjoy the drama and dynamics of a crowd of fans, seating in special VIP boxes or club rooms, often enclosed and above the crowd – if available – is highly desirable. Normally, there will be existing controlled access to these private areas, and the addition of a couple of members of the protective team to the venue security personnel at key entry points will normally help provide defence in depth. Enclosure in a VIP area will also lessen the potential threat of a sniper or armed assassin posing as a fan and taking a shot at the principal from elsewhere in the stadium.

EVACUATION PLAN

Even in a private room, a couple of potential problems remain. It is not unknown for sporting events to result in rioting, although, as a rule, such disturbances take place in the general seating areas. However, the protective team should have a couple of alternate evacuation plans from the VIP area in case rioting breaks out. The team should also be prepared to evacuate the principal to a secure location within the stadium/arena and hold that area if necessary.

DEPARTURE

Another problem will be the large crowd attempting to leave at the end of the event. As with the theatre or opera, normally I would recommend waiting until the crowd dissipates before leaving. Usually, however, there will be a substantial number of police handling traffic at major events, so if it is necessary to leave amid the crowd, try to work with them so that they can clear a path for the limo.

SEATING ARRANGEMENT

If by choice or necessity, the principal is seated in an open box, those bodyguards closest to him or her will seat themselves behind, in front and to the sides to limit direct access. If the manpower is available, I would also deploy a couple of additional bodyguards among the crowd to watch for anyone approaching the principal's box or anyone displaying undue interest.

It might also be advisable to have the principal, his party and the bodyguards assigned to close protection all wear jackets and hats of 'their team' to make it much more difficult for a shooter to identify exactly which member of the group is the principal.

CASINOS

Another specialised area security situation is a casino visit by a principal. Some principals are high rollers who like to gamble. Fortunately, most casinos are very co-operative when such a person is due to visit.

CO-OPERATION

On the positive side, casinos normally have excellent security and will co-operate with the protective team of a serious gambler. It should be possible to have floor security personnel work with the protective team to warn them of anything suspicious in their vicinity. The security personnel who monitor the CCTV cameras covering the casino may also let a member of the protective team into their control room to watch for threats or, if not, may be willing to use the team's radio link to warn of threats.

I've already mentioned the special VIP accommodation available in many casino hotels. Such facilities generally make security much easier.

AUTHOR'S NOTE

One principal for whom I worked often showed up at a casino with a bodyguard carrying a case filled with over a million dollars. We never had any problems getting co-operation from the establishment's security team or approval for us to be armed!

PRIVATE GAMING AREAS

Most casinos have separate rooms for serious gamblers, which are less crowded than the public parts. Even in such private gaming areas, the protective team will need to remain alert, but if for any reason the principal is gambling in the more public area, even more vigilance is required.

BODYGUARD DEPLOYMENT

My experience has been that principals who are gamblers usually like roulette, chemin de fer or baccarat. At any of the table games, especially if a crowd tends to gather, I like to put two bodyguards behind the principal to cover his or her back, one across the table to watch that area and the area behind the principal, and two more at strategic locations near the gaming table, but

Fig. 6.3. *In this casino plan, note that two bodyguards station themselves to protect the principal's back and sides. They will also be the first to react to an attack. One bodyguard is on the opposite side of the table to watch those around the principal, to cover the backs of the two bodyguards close to the principal and to keep a potential threat from having a clear shot across the table. The remaining two bodyguards position themselves to watch the rest of the room.*

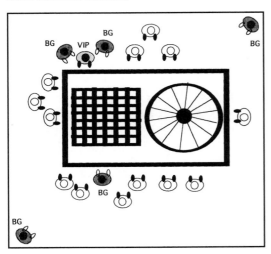

positioned to observe any routes of approach (see fig. 6.3).

OTHER THREATS

Although security is good at casinos, bear in mind that thieves and con men congregate where there are large amounts of money; hence, a protective team cannot become so wrapped up in protecting against kidnapping or assassination that it forgets to guard against burglary or robbery.

SPEAKING ENGAGEMENTS

One of the most complex area security assignments occurs when a principal is attending a large event, such as a political rally or an awards banquet. If it is a speaking engagement for the principal, providing security can become even more complex. The advance team will need to spend a substantial amount of time checking the venue, and there should be substantial liaison with the management of the venue, local police and private security personnel.

LEVELS OF SECURITY

Among the first things that need to be determined are exactly how many tiers of security will be in place and their respective responsibilities. For a typical appearance, there will be security personnel who work for the site of the event. Some may be armed, others unarmed, and the former may include off-duty police officers working at a second job. There will also be local police officers assigned to traffic duties, crowd control, fixed-post security at doors or other entry points and to provide local arrest powers on site. Some plain-clothes police officers may also act as security details if, for example, the local mayor is attending the event. Finally, there will be members of the protective team. If several dignitaries are at the venue, there may be several protective teams.

Lapel pins used by VIP protection teams for identification. The round pin in the centre was used by bodyguards accompanying Henry Kissinger on a trip to Israel while he was US secretary of state.

IDENTIFICATION

The advance team will determine who is handling security for different aspects of the event and with whom it is necessary to co-ordinate security operations. With such a large number of security personnel involved, many of whom the members of the protective team will not know, as well as the various employees at the site, some system of identification is highly desirable. One solution is to employ colour-coded ID cards, which incorporate the wearer's photograph, name and a serial number. The colour codes can indicate the areas to which the wearer has access. Thus, if only employees with a green colour code are authorised to set up the speaker's platform, anyone working in that area wearing a red tag is immediately suspect.

There should also be a method for identifying security personnel. This is particularly important for those who are armed so that if a weapon is spotted, a member of the protective team can look immediately for the identification. Although photo IDs should be worn by security personnel, it may be advisable to have an additional identifier for armed protective personnel or police. Many teams employ a small, but readily visible, lapel button or pin. Often, this will only be worn for one specific event, which prevents a discarded or mislaid ID button from being used in the future by an unauthorised person.

COLOUR CODING

On many protective teams, personnel will have a set of buttons in different colours. The colour to be worn on a certain day will only be announced at the last minute to prevent that information from being compromised.

For the button system to work well, there must be control over their issuance, which should be done as late as possible to prevent counterfeiting. It can be very difficult to enforce controls, however, when a large number of personnel are involved.

One final note on the wearing of ID lapel buttons is that I've found the button tends to draw the eyes of members of the public, although they are unlikely to grasp its significance and, thus, are less likely to notice one's weapon under an arm or on the hip!

AUTHOR'S NOTE

A good example of the need for the close control of the issuance of identification pins occurred when the Pope was visiting a large US city. Local police officers assigned to provide security had a large bowl of pins in their squad room and were told simply to take one as they left. As a result, there was no way of knowing if one or more pins indicating that a person was authorised to be armed had gone astray.

USE OF MAGNETOMETERS

Another consideration in evaluating event security is whether or not magnetometers will be set up at entry points. On many occasions, when political dignitaries are likely to be in attendance, magnetometers have become *de rigueur*. In fact, in Washington, if an event doesn't have magnetometers set up, the assumption is that no one important is in attendance!

I would advise that anyone working in close protection becomes familiar with both portal magnetometers (the type in use at airports) and wand-type magnetometers. Normally, when portal magnetometers are in use, there is a compromise between the sensitivity setting and the volume of people who can be processed per hour. In simple terms, the more sensitive the setting, the more people will set off the alarm, thus slowing the line as they are frisked or checked with a wand. As a result, it is common practice to set the magnetometer to detect the amount of metal present in a handgun or large knife.

IMPROVING DETECTION

There are a few tips that can make those assigned to portal metal detectors better able to spot anyone trying to beat the magnetometer. First, since the device registers the total amount of metal on the person, anyone passing through without any jewellery, belt, etc, could possibly be attempting to smuggle a small knife or even a tiny handgun through the portal. On the other hand, they might be a fashion minimalist.

Since the assumption is that most people with a weapon will carry it on the right side, most portal magnetometers are slightly more sensitive on the right. To allow for this quirk, in some high-security situations, I have seen two portal magnetometers set up, the second being reversed, thus requiring an individual to pass through one with a right-bias sensitivity, then one that was more sensitive on the left.

SHORTCOMINGS

I should give another couple of warnings regarding the use of magnetometers. Although it is a myth that a polymer-framed handgun will pass through a magnetometer without setting it off, experiments have shown that some small polymer-framed handguns, if dismantled, may be taken through in parts, then reassembled on the other side of the magnetometer. Thus, anyone seen passing through the magnetometer several times should arouse suspicion. There are also some quite effective close-combat knives fabricated of plastics that will not set off a magnetometer.

HAND-HELD MAGNETOMETERS

I often carry a very compact magnetometer in a briefcase, just to have it available in case circumstances indicate that someone seeking an audience with my principal needs to be checked. When the protective team is entirely male and a female needs to be frisked, a wand magnetometer can also be useful. I should note, though, that if one is not available, it may be necessary to frisk everyone – I repeat everyone – wanting to approach the principal. Bear in mind, however, that in some cultures, frisking is considered extremely intrusive, which emphasises the advantage of having a hand-held magnetometer available.

When using a wand, develop a pattern for scanning a person so that no portion is neglected, and have the person remove all metal and set it aside. Finally, check that you are not too near furniture or fixtures that will set off the detector. Remember that even small amounts of metal in shoes will register, so practise on different sized metal objects to get an idea of how they will register. Also, practice will indicate how close to the body one needs to scan. Normally, within a couple of inches is best.

One final note on hand-held magnetometers: they can also be useful when checking for letter bombs, since they can be run over thick packets or similar suspicious items to detect the presence of a battery.

WORK OF THE ADVANCE TEAM

Many other aspects of a VIP appearance will be determined by the work of the advance team. For example, the AT will have checked the site for radio dead zones, especially whether or not radio contact may be maintained with the limo while inside the venue. If not, a mobile phone may have to be used to summon the limo driver.

The AT will also have determined the best location for a command post, if one will be set up, and will have decided on the location of a 'safe room' in case the principal has to be evacuated to a point within the site.

An important part of the advance will be determining the precautions to be taken against explosive devices. Will the site be searched by explosives sniffer dogs, then sealed by security personnel? This is the most desirable plan. The AT will also have determined possible evacuation routes in case of fire or bomb threat. Related to this and other evacuation plans will be the location of a secure parking spot for the limo. If there is a secure drop-off/pick-up point where it can wait that is the optimum choice.

ARRIVAL/DEPARTURE ROUTES AND TIMES

From the drop-off point, the advance team should have determined the best route to the rooms where the event will take place and have timed the movement between them. The AT should also have determined alternate routes in case they are needed for moving to or from the rooms housing the event. In any event, the security advance party, which will arrive at the venue ahead of the VIP party and protective team, will advise on the quickest, most secure route based upon the situation just prior to the principal's arrival.

Timing movement will help determine the best arrival and departure times for the principal. Varying arrival or departure by a few minutes can avoid a great deal of congestion and can allow the team to move the principal with the minimum of fuss and disruption to others. Times, of course, will be influenced by the principal's schedule. Does he or she have another appearance that evening? Or want to make a big entrance?

Other considerations concerning arrival and departure times arise if the event includes a banquet. Will the principal dine? Will he or she leave before dinner is served? Or arrive for an after-dinner speech?

It is important to keep arrival and departure times as confidential as possible to make it more difficult for an attacker to anticipate when the principal will be at a certain point. In fact, the protective team will want to look closely at all publicity surrounding the event. The more widely publicised the principal's appearance, the higher the threat level, since more potential attackers will be aware of a location and approximate time at which an attack could be launched.

GUEST AND STAFF LISTS

If possible, the protective team will want to see a guest list, as far in advance as can be achieved. Information about staff members will also be requested, especially those hired recently or hired as temporary help.

Only the highest-level government protective teams will have the resources to run a security check on every guest and every employee. However, an experienced team leader or team intelligence specialist can often assess potential threats among guests or staff. For example, checks will be made for anyone known to harbour bad feelings towards the principal, and for other guests who might attract an assassination attempt, thus endangering the principal as well. Staff will be vetted for anyone who has been fired from one of the principal's companies or, if the principal is a foreign royal or diplomat, any immigrants bearing grudges.

SPEAKING PLATFORMS AND ROSTRUMS

If the principal will be speaking, special precautions should be taken in arranging the podium/speaker's platform. The AT will have examined the room where the principal will be speaking and, if possible, will have advised on the best location for the speaker's platform and/or rostrum. A platform is best because it raises the principal above crowd level and creates an additional barrier to slow an attacker. A well-positioned platform combined with a tall rostrum will also make a shot more difficult.

If the principal speaks often and the threat level justifies it, investing in an armoured rostrum may be worthwhile. If this is tall enough, it should offer almost total protection against small arms or even blast fragments from the front.

The speaker's platform/rostrum should be positioned so that no one will pass behind it. It is quite likely that other dignitaries will be seated on the platform with your principal, but try to position him or her directly behind the rostrum. I always try to arrange for one member of the protective team, normally the team leader, to be seated on the platform next to the principal. Then, if a threat warning comes over the radio, the team leader can quickly begin evacuation procedures and give immediate body cover.

AUDIENCE SEATING

Seating should be arranged so that there is a gap between the speaker's platform and the crowd. I like to place a cordon across the front of the audience, or even around the audience, as well. Even though the cordon will be of something as fragile as silken cord, it still creates a psychological barrier and also slows anyone attempting to approach the platform from the crowd as they go over or under it. Such a hesitation grants the bodyguards enough additional reaction time that they may be able to stop an attack.

To increase the reaction gap even more, the first few rows should be reserved for attendees deemed most secure (ie military personnel, those receiving awards, friends of the principal, etc).

DEPLOYMENT OF PROTECTIVE TEAM

Placement of members of the protective team will have to be adjusted in relation to the layout of the

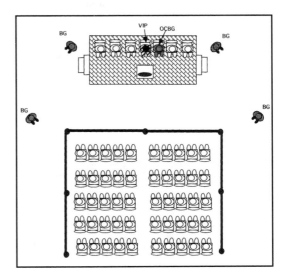

Fig. 6.4. *Speaking engagement security. The speaker's platform is set back from the crowd to allow more time for protective personnel to react. Note that a cordon encloses the crowd to delay anyone attempting to approach the platform. The team leader (OCBG) sits next to the principal. Two BGs cover the stairs leading to the platform, while two others watch the crowd and position themselves to intercept anyone attempting to rush the platform from the crowd.*

room where the speech is being given. Generally, though, in addition to the team leader on the platform with the principal, at least four other members of the protective team will be needed. One should be positioned on each side of the platform, by any stairs, to intercept an unauthorised person attempting to climb on to the platform. Two more should be stationed in front of the platform and to the sides to watch the crowd. If the protective effort is assuming a low profile, they may have to be seated on the ends of the two front rows, or dressed as 'ushers' so that they don't attract attention by standing near the front of the crowd.

If additional personnel are available, they

should be positioned among the crowd, but located on aisles so that they can react to anyone attempting to rush the platform (see fig. 6.4). In large venues, usually there will be a control booth for the lighting and sound systems, etc. It may be advisable to position a member of the protective team in this booth, where he or she can observe the crowd from above and quickly notify those on close-protection duty of anything untoward.

RECEIVING LINES

Normally, as soon as possible after the VIP has spoken, the protective team will escort their principal away from the crowd; however, sometimes a receiving line will have been scheduled. Two procedures exist for providing security in a receiving line – one if the principal is moving down the line; the other if the line is moving past the principal.

Actually, a receiving line where the principal is moving can be more efficient in getting him or her through the procedure quickly on the way to the door. Generally, though, receiving lines will be organised to pass the principal.

POSITION OF BODYGUARDS
If the principal is moving past a receiving line, one bodyguard will normally go ahead of him or her to protect the principal's side and to watch the next person in line. Using peripheral vision, the bodyguard will also watch the person whom the principal is greeting.

A second bodyguard moves down the line on the other side of the principal, protecting that side and watching the person whom the principal has just greeted. He or she will also use peripheral vision to watch the person currently in front of the principal. In addition, this bodyguard may have the duty of disengaging anyone who clamps on to the principal's hand and freezes, a situation that sometimes occurs when meeting the 'mighty'.

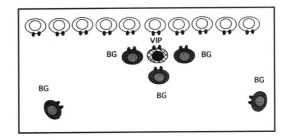

Fig. 6.5. *When the principal must move down a receiving line, three bodyguards provide body protection and are also prepared to react to any threat. The other two bodyguards watch the rest of the room and cover the backs of the three bodyguards giving close protection.*

A third member of the team, usually the team leader, moves directly behind the principal to cover his or her back, watch the person the principal is greeting and pull the principal clear if a threat arises. The person behind the principal will also receive any gifts or other items given to

AUTHOR'S NOTE
In one situation where the receiving line was set up in the corner of a mirrored room, I determined that it would allow faster reaction if the team leader were positioned behind the person greeting the principal and watched him in the mirror. In case of an attack, he would have grabbed the attacker and spun him away from the principal while the bodyguards on each side gave body cover and moved the principal clear. In another situation where we considered the threat level very high, I was positioned beside the principal with a hammer-shrouded Smith & Wesson revolver in an over-the-shoulder leather case. Although my hand appeared to be casually thrust into the case, in reality I had my finger on the trigger and was pointing the gun at each greeter who advanced.

EXAMPLE

EXAMPLE

The Special Air Service developed an interesting tactic while protecting one ruler in the Persian Gulf. Although the threat level was high, it was essential that the ruler appeared very open to approaches by his subjects. As a result, the throne room was designed so that mirrors surrounded the throne. However, they were two-way mirrors, and armed bodyguards watched each person who approached the monarch through them. If an attack had taken place, the bodyguards would have eliminated the attacker immediately by shooting through the mirrors (see fig. 6.6).

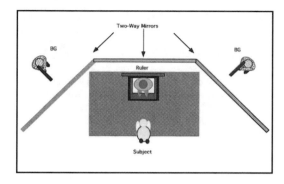

Fig. 6.6. *This technique, originally developed by the SAS, allows a Middle Eastern monarch to give the impression of being very approachable by his subjects. Although there are guards at the doors to the throne room, subjects are allowed to approach the monarch unaccompanied to present petitions, etc. However, behind the two-way mirrors, bodyguards cover each supplicant with submachine-guns. Should he make any threatening move, he can be shot through the mirrors or by opening the doors into which the mirrors are set.*

the principal and will pass them to a support person assigned to remove packages to a secure location until they have been checked. It is preferable, however, to have a system whereby any gifts, etc, are surrendered prior to joining the receiving line.

The other members of the protective team will position themselves to watch the room and the remainder of the receiving line, and to cover the backs of the three bodyguards working close to the principal (see fig. 6.5).

If the principal remains stationary, bodyguards are still positioned on each side of him or her and have the same duties as if they were moving down the line. The team leader will generally be positioned behind the principal and slightly to the side to watch the person greeting the principal.

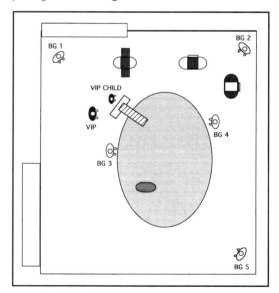

Fig. 6.7. *When protecting a VIP and his family at a pool, the protective team must plan to deal with external threats as well as problems in the pool, which could result in drowning. As a result, the two best swimmers (BG3 and BG4) wear trunks and are prepared to carry out a rescue. They may still keep their weapons nearby in a gym bag. The other bodyguards position themselves to watch approaches to the pool as well as the pool itself.*

ADAPT THE BASIC PRECEPTS

There are, of course, various other area security situations that may arise. Generally, however, an adaptation of the basic precepts discussed in this chapter will allow a well-trained protective team to secure any area. Sometimes, special circumstances may require more adjustment than usual. For example, when protecting a principal or a principal's children at an outdoor swimming pool, deployment of the protective team must take into consideration not only any external threat, but also the possibility of a member of the VIP family or party drowning. As a result, the normal precept that bodyguards watch the crowd or the approaches rather than the principal has to be altered. At least one or two of the protective team who are good swimmers may have to be assigned to 'lifeguard' duty as part of the protective effort (see fig. 6.7).

Whatever the situation, the protective team will want to make sure that they have a defence in depth, an evacuation plan, some idea of potential threats, good communications and a tactically sound plan for dealing with contingencies. It may appear to the uninitiated that the primary duty of bodyguards on area security assignments is to stand around and look tough, but the true test of the professional comes when a crisis arises. At that point, standing around is the last thing he or she should be doing. The good bodyguard combines experience, common sense, training and planning to enable him or her to react decisively in a crisis.

One of the most important and most basic skills for the bodyguard is the ability to provide security for a principal while on foot. The good foot escort formation must allow the principal to move without tripping over his bodyguards, and must be fluid so that it can be adjusted constantly to accommodate changes in terrain, buildings, crowds, barriers or whatever else may be encountered. The protective team must be able to make these adjustments gracefully enough that they will not appear to be a bunch of clowns and without causing their principal to stumble over them.

COMPROMISE

In some cases, the escort formation will be designed to be visible and to act as a deterrent in high-threat situations, while in more casual situations, the formation will need to be as loose as possible and to appear as little like a gang of hulking bodyguards surrounding their principal as possible. The good escort formation will almost invariably be a compromise between security and smothering.

FLEXIBILITY IS THE KEY

Most of all, the escort formation must be flexible, as must the protective personnel providing the formation. During training, bodyguards usually learn the basic escort formations, but practice and experience teach them to adjust to different situations. When I run VIP protection training courses, I normally devote up to a fifth of the time to practising formations and to scenarios employing formations. One of the ways a new bodyguard joining a protective team will be judged is on his ability to function as part of an

escort formation, especially since he may literally have to learn the drills of the team on the job.

TEAM LEADER

The most common number of bodyguards in an escort formation is five, although protective efforts may be carried out with fewer or more. This number includes the team or shift leader, also designated OCBG (Officer in Charge of Bodyguards). The team leader will normally remain close to the principal and will be the decision maker when it comes to adjusting the formation, changing the route or calling the limo to evacuate the principal.

The team leader may be in radio contact with other members of the close-protection team, the VIP driver and others involved in the overall protective effort. However, he may also employ simple visual signals or, when in close formation, arm taps to adjust the formation without alerting members of a crowd to his intent.

BRIEFING THE PRINCIPAL

The principal may have to be quickly informed as well, although principals who have been with bodyguards for some time learn to respond to simple pressure signals from the team leader. In most cases, however, it is not the responsibility of the principal to adjust to the pace of the bodyguards, but their job to match his or hers. However, the principal should have been informed of how escort formations operate and the likely reaction to possible scenarios. Normally, the team leader will brief the principal and any close associates likely to be with him or her so that they will not be surprised if the formation is diverted or other countermeasures are implemented. The principal must also be aware that if an attack is launched, the team will immediately go into their evacuation drill, which will entail rushing him or her to cover or an evacuation vehicle.

FORMATIONS

The two most basic five-man formations are the box and the V (see figs. 7.1 and 7.2).

BOX FORMATION
The box normally places a bodyguard at each corner with the team leader positioned to one side of the principal. As a rule, the team leader will choose the side based partially on whether he or she is right- or left-handed, but will also adapt to the area through which they are moving. If, for example, there are people on one side of a path, the leader will move to that side to be between the principal and the potential threat presented by the people. The leader will also remain ready to grab the principal, give body cover and evacuate

Fig. 7.1. *This box formation is relatively widely spaced, since the group is moving over open ground. Note, however, that as the formation is passing a pathway between shrubbery, the OCBG has taken up position on that side to be between the principal and the area of most likely threat.*

A protective team surrounds a female principal with a four-man box. Note that one of the rear bodyguards watches the people approaching from behind.

Fig. 7.2. *Positioning of bodyguards in a five-man V-formation for escorting a principal.*

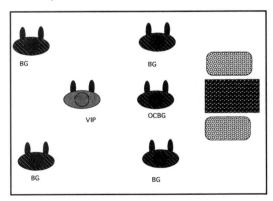

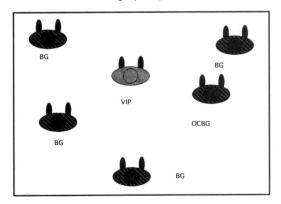

him or her if a threat arises. When moving through a relatively secure environment, or when the protective team is trying to be unobtrusive, the formation can be relatively loose; however, if a crowd is being approached, it will tighten up substantially.

V-FORMATION

The V-formation places the principal in the middle of the V with the point facing his or her rear. This formation allows the principal more open space to the front, and many prefer it because it feels less claustrophobic. Two bodyguards and the OCBG will be positioned on one side, and the remaining two bodyguards on the other side.

Frequently, the V-formation will be used when moving across open ground, but when areas that are more congested or contain more people are approached, the bodyguards will shift into a box escort formation.

FIELD OF VIEW

Whichever formation is used, the bodyguards must maintain a 360-degree field of view. They must also remember to look up when near buildings, high ground or any other areas where the threat may come from above, and down when walking over a bridge or an elevated pathway, or when near any area where the threat might come from below.

When teaching bodyguards, I have found that many trainees have a tendency to neglect looking upward frequently enough. As a result, I sometimes position myself in a window or on some other 'high ground' and pelt anyone not spotting me with water-filled balloons. The constant admonition is 'Check your six,' referring to the pilot's clock system for identifying 'bandits' to the rear, a system also used by many protective teams.

PERIPHERAL VISION

Good close-protection teams will resemble the toy dogs and cats one often sees with heads that bob constantly from side to side and up and down. Members of close-protection teams will also learn to maximise the use of their peripheral vision when searching for threats.

ASSIGNMENT OF BODYGUARDS

Normally, bodyguards who are left-handed will be assigned to the left side of the escort formation so that their gun hands will be towards a threat, thus speeding reaction. Since formations may alter frequently to fit a changing situation, however, it is not always possible to keep right-handers on the right and left-handers on the left. Even so, it is a consideration when assigning basic escort positions.

'TAIL-GUNNER'

Some protective teams employ an additional bodyguard moving behind the main formation, often walking backwards whenever the team slows, specifically to deal with a threat from the rear. Sometimes referred to as a 'tail-gunner', this security man in the US Secret Service often is equipped with an Uzi submachine-gun in a briefcase. Whenever the escort formation comes to a stop, the bodyguards immediately face outward to watch for any potential threat.

OTHER DANGERS

It is important not to forget that there may be dangers other than those posed by assassins or assailants. While moving with the principal, who may be engaged in conversation, waving at a crowd or otherwise occupied, members of the protective team must watch that he or she does not step into a pot-hole, trip over a kerb, become splashed with mud or suffer a dog bite.

A perfect example of the need to guard against accidents as well as attacks occurred when the Duchess of York was visiting her husband Prince Andrew's ship in Australia. A member of the security team noticed a cable stretched very tautly and moved the duchess just before it snapped and lashed across the place where she had been standing.

AUTHOR'S NOTE

I was reminded of the importance of watching for potential accidents when I was working on a protective detail in St Petersburg. Many manhole covers were missing, leaving gaping maws that could swallow a principal or a member of the protective team. Pavements were often in disrepair as well. Consequently, members of the protective team had be constantly alert whenever we were moving on foot.

Guarding the principal from accident and embarrassment is part of the protective team's job as well.

DEALING WITH DOGS

Members of protective teams must learn to be alert to vicious dogs whenever out walking with their principal.

There are a few rules for dealing with an aggressive dog that might prove useful:

- avoid talking to the dog;
- avoid looking into its eyes;
- avoid turning one's back on the dog;
- do not get down on the dog's level;
- do not show fear;
- be aware that dogs will attack the closest extremity;
- if the dog attacks and grabs an extremity, try to lift its back legs from the ground.

Sometimes a sharp blow with the base of the palm against a dog's muzzle will discourage it. Mace may deter a dog, but some hair sprays will work as well or even better. The ASP baton may also be used, but if it is necessary to shoot the dog, try to press the muzzle of the gun against its body and shoot downward to prevent over-penetration from harming someone else. Ex-special forces soldiers will probably have been trained in methods of eliminating dogs with the bare hands. Bear in mind, however, that in many countries there will be a greater outcry over the killing of a dog than a human attacker.

COPING WITH CROWDS

If a closely packed crowd is encountered, the formation will tighten up. Even a friendly crowd can cause serious injury, particularly if they recognise a celebrity and begin to push too close. A hostile crowd, of course, can be even more dangerous.

When facing a hostile crowd, the best option is to move the principal away and into a secure building or the VIP vehicle if it can be summoned. If the only option is to move through the crowd, the bodyguards must close up tightly. When objects are being hurled, or crowd members are trying to reach the principal, the team leader will often push the principal's head forward and downward, using his or her hands and body to shield the principal from serious injury.

PROTECTIVE FORMATIONS
The most commonly taught formation for pushing through a crowd is a tight wedge, the point being towards the crowd. The largest member of the escort team will attempt to force a path for the remainder of the team and the principal to follow

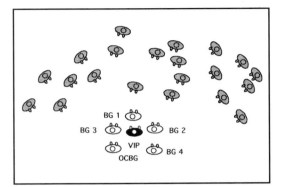

Fig. 7.3. *Wedge formation for approaching a crowd. On nearing a large group of people, the team tightens up around the VIP and assumes a formation that will allow them to 'slice' through the crowd.*

(see fig. 7.3). I have found, however, that with a dense crowd, what I term a 'chisel' formation works best. In this arrangement, the two largest team members force the path, thus giving more impetus to moving the crowd aside (see fig. 7.4).

If the escort team is stopped within a crowd, it is even more important to form a very tight cordon around the principal and turn outward to face the crowd. The team leader may maintain contact with the principal to keep his or her head down and to offer as much body cover as possible (see fig. 7.5).

TYPES OF THREAT

When moving through a crowd, the protective team must be constantly alert for threats and be prepared to make a proportional response to any encountered.

The principal may meet with various types of assault, including:

- verbal;
- unarmed physical;

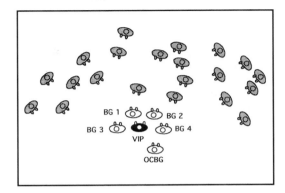

Fig. 7.4. *Modified wedge for moving through a crowd. If a crowd is thick, but not too deep, sometimes this modification of the wedge, in which the two largest team members are in front, allows the team to push through more easily, as it opens a larger gap. With any formation in crowds, if additional personnel are available, either as part of the advance team or perhaps a 'tail-gunner', they move in to help as well.*

Fig. 7.5. *Formation when stopped within a crowd. If a situation arises that requires the escort formation to stop within a crowd, the bodyguards assume positions that allow them to give 360-degree body cover and to watch the crowd. Note that the team leader (OCBG) is placed to observe the VIP as well as the crowd.*

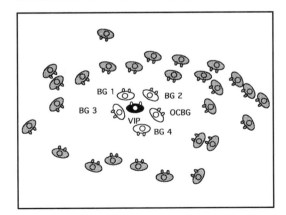

- hurled objects;
- club or knife;
- handgun at close range;
- hurled explosive device (*ie* grenade);
- sniper at a distance.

AVOID CONFRONTATION

In dealing with physical assaults from crowd members that are not life threatening, the protective team should avoid actual confrontation if possible. Not only will a physical altercation slow the progress of the principal, but also it will attract undue attention from the crowd and any members of the media who may be present.

PHYSICAL FORCE

If it is necessary for the protective team to use physical force, it is best to employ quick and dirty techniques, often directed against the assailant's lower body, which will incapacitate the attacker quickly. Many of those in VIP protection wear shoes with steel toe caps. These serve two purposes. First, they protect the feet in the event that the tyres of a vehicle pass over them – a far more common occurrence than one who has never hurried to get a VIP into or out of a limo might imagine. Second, steel toe caps are quite useful for stamping on an attacker's foot, delivering a quick, short snap kick or raking down a shin. If it is necessary to get physical with a crowd member, the basic drill is hit them hard, fast and low (so cameramen have nothing to film!), and move on.

AOP DRILLS

When faced with attacks involving weapons, the well-trained protective team will follow what the US Secret Service terms AOP (Attack on Principal) drills. In simple terms, these are intended to identify and warn against the threat, attempt to counter it, cover the principal and evacuate him or her from danger.

The first member of the escort formation who spots the weapon will normally yell, 'Gun!' or 'Knife!', and move towards the threat, placing his or her body between the attacker and the principal. Most teams like to use directions to indicate from where the threat is coming (*ie* 'Gun, front!'), while others use the clock system (*ie* 'Gun, twelve o'clock!'). I would recommend avoiding fine distinctions when using the clock system. Shouting, 'Gun, 9.30!' will only confuse the other team members. Anything basically forward should be, 'twelve o'clock', anything left, 'nine o'clock', etc.

AGGRESSIVE RESPONSE

A fast, aggressive response will normally distract the attacker from the principal and may give the bodyguard time to counter the threat. Normally, against a knife or a club, or even a handgun at very close range – within arms reach, hand-to-hand combat techniques will be faster than drawing a weapon. When facing an attacker bearing a firearm at very close range, one rule of thumb is that if the weapon is at chest level or above, the bodyguard should attempt to thrust it upwards and back; if the weapon is below chest level, it should be thrust downwards and back. This reduces the likelihood of the principal being hit by a shot fired as the gun is knocked away.

Bodyguards also practise a variety of techniques for very-close-range engagement of targets. These will be discussed in some detail in Chapter 11.

COVER AND DIVERSION

As the protective team moves, its members will be searching continuously for potential cover in case of an attack. Brick or stone walls, ditches, buildings, vehicles, anything that could be used for cover in an emergency should register with the team as they approach or pass its location. I like to constantly keep in mind whether the closest available cover is ahead or behind and how far, and keep updating that information as I look around for any threats.

The team leader particularly, but also all members of an escort formation, must be ready to divert from their route if it becomes blocked. For example, if demonstrators are at a front entrance to a building, immediate diversion to a side or rear entrance is called for. In the case of violent demonstrations, a complete evacuation may be indicated. In this case, the team leader will rapidly divert the formation towards the vehicles.

MEETING AN ATTACK

If the attack from a crowd or from a position of ambush is carried out by more than one person, two members of the protective team may give body cover and engage the attackers, but normally that is the maximum number who will deal with the attackers. The remaining members of the close-protection team must not only keep together to give the principal body cover and carry out an evacuation under fire, but must also remain alert to the potential of another attack still to come.

THROWN EXPLOSIVES

In the case of a hurled explosive device, the team leader or another team member must be ready to act very quickly, as normally only a few seconds will be available to react. The standard drill is to take the principal to the ground, give body cover, and cover his or her ears and one's own if possible. When taking the principal down, an attempt should be made to place the feet towards the device and draw the legs up. If on a raised path or next to a wall – or even a thick hedge – try to take the principal down behind something that will give blast cover. Because of the limited time,

however, if team members manage to get the principal to the ground and covered, they will have performed well.

I try to incorporate thrown-explosive drills into training whenever I can to try to build 'muscle memory', since even a split second saved in performing this manoeuvre can be critical. Note, too, that grenades, although certainly horrific, often have their effects over-exaggerated in films. Gaining a bit of distance and hitting the ground may well prevent serious injury.

COUNTERING SNIPERS

In the case of a sniper, the team will generally only have a chance to react after the first shot has been fired. If the sniper is good enough to have scored a critical hit on the principal with that first shot, there is not much that the team will be able to do. If, however, the first shot misses, moving the principal rapidly to cover is the best reaction.

OBSCURING IDENTITY
Techniques to obscure the identity of the principal can be implemented in many situations where he or she might be a target for a sniper.

AUTHOR'S NOTE
One technique that can help counter a sniper is to make it difficult to identify the target. When I'm giving an initial orientation talk to trainee bodyguards, I often ask if they were protecting a female Asian principal, would they want to have at least one female Asian bodyguard and why? Most answer yes, offering such reasons as, 'To make her feel more comfortable', or 'To show the protective team is multi-cultural'. I agree that these are good reasons, but I want the female Asian bodyguard to make it harder for a sniper to identify the principal!

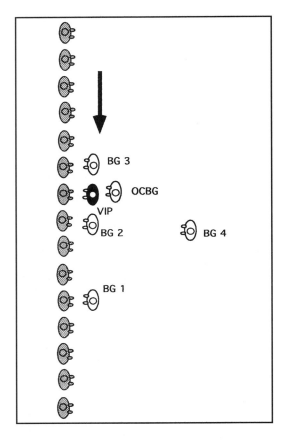

Fig. 7.6. *When moving down a fence line, the protective team must give body cover and watch the crowd for any threats. BG1 walks in advance of the principal, looking for anyone recognisable or who 'sets off alarms'. BG2 moves just ahead of the principal, watching the next person to be greeted and those around the individual. This bodyguard makes sure that no one has a weapon. The OCBG is close behind the principal, ready to pivot him or her away from danger and give body cover. The team leader also watches the crowd directly in front of the principal. BG3 follows just behind the principal, watching the crowd and disengaging anyone who holds a handshake too long. BG4 stands back to gain a wider view of the crowd.*

AUTHOR'S NOTE
Prior to the Gulf War, I trained US Army general officer protective teams. One of their practices, to which I took exception, was the wearing of civilian clothes while assigned to protective duties. If a sniper sees an officer in uniform surrounded by personnel dressed as civilians, isn't it obvious who should be shot?

When jogging, golfing or skiing for example, members of the protective team can wear similar coloured clothing to make target acquisition more difficult.

FENCE-LINE SITUATION

A variation on movement through a crowd will occur if the principal becomes involved in what is known as a fence-line situation – basically an impromptu receiving line. Politicians, particularly, like to move towards a crowd, and the fence line will sometimes arise when a principal is riding in a motorcade and decides to get out to meet the people. Normally, some type of barrier will be in place to keep the crowd back. If possible, when a fence line is anticipated, it is a good idea to place 'safe' human 'barriers' nearest the principal (*ie* police officers, military personnel, local school children, etc). If a fence line is planned, it is best if the crowd is positioned so that there is some type of cover opposite them to protect the principal's back. In an impromptu situation, however, this will not be possible.

DEPLOYMENT OF BODYGUARDS
The actual formation for dealing with a fence line is somewhat similar to that for a receiving line (see Chapter 6). One of the bodyguards will move quite a way ahead of the principal, watching the crowd. Another member of the protective team will move directly ahead of the principal, observing the crowd and particularly the

individuals nearest the principal. The team leader will be directly behind the principal, ready to pull the VIP clear and pivot him or her away from a threat while giving body cover. Another bodyguard will be moving down the line immediately after the principal, watching those closest to the principal and also prepared to break any lengthy handshakes to keep the principal moving.

Different team leaders position the fifth bodyguard according to their own tastes. I like to place him or her just ahead of the principal, but back from the line a bit to be able to see into the crowd near the principal (see fig. 7.6).

If possible, a member of the principal's staff should be near the team leader to receive any flowers or other gifts handed to the principal so that they can be quickly taken away to be checked. If enough protective personnel are available, I like to put two or three into the crowd, moving along the route and watching the people from the rear. In a dense group, however, this may not be possible.

WATCH FOR STALKERS
When moving through the crowd, protective personnel should be especially alert to anyone who seems to be stalking the principal, keeping pace with and observing him or her. If such a person is carrying a parcel, wearing a long coat or displaying any other incongruities, they should be watched even more carefully.

EYES AND HANDS
When watching a crowd, attention should be paid to their eyes and hands. Watch to make sure that

EXAMPLE
When Mikhail Gorbachev visited New York City during his tenure as leader of the Soviet Union, at one point he got out of his motorcade to mingle with the crowd. His KGB protective team made it a point to pull the hands from the pockets of anyone near their principal, saying, 'Hands!'

nothing is in the hands and that nothing is being thrust towards the principal.

CORNER ADJUSTMENTS

When carrying out a movement on foot, members of the protective team must be trained to adjust the formation to fit various circumstances. When approaching a blind corner, for example, the bodyguard in the lead position, opposite the corner, may move ahead to observe that it is clear

Fig. 7.7. *Adjustment of formation for a blind corner. Note that the team member in the right-hand lead position moves forward to look for any threat at the corner. Since that bodyguard is farther from the corner than the left-hand lead bodyguard, he or she can observe any danger slightly earlier. Note also that the OCBG moves up slightly to fill some of the gap left by the bodyguard who has moved forward.*

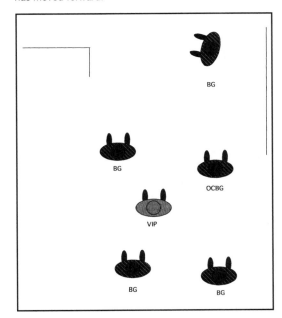

(see fig. 7.7). As the formation passes the corner, the rearmost member nearest the corner will hang back to provide cover until the remainder of the formation is well past it.

DOUBLE CORNERS

If approaching a double corner, the situation may be handled in either of two ways. One of the lead bodyguards may move ahead and check in both directions, or the two leaders can move forward, each covering one direction. The latter method is most likely to be used if people on foot are

Fig. 7.8. *This illustration shows a typical escort formation for a multi-flight stairway. The formation opens up on the stairway so that the bodyguards won't trip over each other and to allow coverage of several levels. BG1 covers the rear and watches the entrance to the flight of stairs they have just ascended. BG2, BG3 and OCBG remain with the VIP, although with greater spacing to allow ease of ascent. BG4 has moved ahead to secure the next landing and make sure it is clear of threats.*

approaching from around the corners. If both corners are covered, the two rear bodyguards can move to the lead as the formation passes, while the pair covering the corners can fall in at the rear once the formation has passed, or the two leaders can pass control of the corners to the two rear bodyguards as they approach. Either method will work, but a team should have determined in advance how they will handle this manoeuvre.

STAIRCASES

Another common situation that will be encountered when escorting a principal on foot is the need to navigate staircases. Normally, the escort team will attempt to secure one level below and one level above the principal during the ascent or descent. Therefore, the formation will remain relatively open, which is necessary, in any case, to prevent tripping over each other (see fig. 7.8). If others are encountered on the stairs, the formation will tighten up. Generally, however, one mission of the bodyguards moving above and below the principal is to prevent anyone else from being on the stairs at the same time as the principal.

When negotiating open stairways, bodyguards on the outside of the formation will need to constantly look upward to watch for dropped objects or even a shooter.

NEGOTIATING DOORS

One of the most frequently encountered situations when carrying out foot escort assignments is passing through doors. Although good manners dictate deferrence to an employer in normal circumstances, this is not always the case in VIP protection. As a result, it is important that at least one bodyguard precedes the principal through the door to check for any threats. Even when a principal is being escorted

Protective personnel practising escort formations on stairs. Note the vests to designate position within the formation; this technique was developed by the SAS for training bodyguards in Third World countries.

by only one bodyguard, he or she will normally take a quick peek through any door before ushering the VIP through.

FIVE-MAN TEAM

With a five-man escort team, normally two bodyguards will precede the principal through the door. If it is a single door, the lead bodyguard nearest the door will normally hold it to allow the other lead bodyguard to pass through. Then the team leader takes the door, allows the principal to enter and follows. Finally, the two rear bodyguards pass through the door (see fig. 7.9). This provides body cover in front and behind, and allows quick evacuation if the first two bodyguards through the door encounter a problem.

DOOR OPENING DIRECTION

The advance team may have noted which way the door opens – in or out, right or left – but normally the lead bodyguards will also have observed the location of the hinges during the

approach and will be aware of the way in which the door will open.

DOUBLE DOORS

When double doors are encountered, the two lead bodyguards open the doors and proceed through, while the two rear bodyguards secure the doors so that the principal can pass. The team leader takes up a position to give body cover from the rear until the principal is through the doors (see fig. 7.10).

When the doors open outward, the two lead

Fig. 7.9. *When escorting a principal through a single door, the lead bodyguard on the side on which the door is hinged will open the door, allowing the lead bodyguard on the other side to enter and check the interior. Then the OCBG holds the door while the other lead bodyguard moves through, followed by the principal. The two rear bodyguards continue to 'watch the six' and give rear body cover to the principal until they follow the OCBG through.*

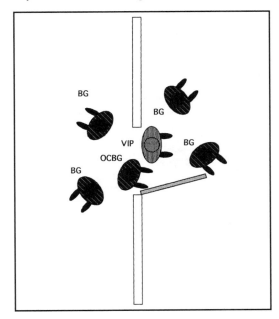

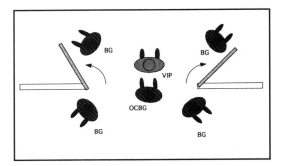

Fig. 7.10. *When an escort team encounters double doors, the two lead bodyguards move through the doors and hold them open to allow the principal to pass through. The OCBG gives body cover from the rear while following the principal through the doors. The two rear bodyguards secure the rear until the principal is moving away from the doors inside the room. If the double doors open outward, the easiest way to deal with them is for the two lead bodyguards to open them and watch the rear of the formation, while the two rear bodyguards shift position and move into the room to secure it. Otherwise, the formation will operate as shown here.*

bodyguards hold them open and turn to watch the rear of the formation. The two bodyguards who had been at the rear pass through the doors to assume the lead and secure the area beyond the doors. Then the VIP and team leader proceed through, while the two bodyguards holding the doors take up position as the rear members of the formation.

SECURITY ADVANCE PARTY

When entering a venue where a security advance party has preceded the close-protection team, one of the SAP will normally be at the door to signal that the area beyond is secure. As a result, the two lead bodyguards may not have to penetrate as far into the building as when entering an establishment that is assumed to be unsecured.

ADDITIONAL BODY COVER

Frequently, the principal will be met upon arrival by a doorman or another dignitary. It is

acceptable to position this person ahead of the principal when passing through a door so that they can act as a 'bullet catcher'. This term is often used, incorrectly, to refer to bodyguards, but in my experience those in VIP protection apply it to people around a principal who are not part of the actual protection team, but because of their propinquity end up giving body cover. I will discuss using 'bullet catchers' in more detail later in this chapter.

LIFT PROCEDURES

Although I have already described techniques of escort on a stairwell, other types of upward and downward movement will occur when protecting a VIP. Probably the most common is the lift, although escalators and even ski lifts may require specialised escort formations as well.

Most members of protective teams are particularly suspicious of lifts, since they are entering what is, in effect, a box with their principal, a box that has no alternative exit. As a result, team members tend to be particularly alert during lift movements. Where available, an express lift that does not stop at intermediate floors is preferable. Even better is a private lift serving a penthouse or VIP floor. When neither of these options is available, it will be necessary to take a public lift.

Escort formations for lifts are designed to protect the principal while entering, leaving and riding in the lift with other passengers on board. Having said that, in my experience, many people, seeing an individual surrounded by five burly bodyguards, will wait for the next lift.

Although it seems obvious, the protective team should not let the principal enter a lift going in the opposite direction from his destination. Riding a lift up, when the intent is to go down, only increases the level of exposure in a contained area.

ADVANCE GUARD

When leaving a hotel room or other location to

take a lift, the team will normally form up in the corridor to await the signal from the team leader that the principal is coming out (see fig. 7.11). I prefer to have at least one member of the protective team already in position on the ground floor, in the underground car park or on whatever floor is the destination for the principal. This bodyguard's job is to make sure that the lift door does not open on to an unpleasant surprise. If a sixth bodyguard is available, that is his or her

Fig. 7.11. This illustration shows the technique for escorting a principal from a secure room to a lift; the same basic technique is used to begin many other types of movement. In this case, note that the OCBG is with the principal and is giving the order, 'Prepare to move.' The four bodyguards are securing the corridor and are prepared to move into the lift in the positions they will assume inside. In a non-lift movement, BGs 1 and 2, and 3 and 4 would switch positions so that they could form more readily into the escort formation.

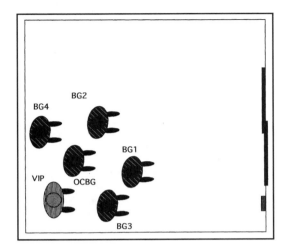

Fig. 7.12. When guarding a principal in a lift, the close-protection team adopts an approximation of the formation in which they will leave the lift, adjusted as necessary to give body cover to the VIP.

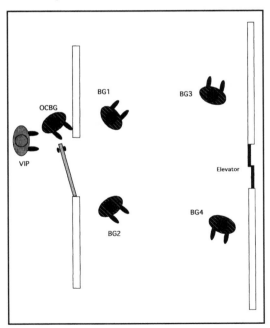

function. If not, one of the five close-protection team members can be sent ahead.

BODYGUARD FORMATION
When entering the lift, most teams position themselves so that it will be easy to move into formation upon leaving; thus the two rear bodyguards will be at the back of the lift. Normally, the team tries to place the VIP towards a rear corner of the lift so that anyone firing through the door as it opens will have more difficulty in hitting the VIP (see fig. 7.12).

LEAVING THE LIFT
When the door opens, the first two bodyguards will look for an all-clear signal from the team member sent ahead to the destination floor before stepping out of the lift. If it was impossible to send someone ahead, the first two escort personnel will move out to secure the immediate area before the rest of the party leaves the lift (see fig. 7.13).

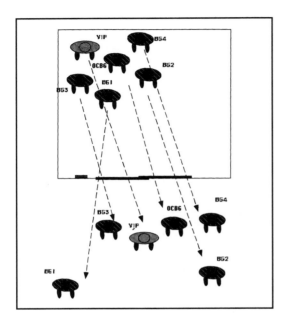

Fig. 7.13. *When escorting a principal out of a lift, BG1 and BG2 will look first for an all-clear sign from the bodyguard sent ahead to the destination floor. Then they will leave the lift and move far enough away to clear an exit for the remainder of the formation and also to look around. As the VIP leaves the lift, the team forms around him or her and begins to move to the vehicle, building exit, room or other destination.*

ESCALATORS

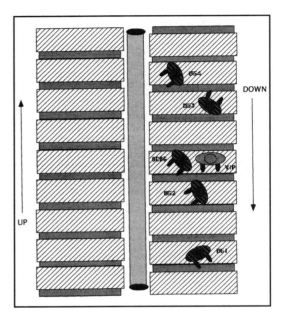

Fig. 7.14. *When escorting a principal on an escalator, the formation must remain flexible, yet cover the various potential areas of attack and ensure that the bodyguards give body cover. In this example, the team is formed for a movement on the 'down' escalator. Note that BG1 is near the bottom, ready to step off and check the landing. He is also looking around as he approaches the bottom. BG2 helps give body cover and watches anyone on the 'up' escalator. The OCBG gives direct body cover and watches the 'up' escalator as well. BG3 watches the formation's rear and gives body cover for the principal. BG4 watches upward towards the 'up' escalator.*

When moving through some open areas in office buildings, airports, shopping centres, etc, the close-protection team may have to deal with escalators. From the bodyguard's point of view, the greatest problem with an escalator is that there is an added threat posed by people passing close to the principal on the adjacent escalator, which will be travelling in the opposite direction.

Although it would be possible to send a team member to ride the neighbouring escalator and watch anyone on it, timing would be quite difficult to ensure that the bodyguard was in the right position. I have found instead that it is best to adjust the basic formation so that the team leader gives body cover between the principal and the adjacent escalator, while the rest of the team position themselves to watch upward and downward for threats (see fig. 7.14).

SKI LIFTS

When protecting a principal on the ski slopes, using a ski lift presents a variant of the problem encountered with an escalator. Normally, one member of the escort team will be sent ahead to secure the point of debarkation at the top of the slope. Another will remain at the point of embarkation until the lift carrying the principal has arrived safely at the top of the slope. The remainder of the team will ride the lift just ahead of, or behind, the principal.

If the lift allows two skiers to ride next to each other, the team leader will accompany the principal and take the side most likely to present a threat. In most cases, this will be wooded areas or

Fig. 7.15. *Escort formation for moving between two buildings. Note that one of the two lead bodyguards has moved forward to check the two blind corners, towards which the formation is moving. One of the two rear bodyguards has hung back to secure the blind corners at the rear. Normally, the OCBG will move to the side where there might be a greater threat (ie windows, doors, etc).*

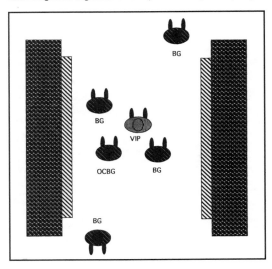

other points from which a sniper might fire. If the protective effort is large enough, protective personnel on skis may be sent to secure the most likely sniping sites until the principal reaches the top of the slope.

SHOPPING TRIPS

When escorting a principal on a shopping jaunt, the type of shop entered will determine how tight the protective cordon should be. In a large crowded store, the team leader and perhaps a couple of bodyguards, will remain close to the principal. In a small shop with fewer customers, a member of the protective team will check the premises before the principal enters, but the team will probably wait outside, observing anyone going into the shop. In some cases, the team leader will accompany the principal into the shop while the remainder of the team remains outside.

CORRIDORS AND ALLEYWAYS

One situation that may arise indoors or outdoors is the need to escort a principal along a lengthy corridor, between two buildings or down a path with hedges on both sides. In each case, there will be blind corners to the front and rear. As a result, some adjustment to the formation will be necessary so that one of the lead bodyguards moves ahead to cover the blind corner in front, and one of the rear bodyguards lags behind to cover the blind corner to the rear (see fig. 7.15).

BULLET CATCHERS

I mentioned the use of 'bullet catchers' earlier in this chapter. One of the most common situations

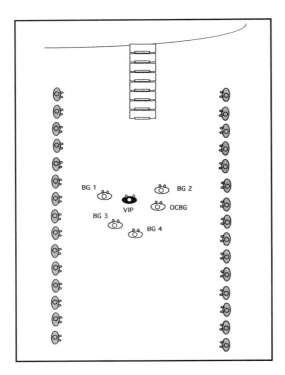

Fig. 7.16. *When it is necessary to escort a principal across open ground, perhaps when boarding an aircraft, an honour guard formed of local dignitaries, police or military personnel may be placed in such a way that they give body cover for the VIP and act as 'bullet catchers'. Note that the aircraft blocks the view of the VIP from the front; the escort formation covers the rear; and the honour guard covers the sides.*

where people surrounding a VIP are employed as additional body cover – even if they aren't aware that they're giving body cover – occurs when a sniper might pose a threat. For example, when escorting a principal into a building from a vehicle – techniques for which will be discussed in Chapter 8 – or on to a waiting aircraft that is not parked at the terminal, a double line of 'honorary greeters' can offer quite useful cover (see fig. 7.16).

TEAM SIZE

Although those in close protection would prefer to have at least five bodyguards available for a foot escort detail, often this is not possible. Top-level official protective teams will normally have substantially more protective personnel on each shift, but smaller details may rely on a very limited number of personnel. As a result, escort formations must be adjusted accordingly.

FOUR-MAN TEAM

With a four-man detail, formations remain quite similar to those with five members. In the box formation, for example, the four bodyguards at the corners remain, but instead of functioning within the box, the team leader handles one of the corner assignments. In this situation, I recommend that the leader occupies one of the two rear positions to obtain a good view of what is going on around the team and also to be able to see the principal if a crisis arises.

The V-formation can also be adjusted for four bodyguards – two on each side and the point of the V left open. One formation that is considered

Fig. 7.17. *Four-man diamond escort formation.*

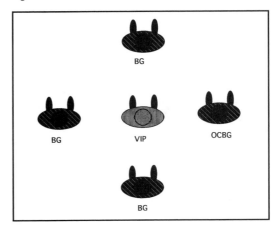

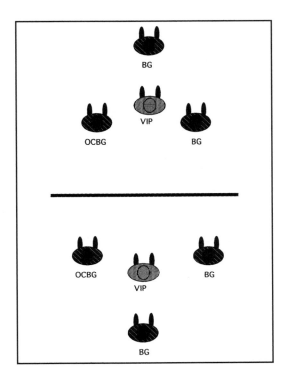

Fig. 7.18. *Three-man triangle escort formations.*

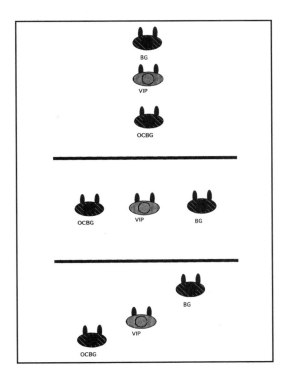

Fig. 7.19. *Two-man escort formations.*

particularly applicable to the four-man team is the diamond, which has one bodyguard in the lead, one in the rear and one on each side of the principal (see fig. 7.17). This formation has the advantage of giving loose body cover from each direction.

THREE-MAN TEAM

When only three bodyguards are available, it is still possible to provide reasonable cover while walking, using either a triangle or inverse triangle formation. In the former, one bodyguard assumes the lead, while the other two act as flankers, usually spaced a little behind the VIP. In the latter, the open end of the triangle faces forward with two lead bodyguards, while the third bodyguard acts as rear security (see fig. 7.18).

Many in close protection actually like the three-man escort formation, as it is very flexible, yet still allows reasonable cover. It provides two bodyguards to cover and evacuate the principal while one deals with an attacker. However, three bodyguards are considered by most professionals to be the minimum necessary to give an acceptable degree of protection against a significant threat – and they will be stretched very thinly.

TWO-MAN TEAM

When carrying out escort duties with only two bodyguards, the formation must be very fluid, since the two protectors must constantly shift position to fit the circumstances. On some occasions, one will take the lead while the other covers the principal's back. If they move through an area with people on each side, the bodyguards may become flankers. In yet other situations, one will take up position to the front and side of the principal, while the other is behind and to the other side (see fig. 7.19).

Whenever a protective team is engaged in foot escort duties, everyone must be extremely alert, but this requirement is magnified with only two bodyguards, as each must try to cover more than 180 degrees while looking for danger. At least with two bodyguards, when passing through a doorway, one can move ahead of the principal, while the other remains behind the VIP. If an attacker is encountered and one bodyguard becomes involved in countering the attack, the other can still attempt to cover and evacuate the principal.

SOLO BODYGUARDS

When only one bodyguard is available, he or she still may be a deterrent and be able to counter an attack or move the principal to safety, but will not be able to do both. When approaching a doorway, the bodyguard will have to move forward to take a quick peek before leading the principal through the door. The lone bodyguard will have to remain ever active and ever vigilant, but will lack any ability to provide defence in depth and will be able to offer little versatility when reacting to a threat.

A FLEXIBLE APPROACH

Although I have tried to explain a diverse group of escort formations in this chapter, by no means have I covered all the situations that may be faced by a protective team when carrying out escort duties on foot. Instead, I have attempted to illustrate typical scenarios that are likely to be encountered. An experienced protective team will have learned to adjust their formation to fit all contingencies.

AUTHOR'S NOTE

I was working as part of a three-man detail in Amsterdam, and we had to cope with a fairly lengthy walk along a canal while worrying about traffic passing nearby. We determined that the traffic was a greater danger than falling in the canal and arranged our formation accordingly, positioning one bodyguard in the lead, one on the traffic side and one – the best swimmer – behind the principal with the duty of going into the canal after our charge if necessary.

CONSTANT VIGILANCE

Although it is difficult to set aside time for training, unless one serves on a large protective team that actually builds in a rotation for training, it is important for members of a close-protection team to practise their close-combat skills, their powers of observation and their AOP drills whenever possible. Foot escort assignments can be extremely stressful because the bodyguards must remain constantly vigilant to all types of danger – assassins, unruly crowds, dangerous dogs, vehicles splashing mud, unexpected kerbs and so on. The bodyguard must be ready at all times to make a split-second decision that can affect the principal, the members of the protective team and innocent bystanders.

Foot escort duties graphically illustrate why those in close protection need to be in excellent physical condition and mentally alert. The bodyguard in most situations, but especially when engaged in foot escort duties, must be able to make an immediate assessment of threat, decide rapidly upon the best course of action and implement that course of action decisively. That's why for those in VIP protection, even a walk in the park isn't really 'a walk in the park'.

Because a VIP is particularly vulnerable when travelling by car, particular emphasis must be placed on security while in transit. The number of VIPs who have been kidnapped or assassinated while driving or being driven is very large. To name two well-known examples, Aldo Moro was kidnapped from his vehicle and later killed, despite the presence of a substantial protective team; and US President John F. Kennedy was assassinated while riding in a motorcade. Dozens of similar examples could be cited very easily.

IMPORTANT CONSIDERATIONS

Assassins and kidnappers often choose vehicle assaults for the simple reason that they allow them to select the time and place of the attack. Those in VIP protection must give serious consideration to the choice of VIP vehicles, the training of VIP drivers, the planning of travel and motorcade routes, the organisation of motorcades, the drills for getting into and out of a vehicle, and the methods for dealing with an assault against a VIP vehicle. In this chapter, I will discuss each of these aspects of the protection team's job and show how they are interrelated.

SUITABLE VEHICLES

One of the first considerations, on which the head of protective security is likely to be consulted, is the choice of VIP vehicles. I say 'vehicles' as opposed to 'vehicle' because if more than one bodyguard and one VIP driver are involved in the protective effort, at least two vehicles will be required. For most full-scale protective efforts, a minimum of three vehicles is considered standard.

I have been consulted on the selection of VIP vehicles on numerous occasions and have determined some very basic considerations for selecting a vehicle and hardening it to give maximum protection. Normally, a vehicle chosen for VIP transport should be a large, powerful, four-door saloon or an equivalent sport utility vehicle (SUV). Among those makes that have served well are Cadillac, Lincoln, Mercedes, BMW, Jaguar, Rover and Rolls Royce. Where SUVs are concerned, any of the models of Range Rover or even something of Chevrolet Suburban size will usually work well. Note, however, that the Rolls Royce is uncommon enough in many parts of the world that it attracts undue attention. Stretched limos should also be avoided, as they are too ostentatious and too 'visible'.

The more a vehicle can blend in, the better. Therefore, a model that is relatively common in the country where it will be used is probably the best choice. If possible, two or three examples of the same make, model and colour should be acquired so that it will never be obvious which vehicle is carrying the VIP in motorcades. If the principal lives in a country where the government is unpopular, or where an insurgency is taking place, I would advise against choosing the same type of vehicle as used by senior government officials, since this might invite attack on the mistaken assumption that a member of the government is being 'hit'. Avoid 'official' colours, too. In some cases, for example, black vehicles are assumed to be official. Do not, however, choose a bright colour, which will attract attention.

VEHICLE SPECIFICATION

It is important when selecting the vehicle to ensure that it retains sufficient power for evasive driving and pushing through barricades even after weight has been added during the 'hardening' process. Be sure that the transmission/engine combination provides substantial torque at low speeds so that the driver has enough acceleration to clear an ambush or other danger quickly.

Other important options include heavy-duty suspension, brakes, transmission, steering, etc. I have found it useful, too, for the bumpers to be discreetly reinforced so that the driver can punch through road-blocks if necessary. Among other useful features are twin side mirrors with power adjustment as an aid to spotting surveillance, a locking fuel filler cap, locking bonnet, remotely operated boot lock and a heated rear window. Enhanced vehicle lighting is also advisable, including fog lights, high-intensity headlights and reversing lights, and a spotlight mounted on the front passenger side.

ORDERING

When ordering vehicles, release their specifications on a need-to-know basis. This will prevent any potential attacker from knowing the vehicle's capabilities in an emergency. It is even more important to keep the various steps in the hardening, or armouring, process classified.

HARDENING THE VEHICLE

When planning the hardening of a vehicle, members of the protective team, particularly the VIP driver, will work closely with a firm that specialises in armouring vehicles. This company will advise on the options available and their pros and cons. It is always a good idea, however, to have some idea of the basics of vehicle hardening to ensure that the principal obtains the best vehicle possible.

TYPES OF ARMOUR

Armour will normally be chosen from three basic types – steel, light alloy and composite. As a rule,

steel will be used for large, flat areas such as roofs and doors. For roofs and sides, hard steel usually works best, while less brittle, tougher steel is more desirable in floors to provide greater blast resistance. One of the best designs incorporates steel bands that form a cage to prevent the passenger compartment from collapsing even if the vehicle is blown over.

When alloys are used for armouring a vehicle, they usually comprise a steel and aluminium laminate, sometimes with the addition of a ceramic laminate. A lot of armouring today is done with Kevlar, a composite material; however, carbon fibre is stronger, but more expensive. Glassfibre is also used, specifically to protect against blast, especially in vehicle floors. When overseeing the construction of a hardened vehicle, it is important to ensure that when Kevlar is used, it is waterproofed with resin so that moisture, which is likely to seep into crevices, cannot lower its protection level.

CONSTRUCTION

Armour plate is available in pre-cut sections, particularly for vehicles that are frequently armoured, but flat sheets may be purchased and formed in the workshop to fit the vehicle. I have seen pre-cut sections for some Mercedes vehicles, which may be installed relatively quickly. If expense is a major consideration, choosing a vehicle that allows the use of pre-cut sections will produce substantial savings.

During the fabrication phase, captive bolts should be used to attach the armoured panels, preventing the fixings themselves from becoming projectiles. Note that the firm building the vehicle may advise overlapping the armour so that an angular shot cannot slip between panels.

Fortunately, modern ceramic panels combined with Kevlar offer as high a level of protection as that provided by very heavy steel plate. Thus, much lighter, more compact vehicles may be hardened to the same level that previously would have required a very heavy saloon.

There are some choices when it comes to armouring doors. Many prefer panels that may be

Armoured Rolls-Royce used by London's Metropolitan Police for transporting VIPs.

Note the thickness of the windows in the Metropolitan Police armoured Rolls-Royce.

removed or slid to one side to create gun ports so that protective personnel can fire from within the vehicle. Usually, though, it is best not to break the integrity of the armour in this way, since it also offers a point through which bullets can enter the vehicle. Some VIP vehicles have gun ports only on the front passenger side, as this is normally where the team leader rides.

ENGINE COMPARTMENT

To make it more difficult to disable the engine with gunfire, a hardened vehicle will usually incorporate protection for the bulkhead, battery and radiator as well as other portions of the engine compartment. Note, however, that in hot climates, armouring the radiator can increase the likelihood that it will overheat. If it is not deemed feasible to armour the radiator, bear in mind that even if the radiator is punctured during an ambush and all the coolant drains out, the vehicle should be able to run far enough to leave the area of an attack and reach safety before seizing up.

WINDOWS AND DOORS

Although it would be possible to have armoured panels covering windows, this would restrict visibility and attract attention to the vehicle. Instead, bullet-resistant glass is used on hardened vehicles. Normally, this is actually a laminate of glass and polycarbonate, with polycarbonate film on the inside to protect against shattering and fragments. An air gap is incorporated between the glass and the polycarbonate to allow for expansion caused by temperature changes.

Underwriters Laboratory Rating 752 sets out specifications for bullet-resistant glass in levels between 9mm Parabellum and 7.62 NATO or .30-06. Note that glass designed to stop the more powerful rifle cartridges may be two inches thick or more.

To handle heavy bullet-resistant glass as well as armoured panels, doors of hardened vehicles will probably need extra hinges and reinforced pillars. Special framing will be necessary for the panels as well, and normally the windows cannot be lowered. Bodyguards will have to be very aware of the weight of these doors, too, since they may cause injuries if they hit anyone as they open or close.

Front and rear windows usually receive the thickest glass, as they are most likely to suffer from multiple hits. Windows should be tinted, as well, to make it more difficult for a shooter to spot a target.

One point about heavy bullet-resistant glass that must be noted is that the driver's window may have to incorporate a small port, which may be opened or lowered, as the driver may have to use a key card to enter a garage. It would be an invitation for attack if he had to exit the vehicle to use the card.

TYRES

Once the body, glass and power train have been selected and designed to complement each other, the tyres must be considered. Although a standard tyre will continue to hold air for longer than is usually assumed when punctured by a bullet, caltrop or other sharp object, 'run-flat' tyres are a virtual necessity when designing a hardened vehicle. They are made by Michelin and Dunlop among other manufacturers.

Some run-flat tires incorporate a foam filling, but it must be borne in mind that the foam can liquefy, thus flattening the tires. Check what conditions will have an adverse effect on the foam filling if these are chosen. More modern run-flat tires have an internal sealant that quickly closes any punctures to the tyre.

SAFETY BANDS
Normally included in the tyre package are steel safety bands, which cover the well of each wheel between the two rims, preventing the tyre beads from entering the well and, thus, coming off the wheel. One of the great advantages of these safety bands is that they can be used with conventional tyres to allow a vehicle to keep going even when the tyres have lost pressure. They work best, though, in conjunction with run-flat tyres.

AUTHOR'S NOTE
Run-flat tyres are now offered as an option on some US saloons and should be considered if buying non-hardened vehicles as part of the fleet for a VIP family, since they preclude the need to stop to change a tyre if it goes flat in a dangerous area. This happened to Bill Cosby's son, resulting in his death.

PROTECTING FUEL TANKS

Since fire is always a danger during an attack, and particularly in cases of civil unrest when fire bombs may be thrown at the vehicle, fuel tanks must be protected. For many years, a material that expanded to seal leaks was commonly used in fuel tanks, but subsequently the company that manufactured this sealant went out of business. At the time of writing, I am not aware of any firm that is making anything similar. However, another material named Explosafe can be employed instead.

Explosafe is an aluminum foil that forms a honeycomb inside the tank; it channels heat away from a fire so rapidly that the flame is extinguished instantly. Additional points in Explosafe's favour are that it is very light in weight and low in volume. Another option, often used in addition to Explosafe, but sometimes without it, is a remote fire extinguisher for the fuel tank.

AUXILIARY TANK
Some type of protective panel will usually be incorporated to make puncturing the fuel tank difficult, but another feature added to some hardened vehicles is a separate auxiliary tank, which contains enough fuel to get well clear of an ambush if the main tank is ruptured.

AIR CONDITIONING

Since armoured windows normally cannot be opened, air conditioning is a must. The system should offer the facility of pressurising the interior of the vehicle so that CS gas or other anti-riot agents will not be sucked inside when driving through a demonstration. Such a system will also help protect against an actual chemical or biological attack against the vehicle.

ADDITIONAL VEHICLE PROTECTION

Vehicles intended for use in areas where civil unrest is common often incorporate a variety of other features. They may, for example, have their own dispensers for CS gas or smoke. Such vehicles may also have a razor-sharp moulding around the lower panels to slash members of a crowd attempting to tip the vehicle over. Some incorporate the capability of sending an electric charge through the vehicle's exterior. Yet another option is an automatic fire extinguisher in the vehicle's boot.

COMMUNICATIONS

Additional features may be provided to help ensure the VIP's safety. Communications equipment should be incorporated to allow continuous contact with other vehicles and the ability to summon the police. Official VIP cars often have a radio tuned to the police frequency to be able to call for help. A hands-free car phone should be added, and the VIP driver and team leader – as well as the principal – should have mobile phones as a back-up. A public address system is also useful, since it allows those inside the vehicle to communicate with anyone outside without opening a window.

LIGHTING

Sirens and searchlights may be desirable, especially if the VIP has official status. When snipers or attackers armed with anti-tank rockets are considered a danger, some protective teams like to fit a strobe light on the roof of the vehicle to make it more difficult for anyone using an optical sight to acquire the vehicle as a target.

AUTOMATIC FEATURES

Other useful options include automatic locking doors, an automatic alarm, a remote starting capability and high-quality mirrors that are adjustable from within the passenger compartment.

RUNNING BOARDS

Vehicles that will be used by political figures who may often take part in parades or slow-moving motorcades may also be equipped with running boards so that protective personnel can ride on the outside of the vehicle.

TAMPER PROTECTION

Another system that I recommend is the Maxim Detection Device (MDD), or its equivalent. The MDD is designed to monitor a group of sensors affixed at critical points to the vehicle. This system allows the chauffeur to quickly determine via a remote receiver whether the vehicle has been tampered with while left unguarded. The MDD may, in fact, be linked to the driver's pager so that it sends a signal if triggered.

Among the types of tampering detectable by the MDD system are:

- door, bonnet or boot being opened;
- something having been placed beneath the vehicle;
- battery failure;
- battery disconnection (likely in the event of a bomb having been wired into a vehicle's electrical system);
- system failure, tampering or destruction.

The MDD system is particularly invaluable when only a single bodyguard/driver is employed or when the team is so small that the vehicle will be left unattended at times.

WEIGHT CONSIDERATIONS

The total hardening package should not increase the vehicle's weight by more than twenty-five per cent, otherwise its performance will suffer to an unacceptable degree. A hardening package that grants the protection level desired with the minimum of weight gain is preferable.

To give a rough idea of the weight added by armouring, one estimate is that Threat Level III armouring, which will defeat .44 Magnum, adds 4.3 pounds per square foot; Level IV armouring, which will defeat .308 NATO or .30-06, adds 8.4 pounds per square foot; and Threat Level V armouring, which will defeat .50 Machine Gun, adds 11.9 pounds per square foot.

During the design stage, therefore, whenever there is a choice between two options that offer equal protection, but a difference in weight, the lighter option should be chosen. For front-engined vehicles, weight distribution should remain at fifty-five per cent on the front so that handling is not affected adversely.

VALUE FOR MONEY

When determining the extent of vehicle hardening required, the threat level faced by the principal will play a critical role. Cost may be a factor, but the team leader should put cost into perspective for the principal by explaining how often attacks take place on vehicles. Bear in mind, though, that the cost of a vehicle incorporating all, or most, of the features I've discussed would be in the region of £170,000 ($250,000) or more. With an investment of this size, the head of security, the VIP driver or even the VIP should monitor the vehicle's construction to make sure no corners are cut and that the criteria set out for the vehicle are met.

CARRY OUT A TEST
I recommend having a window or panel pulled from the vehicle at some point and shooting at it with the type of weapon it is designed to stop to make sure that it performs as advertised. The principal will be charged for the item, but I think it is money well spent for peace of mind. I would equate this with the bullet dent normally

encountered on Renaissance breast plates to show that a bullet had been fired at the plate and that it had succeeded in stopping the projectile.

VIP DRIVER

Before taking delivery of the vehicle, a trained VIP driver should put it through its paces to ensure it retains acceptable handling and performance. In fact, a trained VIP driver is an important aspect in the provision of secure VIP transportation.

AUTHOR'S NOTE
To give an idea of the importance of a trained VIP driver, the King of Kuwait managed to escape from his country during the Iraqi invasion largely through the skills of his driver.

To be sure that a VIP driver is capable of carrying out this stressful and critical job, an individual who is decisive and cool in a crisis must be chosen so that he will not hesitate to take action if necessary. However, he must not be reckless or impulsive.

PRE-EMPT PROBLEMS
One of the first skills a VIP driver learns is the ability to recognise and prevent problems rather than simply reacting to them. In fact, the good driver must constantly scan ahead to anticipate potential threats and dangers. One of the most critical factors in countering an ambush is early recognition to give the driver time to react. The driver must also be aware at all times of potential escape routes in case he has to use them.

VIP drivers must be trained in a number of skills, including:

- carrying out route surveys;
- vehicle explosive recces;
- surveillance recognition;

- selection of vehicles;
- early recognition of attacks;
- vehicle ambush/counter-ambush techniques;
- vehicle safety.

DRIVER TRAINING

While many drivers receive their initial training individually, they will also learn to work as part of a protective team, unless they are functioning as a lone driver/bodyguard. This is a relatively common practice, but not one I would recommend, since it is much better for the driver to concentrate solely on the skills necessary for being a protective driver, even though that may entail using firearms at some stage. It is important, however, to differentiate between a chauffeur and a trained VIP driver.

By training and inclination, a chauffer is concerned primarily with the vehicle's appearance and with smoothly transporting the VIP from place to place. A chauffer is not attuned to taking decisive evasive action, which may damage the car's pristine paintwork, even though this may save the principal's life. It is

also important that a VIP driver receives at least basic bodyguard training so that he or she understands how a protective team operates and the part the driver plays in the overall protective effort.

ESSENTIAL TECHNIQUES
Specific driving skills are obviously an important part of VIP driver training. Among the techniques to be employed when an attack cannot be avoided and must be countered are evasive driving, J-turns, bootlegger turns, counter-ambush, ramming and various other manoeuvres.

OFFENSIVE DRIVING
The VIP driver must also learn to drive offensively when facing situations that may not be avoided. Normally, for example, he or she will drive in the centre lane on multi-lane roads to make it harder to run the car off the road. If an attempt is made to force the vehicle from the road, the trained driver may counter this by forcing the attacking vehicle off the road by spinning the steering wheel through about ninety degrees.

VIP drivers learn techniques for ramming other vehicles. (Scotti Driving School)

Fig. 8.1. *When using the J-turn* (top) *to escape an ambush, the driver stops (A), reverses the vehicle in a 180-degree turn (B), then accelerates forward (C). The J-turn is normally used when there is only limited manoeuvring room. Note that in this case, the turn is covered by the trail vehicle, which has accelerated forward to give the VIP vehicle cover while it escapes (D). The driver of the cover vehicle will take evasive measures once the VIP car is clear.*

The Y-turn (bottom) *is used when there is a bit more room. The driver stops (A), reverses in a ninety-degree turn (B), then begins to accelerate (C) as the turn is completed.*

DEALING WITH AMBUSHES

The driver must be constantly alert for signs of an impending ambush. Not only must he or she watch for stationary road-blocks, but also for moving cut-offs, in which two or more vehicles attempt to box in the VIP car.

To counter the moving cut-off, the VIP driver may slow, but not stop, to provide manoeuvring room, or may use controlled braking to let the blocking cars overshoot, then use a J- or Y-turn (see fig. 8.1) to quickly leave the area. If this is not possible, the driver should be prepared to take evasive action, and should know how to force the other vehicle off the road by bringing the front three feet or so of the VIP vehicle into contact with the area between the rear wheel and bumper of the opposing vehicle.

RAMMING

If, however, the road-block is stationary and there is no other escape, the driver will use the offensive technique of ramming. When possible, prior to ramming, it is best to slow down and change into low gear, then, after choosing the optimum impact point, to accelerate. Many trainers of VIP drivers advise that prior to ramming, the driver should make sure that his or her thumbs are not hooked on the wheel so that they are not injured by the impact.

The best point to ram is usually where the target vehicle is lightest so that it will pivot away from the impact. Thus, in a front-engined vehicle, the best ramming point is usually just behind the rear wheel. Care must be taken, though, not to hook the bumper of the vehicle being rammed.

MAKING THE MOST OF THE VEHICLE

Sometimes a road-block may be avoided by driving across a kerb and pavement. If the VIP vehicle is a four-wheel-drive model, it will have a much greater capability of avoiding blocks by travelling cross-country. The VIP driver should remember, too, that the vehicle can make a formidable anti-personnel weapon. If a portion of the attacking force can be taken out by running them down, so be it!

COLLISION AVOIDANCE

The trained driver must know how to deal with attempts to ram the VIP vehicle. He or she should make whatever manoeuvres are necessary to avoid being hit at a ninety-degree angle, as this will be more likely not only to shove the vehicle off the road, but also to injure the occupants. If the attackers attempt to ram the car from the rear, the VIP driver should try to hit the brakes just prior to impact to raise the rear of the VIP vehicle so that the bumpers of the two vehicles do not become entangled.

RAPID MANOEUVRING

The trained driver will learn many tricks that will allow rapid evasive manoeuvres to be carried out efficiently. For example, VIP drivers are taught to employ the left foot for braking so that time is not wasted in removing the right foot from the accelerator. This also permits the car to be driven through the simultaneous use of the accelerator and brake. The most effective control of the steering wheel can be achieved by placing the hands at the ten o'clock and two o'clock positions on the rim.

MULTI-VEHICLE TACTICS

When the driver is operating as part of a full-scale protective team, he or she will also train in manoeuvres involving several vehicles. For example, a trail car will often turn wide to protect the VIP vehicle as it turns, or swing into the passing lane before the VIP car pulls out to pass another vehicle. The VIP driver, however, must signal his or her intentions and co-ordinate manoeuvres with the driver of the trail car. These will include clearing an ambush site while one of the other vehicles offers cover, and evacuation under fire. Each of these tactics will be covered in detail later in the chapter. The trained VIP driver must also know how to function as part of a motorcade.

UNDERSTANDING THE VEHICLE

A key part of driver training is learning to employ the vehicle's capabilities to the full. As a result, studying the vehicle's dynamics in conjunction with developing proper control of the steering and brakes enables a good VIP driver not only to drive through a terrorist attack, but also to be a safer driver under all sorts of conditions. Thus, even if the VIP driver never has to use evasive driving

skills, he or she will still be a safer, more effective driver for the principal.

One of the driver's responsibilities is to inspect the vehicle to make sure that it is safe and well maintained. Normally, he will ensure that any fire extinguishers are charged and medical kits fully stocked. The fuel tank should never be allowed to drop below half full. The driver will also inspect the vehicle for tampering and will know how to carry out a full explosives recce of the vehicle, an aspect that will be discussed in Chapter 10.

A BALANCED APPROACH

A good VIP driver will balance the skills of defensive, evasive and offensive driving.

The basic rules that apply to defensive as well as evasive or offensive driving are:

- If it is necessary to take evasive action to avoid trouble, head away from oncoming traffic.
- If the choice is between an uncontrolled skid and leaving the road under control, leave the road.
- If it is necessary to hit something, choose the softest possible object (ie bushes rather than a lamp post or concrete barrier).
- If it is necessary to hit something, hit something moving in the same direction as the VIP vehicle rather than something stationary or moving in the opposite direction.
- If it is necessary to hit something, try to hit it a glancing blow.
- Don't hit anything head on.

In simple terms: apply the laws of physics in a practical manner.

EMBUS AND DEBUS DRILLS

One occasion that requires co-ordination between the VIP driver and the protective team is when the

VIP is entering or leaving the vehicle and the protective team is forming up around him or her. This combination of vehicle and foot escort techniques is frequently referred to among bodyguards as an 'embus' or 'debus' drill. These drills require a great deal of co-ordination, since the escort personnel must protect their principal until he or she is safely in the vehicle, yet must be able to move quickly to take up position in their own vehicle.

MULTI-VEHICLE FORMATIONS

As a rule, if a principal has a protective team consisting of more than one driver and one bodyguard, at least two vehicles will be employed. The use of a second – and often third – car allows the principal privacy within his or her vehicle, since the driver and one bodyguard can ride in the front, leaving the rear free for the principal and family or associates. Moreover, the second vehicle can also be used as a back-up if the VIP vehicle becomes disabled.

The team leader will make sure that the VIP is safely in the vehicle before entering. Note that the author has his Glock in a holster designed to allow a draw while seated.

In addition, a second vehicle can be used to head off any vehicle attempting to pursue the VIP and can provide cover during an extraction from an ambush.

If possible, the VIP vehicle and escort vehicle, or vehicles, should be of the same type, colour, etc. This not only makes it more difficult for an attacker to determine exactly which vehicle carries the principal, but also ensures that the vehicles will have similar performance characteristics. In fact, if an escort vehicle is more lightly armoured than the VIP vehicle, this will normally give it better performance, which is useful, since in some circumstances it will have to be able to move ahead of the VIP car quickly or accelerate to catch up in others.

TWO-CAR TECHNIQUES

When two cars are used, the second vehicle will usually carry up to four bodyguards in addition to the driver and will follow the VIP car most of the time. Under normal circumstances, it is considered better to be in the trail position so that any attack on the VIP vehicle or attempt to cut it off will be immediately obvious. If an escort travels ahead of the VIP car, it may be allowed to pass before an ambush is sprung on the VIP.

EMBUSSING
Normally, when embussing the VIP, the car will pull into a parking spot that allows the most secure approach for the principal. Before moving the principal to the vehicle, however, the team leader or another member of the protective team will make a quick check of the area for any signs of danger.

As the protective team approaches the vehicle, the two lead bodyguards will move around it, then position themselves to give body cover to the front and rear windows on the driver's side. Not only does this make a shot at the principal more difficult, but also it protects the driver if a quick evacuation is necessary, a difficult task if he or she has been 'capped' by a sniper!

The two rear bodyguards position themselves just in front of the front door and just behind the rear door to give as much body cover as possible without blocking the door. The team leader holds the door for the principal, then, when the latter is safely inside, jumps into the front passenger seat and gives the driver the 'Go!' order.

DON'T BE WRONG-FOOTED

When jumping into vehicles, bodyguards learn always to put the inside foot into the vehicle first. When leaving the vehicle as it comes to a stop, one should always let the outside foot hit the ground first. On no account should the bodyguard allow his or her feet to become crossed when entering or leaving a vehicle in the process of starting or stopping.

TRAIL CAR

As the VIP vehicle pulls away, the trail car (sometimes known as the chase car) pulls into the formation that the bodyguards have held, allowing them to enter the vehicle quickly, the two driver's-side bodyguards through the rear door, and the passenger-side bodyguards through the front and rear doors (see fig. 8.2). Many teams like to have the driver of the trail car park with the front protruding slightly to force any passing traffic to swing wide of the VIP car.

DEBUSSING

The debus drill is the reverse of the embus drill. The trail car pulls ahead of the VIP vehicle upon arrival at the destination, and the four bodyguards riding in it leap out and take up their formation facing outward, although a little looser than if the VIP car were stationary. The VIP car pulls into the formation, whereupon the bodyguards close up a bit to offer body cover to the VIP and driver. The team leader gets out, checks that everyone is in position, then opens the VIP's door to allow him or her to get out.

Note that the normal practice is to leave the door open until the principal is in the building, in case an emergency evacuation is necessary. The

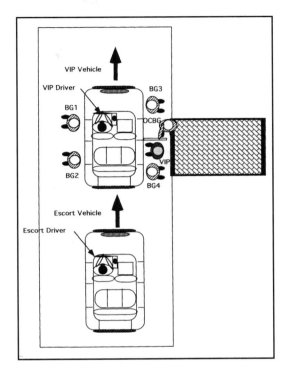

Fig. 8.2. *When embussing, the two lead bodyguards (BG1 and BG2) stay in a box formation until the VIP is near the car and the team leader (OCBG) opens the door. At this point, they move around the vehicle to give body cover at the front and rear driver's-side windows. The two rear bodyguards (BG3 and BG4) give the principal body cover until he or she has entered the vehicle, at which point they move to give body cover at the passenger-side windows. The OCBG jumps into the front passenger seat and gives the 'Go!' order. As the VIP vehicle pulls away, the escort vehicle moves forwards so that BGs 1–4 can quickly enter. Then the escort vehicle follows the VIP vehicle.*

driver also keeps the engine running during embus and debus procedures.

MOVING OFF

As the VIP begins to move, the two bodyguards

on his or her side of the car move out in the lead postions of the escort formation, while the two on the far side of the vehicle hustle to assume the rear escort positions (see figs. 8.3 and 8.4).

THIRD CAR
If the protective team likes to have the trail car park so that it forces traffic to swing wide of the VIP car, then three cars will be best for the debus procedure, since in a two-car formation, the trail car will have swung ahead to allow the bodyguards to get into position to debus the principal.

ONE-WAY STREETS
These drills are normally practised on the assumption that the principal will be leaving the

vehicle on the passenger side; however, when stopping on a one-way street, the debus drill might have to be carried out from the rear door on the driver's side. Therefore, teams should have rehearsed this possibility as well.

THREE-CAR TECHNIQUES

When three cars are used, if each escort vehicle carries a full four-bodyguard team, one acts as a lead car and one as a trail car. The bodyguards in the lead car will form up and act as the escort

Left, fig. 8.3. *The lead, or sole, escort vehicle pulls up at the debus point, and the bodyguards quickly jump out to form a protective box into which the VIP driver pulls.*

Below, fig. 8.4. *Once the VIP vehicle has pulled into the box, the OCBG holds the door for the VIP to get out. As he or she does so, BG1 and BG2 move forward to assume the lead in a box escort formation. The OCBG moves alongside the VIP, while BG3 and BG4 come around the vehicle to assume the rear positions in the box. The VIP driver keeps the vehicle in position until the VIP is safely inside the building so that it is available for evacuation if needed. If allowed to park in front, the driver will remain there or may move to a less obvious parking spot, yet one that ensures the vehicle is readily available.*

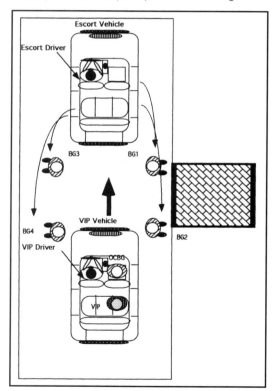

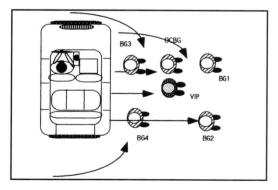

US Army general officer protection personnel practise vehicle debus techniques; faces obscured for security.

formation for debussing, while those in the trail car get out as soon as they arrive and take up positions to secure the area farther away from the vehicles.

When embussing, the bodyguards in the lead car get directly into their vehicle, while the bodyguards escorting the VIP form their box around his or her vehicle and enter their trail vehicle much as if it were a two-car formation. In fact, usually the same four-man team does the actual escort, while the support team's vehicle switches from lead to trail to fit the situation.

EXTRA MANPOWER
The great advantage of this system is that it provides an additional vehicle for evacuation or cover, and puts four more trained bodyguards on the scene to handle whatever situations might arise and give additional security during arrival and departure. It also ensures that there is always one support car moving with the VIP car and offers extra manpower in case one of the two escort cars comes under fire, must stop and fight, or is disabled.

TRAIL-CAR DRIVER

The driver of the trail car must be as skilled as the VIP driver. In fact, normally, he will have been through the same training courses as a VIP driver.

TRAIL-CAR TACTICS

Most of the other missions the trail car performs are aimed at placing it between the VIP car and danger. For example, the trail car will normally position itself so no other vehicle can pass the VIP car until it has been looked over. Since the middle bodyguard in the back seat of the trail vehicle usually has responsibility for watching the rear, he will usually give the driver the 'All clear' to let an approaching vehicle pass.

One reason that Chevrolet Suburbans and some other sport utility vehicles make good trail cars is that usually they can be configured so that the back seat faces rearward to allow easier observation of any approaching vehicles. Of course, an SUV trail vehicle does not fit the criteria of being the same make and model as the VIP car.

POSITIONING
The trail car will also try to prevent any vehicle from coming between it and the VIP car. In the realities of traffic, however, occasionally entirely innocent vehicles will end up between the trail car and VIP vehicle. In this case, the trail driver will move back into position as soon as possible.

RUNNING WIDE
Although I have found the tactic impossible for much of the time, many teams like to have the trail vehicle offset slightly at the rear of the VIP vehicle. The theory is that this allows the trail driver to spot any threats ahead more readily, and also to block a rear approach more effectively.

A similar tactical manoeuvre on two-lane roads is to have the trail car offset slightly towards the oncoming lane, to force any approaching vehicles to give the VIP car a wider berth. In my experience, however, constant use of this technique will not only attract the attention of the police, but also irritate other drivers. Since 'road rage' may be a greater danger in some countries, such as the USA, than assassins or kidnappers, I

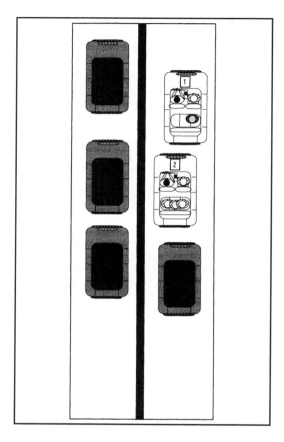

Fig. 8.5. *A common method for positioning VIP and trail vehicles at traffic lights. The VIP vehicle (1) stops so that the VIP is not exposed to either of the vehicles in the other lane. The VIP driver has also chosen the inside lane so that the VIP is farther away from those vehicles. In addition, this lane allows a quick right turn if evasive action is necessary, while the gap the VIP driver has left in front grants a certain amount of manoeuvring room. The trail vehicle (2) is positioned slightly towards the outside lane to shield the VIP vehicle from as many of the other vehicles as possible. Note that it is placed so that it blocks line of sight to the VIP vehicle from the vehicle behind.*

recommend this tactic only be used in special circumstances.

A variation of the technique places the trail car in the lane next to the VIP car on multi-lane divided roads to prevent anyone from passing and to observe ahead. Generally, as long as the trail car doesn't hold up traffic unduly, this tactic works quite well.

SCREENING

The trail car can also provide an invaluable screen when stopping in traffic. Normally, to provide privacy for the principal and to make an attack from a neighbouring vehicle more difficult, the VIP driver is trained to stop so that the car is not directly next to another vehicle. Instead, the driver will usually position the VIP vehicle so that it is slightly ahead of, or slightly behind, a vehicle in the adjacent lane. The trail car may also position itself to prevent another vehicle from pulling up next to the VIP car in a line of traffic (see fig. 8.5). The VIP driver and drivers of escort vehicles should leave their vehicles in gear so that they are ready to take immediate evasive action if necessary.

ROUTE SURVEYS

Whether the principal is travelling to or from work, is being shuttled from an airport to a hotel or is taking part in a motorcade, it is most probable that the route will have been surveyed in advance. Although I discussed route surveys in Chapter 4, it is important to mention some of the primary information a survey should contain and how that information is used in preparing the actual route.

One of the first considerations in actual route planning, which will play a part in the route survey, is the exact time that the principal wants to arrive at his destination. Once this is known, the team leader can begin filling out his operations order (see Appendix).

When preparing a route, if the journey is one that the principal makes every day, such as to his office, the route and time should be varied.

When surveying a route, attention should be given to:

- width of streets;
- number of traffic lights;
- speed limits;
- vulnerable points (*ie* overpasses, tunnels, construction sites, etc);
- street lighting if travelling at night;
- parked vehicles;
- communication dead spots;
- sharp bends;
- high-crime areas where hijackings may occur;
- thick trees or undergrowth;
- railway crossings (if possible, note when trains usually block the road);
- one-way streets;
- any other information deemed useful in planning the route.

TROUBLE SPOTS

The advance team should have driven the route at the time the principal will be using it so that some idea of the journey time can be gleaned. Particular attention should be paid to points on the route that cannot be avoided, especially areas close to the business or residence that will have to be traversed no matter which route is taken. These are prime ambush sites. If one of these is a narrow or one-way street, it will be an even more attractive location for an attack.

SECURITY REQUIREMENTS

If the route is being used for an official motorcade, it may have been planned to pass through areas where residents can glimpse the motorcade. Normally, this will be determined by whether or not the visit is political. Even in the case of a motorcade intended to be 'visible', however, the security requirements may have some bearing on route selection.

DIVERSIONS

Whichever type of route is being planned, it is important to be aware of points along it that allow a diversion to be made and where that diversion

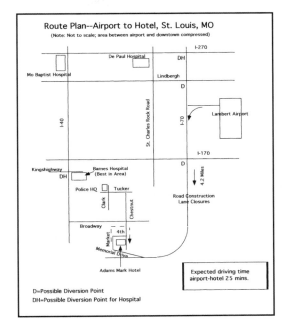

Fig. 8.6. *A typical route plan.*

will take the VIP. The route should also be chosen with consideration to the location of the nearest police stations and hospitals with accident and emergency units.

PRINT-OUTS

All of the information relevant to the route should be assembled in the most usable form, preferably with the aid of a lap-top computer, and printed out for each driver, the team leader and any other members of the protective team who may need it.

Some teams like to prepare the route map as a linear chart with a running commentary about each intersection, etc (see fig. 8.6). Others prefer a computer generated map with comments printed directly on it. I like a combination comprising a linear/descriptive outline of the route backed up by a map in case of confusion. I also use a mapping program on my computer, which can interface with a GPS (global positioning system) device to show me on screen where we are at any time.

DECISION MAKING

The team leader will normally act as the 'navigator' and will make any decisions about diversions. As the journey is made, if enough personnel are available, a security advance party vehicle will travel 3–5 minutes ahead of the VIP vehicle to radio back any problems along the route and allow early diversion.

MOTORCADES

If one is protecting a principal who is a political figure or otherwise is very well known, it is possible that, at some stage, he or she will take part in a formal motorcade, which entails many special considerations. Informal motorcades, when the route is not predetermined and there is no prior publicity, are best from a security point of view. An informal motorcade is virtually identical to a standard VIP multi-car movement in that there will be fewer vehicles – normally only two or three; it can move fast, and there will not be waiting crowds along the route.

A formal motorcade, on the other hand, will have been announced in advance, will follow a

AUTHOR'S NOTE

VIP vehicles for the US and Russian presidents normally incorporate running boards, and a friend of mine tells an interesting story about KGB bodyguards in the days of the Soviet Union riding the small running boards at the rear of their principal's vehicle while it travelled at speed into London from Heathrow Airport! In the past, Russian VIP vehicles have also incorporated compartments in their sides that contained heavy weapons, which were accessible through a small door.

published route, will travel at a slow pace, may entail stops for the principal and/or other VIPs to be seen, will move through crowded areas and probably will pass tall buildings. Formal motorcades require detailed planning and a great deal of co-ordination with local law enforcement agencies. If the VIP vehicle stops in the middle of the crowd, bodyguards from the trail car will have to get out to surround it, unless it is a specialised VIP 'parade' car with running boards for the bodyguards to stand on while it is moving.

WALKING BODYGUARDS

When bodyguards dismount to walk alongside a VIP vehicle, normally the team leader walks by the principal's door, while other bodyguards take up positions just in front of the front doors and outside the other rear door. Some teams vary this arrangement, however, leaving the team leader inside the vehicle to maintain overall control of the protective effort. I prefer this second option and assign the senior bodyguard in the trail car to the position at the principal's door. If the parade/motorcade route is very long, extra bodyguards should be available in a trail car to take over from those walking alongside the vehicle.

When a hardened vehicle is used, which is likely to be the case in this situation, the walking bodyguards are really more a show of power and strength than a necessity. The exception, however, is when the principal is riding in an open vehicle.

POLICE INVOLVEMENT

Normally, along a motorcade/parade route, there will be local police assigned to crowd control. One important point the advance team should make to the local police liaison officer is that officers assigned crowd duty should face in towards the crowd rather than out towards the principal. Their job is to watch the crowd, not the motorcade!

POSITIONS OF VEHICLES

When arranging vehicles for a formal motorcade, some aspects are standard and some will vary. Normally, there will be a pilot or scout car, which will travel a reasonable distance (*ie* a hundred yards) ahead of the motorcade As a rule, this vehicle will contain a local police officer and a member of the protective team. Its job is to give early warning of any problems along the route. There may also be a security advance vehicle, which runs about 3–5 minutes ahead of the motorcade. After the pilot car, and at the head of the actual motorcade, will usually be the lead vehicle, which is driven by a member of the protective team and carries a ranking local law enforcement officer. The VIP vehicle will frequently be positioned next, followed by a trail car filled with bodyguards.

If the motorcade is for a head of state or other high-ranking official, such as the US secretary of state, the next vehicle may be a heavy weapons carrier, designated the CAT (counter-assault team) vehicle by the US Secret Service. In this vehicle will be bodyguards trained and armed to lay down heavy fire to break an ambush. Official US teams normally use a large SUV, such as a Chevrolet Suburban, with the rear seat designed to allow one or two members of the team to face rearwards.

In some cases, the local police SWAT (special weapons and tactics) team will supply a heavy weapons vehicle, but if this is the case, members of the protective team must be absolutely certain that they understand and are trained for their mission. If no heavy weapons vehicle is available, the trail car should carry at least one or two assault rifles.

After the heavy weapons vehicle will usually come the vehicle or vehicles carrying the VIP's staff. In many motorcades, a Press bus follows the VIP staff vehicles. Some protective teams, however, place the Press bus just after the lead vehicle and ahead of the VIP vehicle. The Press are told that this allows them to set up their equipment at any venue before the VIP arrives. Although this is true, protective teams, who can be draconian when it comes to protecting their principal, also assume that the heavier bus will set off any pressure-sensitive explosive devices before the VIP vehicle reaches them!

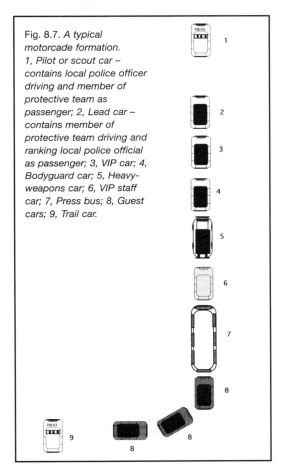

Fig. 8.7. *A typical motorcade formation. 1, Pilot or scout car – contains local police officer driving and member of protective team as passenger; 2, Lead car – contains member of protective team driving and ranking local police official as passenger; 3, VIP car; 4, Bodyguard car; 5, Heavy-weapons car; 6, VIP staff car; 7, Press bus; 8, Guest cars; 9, Trail car.*

Assuming that the Press bus is in the standard position, however, behind the staff vehicles, cars carrying guests of the principal and other local VIPs will normally follow it. At the rear will be another local police vehicle to mark the end of the motorcade and to prevent anyone from attempting to pass it. Additional police motorcycle outriders may be employed to leap-frog ahead of the motorcade and block side streets before it passes (see fig. 8.7).

AIRPORT PICK-UP

A situation that often arises with a high-ranking political or military VIP is that he or she lands at the airport in a private aircraft. In this case, the VIP will often disembark directly into a motorcade, which will rush him or her to the destination.

HARDENED MOTORCADE

A standard motorcade may not be viable in countries where a guerrilla war is raging or urban terrorism is a constant threat. In this situation, a 'hardened' motorcade may be necessary. Advance work will also have to reflect the more extreme threat level and include an assessment of terrorist/guerrilla order of battle, tactics and weapons so that the protective effort can be geared to the potential threat.

ADVANCE GUARD

In a hardened convoy, a paramilitary element may be added to the normal protective team. These additional personnel, preferably with substantial light infantry training, will be employed as an advance guard and as a reaction force. A gun jeep, such as a Hummer, will usually act as the lead vehicle, running 100–200 yards ahead of the rest of the motorcade. Some teams I've known have included at least one or two ex-military combat engineers in the advance team to search for mines and explosive devices. The lead unit travels far enough ahead that if it springs an ambush, the VIP vehicle and its support will be outside the ambush.

POSITION OF VIP CAR

The VIP car will be between two vehicles containing bodyguards. An ambulance or vehicle containing trained emergency medical technicians will often follow the VIP contingent. Any VIP staff cars will be slotted in before or after the ambulance.

REACTION FORCE

Bringing up the rear will be a truck and/or gun jeep carrying the reaction force. This unit will follow at a sufficient distance that it will not be caught in an ambush of the VIP vehicles, thus allowing it to bring its firepower to bear where it will be most effective. A four-wheel-drive vehicle is highly preferable for the reaction force so that they can flank any attackers.

AERIAL SUPPORT

Ideally, liaison with the local military and police should be strong enough that a helicopter gunship or other support can be called for if facing a heavy attack. If the principal has a private helicopter, it may be incorporated into emergency evacuation plans, or even fly cover for the convoy to provide early warning of potential trouble.

SUITABLE ROUTE

Whenever possible, the convoy should move on main roads, but avoid built-up areas. It should be

The mobile phone can be invaluable if radio communications have been knocked out and a team is under fire.

borne in mind that tunnels, bridges and passages with high ground on both sides present prime ambush sites. I should emphasise, too, that all vehicles should have four-wheel drive so that they can leave the road if necessary. Possible diversion points and contingency plans should have been studied religiously so that evasive action can be taken quickly if called for.

COMMUNICATION FACILITIES

All vehicles should be fully fuelled and checked rigorously for mechanical condition prior to beginning the convoy/motorcade. Advance work should have determined any areas that will cause communication problems. At least three levels of communication should be available, too. Each vehicle should be able to call for help on the local police frequency and should also have a vehicle-to-vehicle communication facility. As a back-up, at least a couple of mobile phones should be in each vehicle.

ABILITIES OF BODYGUARDS

It is important that at least some members of the protective team speak the local language fluently, and it is even more desirable for members of the team to have trained, or trained with, local police and military personnel so that they understand their response capabilities and tactics. The VIP vehicle and the bodyguard vehicles should carry heavier weapons than they might normally use, particularly assault rifles.

Although it is a specialised type of motorcade, the well-trained bodyguard should still know how to organise and deploy a high-threat convoy. In many cases, the very appearance of well-organised firepower will cause potential attackers to look for a softer target. Nevertheless, plenty of spare magazines should be carried for the assault rifles, and everyone should be wearing ballistic vests with hard plates inserted. If a guerrilla or terrorist group decides to hit a heavily armed convoy of the type I've described, the protective personnel must be very well trained in counter-ambush techniques and ready to 'go to war'.

AMBUSH TECHNIQUES

So important is the ambush as a tactic in guerrilla warfare that Carlos Marighella, in his classic *Mini Manual of the Urban Guerrilla*, devotes substantial space to its uses. He argues that the guerrilla has various advantages in carrying out an ambush, including surprise, better knowledge of the chosen terrain, mobility, information/local intelligence and the ability to take decisive action.

Marighella sets out twelve steps for the successful ambush:

1 Intelligence gathering and analysis.

2 Observation of the target.

3 Reconnaissance of the site.

4 Study and timing of routes.

5 Mapping of routes.

6 Choice of transportation.

7 Selection of personnel.

8 Selection of weapons.

9 Rehearsal of the attack.

10 Execution of the attack.

11 Cover for those carrying out the attack.

12 Withdrawal.

Ambushes against vehicles can normally be broken down into the following types:

Stationary Ambush: The ambushers are in fixed concealed positions awaiting a moving target. When the target enters the killing zone, the ambush is triggered with overwhelming firepower. This type of ambush is usually intended to kill the target.

Rolling Ambush: This type employs automobiles, motorcycles or other vehicles to intercept the target. Firearms and explosives are used to either kill the occupants of the target vehicle or to immobilise the vehicle so that its occupant may be kidnapped.

Explosive Ambush: Intended to kill the target, this type of ambush employs explosive charges to destroy the vehicle carrying the target. Charges may be detonated remotely, command detonated or fired from an anti-tank weapon such as an RPG.

Deception Ambush: Especially useful in kidnappings, this type of ambush employs a ruse to halt the vehicle. For example, female guerrillas pushing baby carriages have been used to force a VIP vehicle to stop. A member of the terrorist group posing as a police officer might also be used to flag down the vehicle. It is advisable for the VIP driver and other members of the protective team to study the correct police uniforms and police vehicle markings for any area that they will visit, particularly in foreign countries. This will make spotting fakes easier. Also pay particular attention to news reports about stolen police vehicles and find out their ID numbers if possible. Faked accidents blocking the road have also been used to stop convoys.

Well-set ambushes will usually adhere to most or all of the following principles:

All exits must be covered: This requires enough manpower not only to stop the VIP vehicle, but also to block possible escape routes.

The ambush must be sited in depth: Once again, sufficient manpower is needed to block escape routes and set secondary ambushes to prevent possible reinforcement from the military,

police or members of the VIP protective team. Blocking vehicles may have to be pulled into position to stop the VIP driver from escaping the kill zone.

Overwhelming firepower: The ambushers must have effective weapons and be skilled in using them. They should include weapons heavy enough to penetrate a vehicle's armour plating. The weapons should be sited so that they deliver a great deal of fire without endangering other members of the ambush team. Those carrying out the ambush should be disciplined and accurate in their fire so that they can eliminate protective personnel without killing the VIP if the object is kidnapping.

Ambush personnel must be dedicated and disciplined: They must display not only fire discipline, but also communications discipline. They must be able to stick to the plan and to display extreme ruthlessness if necessary.

Detailed planning and thorough briefing: The leader of the guerrilla/terrorist group should exhibit good target selection, carry out thorough recconaisance and obtain good intelligence. Sufficient time must be allowed for preparation. Good sources of information must be developed and utilised. Safe houses and caches for weapons and vehicles must be arranged. Traffic patterns along the routes must be studied, as should timing along the routes. Sufficient funds should be available to finance the operation. Extra vehicles should be positioned to allow switches to be made during the escape phase. Good communications should be developed, including simple radio and telephone codes. Planning should be thorough, but flexible, to allow for adjustments before, during and after the ambush. Those taking part should be fully briefed and well rehearsed, but not on the actual site, since that could compromise the operation.

Tight security: Personnel should be selected carefully and any security risks should be eliminated. Some key details should be withheld until the last minute. Planning and action should be kept compartmentalised. Communications should be coded.

Ambush should be well sited: Routes should be investigated carefully so that natural obstacles can be incorporated into the ambush plan. Traffic patterns should be considered. The least obvious site for the ambush is highly desirable. Fields of fire should be calculated in advance. Stop groups should be well sited. Be aware of the target's routine and use it against him or her. Remove any obstructions that could hinder the operation.

Concealment: Good hiding places should be chosen for personnel, weapons, vehicles and stop groups. If disguises are to be used, acquire them as clandestinely as possible. Maintain radio silence.

Patience to wait for the best time to launch the ambush: Personnel with zeal for the cause should be chosen. They should be stable and unemotional. Everyone must be willing to wait for weeks if necessary for the right moment to launch the operation.

Follow the KISS (Keep It Simple, Stupid) principle: Do not make the plan any more complicated than necessary.

Good escape routes: Evaluate potential escape routes for traffic, police patrols, road construction and choke points such as tunnels, etc. Determine a location for switching vehicles. If personnel are available, assign them to keep the primary escape route clear. Use evasive tactics. Know the route in detail and plan alternate escape routes.

Deception: Plan diversionary tactics to draw off police or other possible pursuit. Use disinformation.

Safe houses: Decide on boltholes in advance, both primary and secondary.

AMBUSH FACTS

From studying ambush patterns, other conclusions can be drawn about terrorist/guerrilla ambushes. Overwhelmingly, they take place when the target is travelling between home and the office. A substantial portion occur when the principal is entering or leaving his or her vehicle at home. Note, too, that the bodyguards are usually eliminated as part of these attacks.

Ambushes normally succeed because the target has not taken precautions or the protective personnel are lax. Since most terrorist groups gather intelligence prior to an attack, a well-trained protective team that gives the impression of effectiveness is a real deterrent and may well cause potential ambushers to look elsewhere for a target.

In a substantial number of ambushes, the actual attacking group consists of five or six individuals, although they may be backed up by another six to twelve drivers, scouts, observers, etc.

UNDERSTANDING TERRORIST TACTICS

Terrorists study protective teams and their principals before attacking them. It is even more important that members of protective teams study terrorist tactics and incorporate them into their training. When I train protective teams, normally I divide them into two groups during the phase on ambush/counter-ambush techniques. Once all personnel have learned the basics of ambushes, one of the two groups plans a protective operation, while the other plans to ambush them at some point along their route. When the training exercise is complete and both groups have been debriefed, they switch roles and repeat the exercise. As part of training, ambushes will also be planned by some of my instructors, normally ex-special forces soldiers, and sprung on trainees doing vehicle escort exercises.

DETECTING SURVEILLANCE

Because terrorist groups will study potential targets, bodyguards must be particularly alert to possible surveillance. The VIP driver, team leader and other members of the protective team should carry mini tape recorders into which they can dictate the licence numbers and descriptions of vehicles they encounter, as well as the descriptions of individuals who may be observing the VIP residence, business or route. By quickly recording this information at the time, comparisons can be made to determine if the same vehicles or individuals turn up on more than one occasion.

COUNTER-AMBUSH TECHNIQUES

Part of bodyguard training is learning counter-ambush techniques. One of the most important steps in breaking an ambush is spotting it as soon as possible. Consequently, vigilance on the part of drivers and bodyguards is very important.

ALL CARS MOBILE
Once an ambush has been launched, if all cars in the VIP party are still mobile, drivers should attempt to continue right through it. The team leader should climb over the front seat into the back of the car with the principal to give him or her body cover. However, if the vehicle is heavily armoured, it may be more advisable for the team leader to stay put and use the radio to co-ordinate action among the escort vehicles.

If the VIP convoy consists of three cars, the lead vehicle should punch on through, followed by the other vehicles. Likewise, if only two cars are involved, the VIP car should force its way through. The trail car will follow, but will block pursuit.

LEAD CAR OUT OF ACTION
If, in a three-car convoy, the lead car is put out of action by the ambush, the driver and bodyguards will normally jump out of the vehicle and engage the attackers while using the vehicle as cover. However, if the attackers are rushing the vehicle, at least some members of the protective team will have to engage them while

Fig. 8.8. *In this scene, the VIP vehicle has been disabled. The trail vehicle has pulled up on the side away from the ambush. The team leader (OCBG) has extracted the VIP from the back seat and is ushering him or her into the trail vehicle. BGs 1–4 have left the trail vehicle and taken up positions to give covering fire during the transfer. The VIP driver (VIP D) has left the VIP vehicle and is also giving covering fire. The OCBG, BG3 and BG4 will evacuate the VIP in the trail vehicle.*

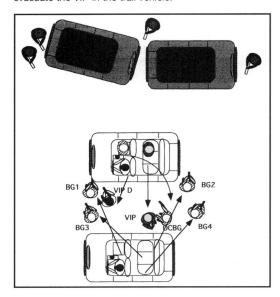

Fig. 8.9. *In this scene, the VIP motorcade encounters an ambush blocking the road with a truck (1). At least one ambusher is armed with an RPG (2). As a result, the lead-car bodyguards (3) engage the ambushers. The trail car (5) speeds forward to cover the VIP car (4).*

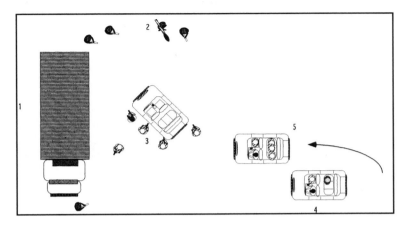

the others debus. The VIP and trail cars will accelerate through under the covering fire of the bodyguards from the lead car. The team leader will radio for assistance for those who have had to stand and fight.

DISABLED VIP CAR

If the VIP car is put out of action, it will be necessary to initiate an evacuation-under-fire drill. Normally, this will involve the trail car pulling up on the side of the VIP car away from the ambush to use it as cover. The four bodyguards in the trail car will leave the vehicle and take up positions to give covering fire, while the team leader, if he can get over the front seat of the VIP car and into the back, moves the principal to the trail car. Once the principal is in the vehicle, the team leader and two of the bodyguards jump in the vehicle and it accelerates away (see fig. 8.8). The VIP driver and two remaining bodyguards will normally stay in position to give covering fire until they can be extracted.

If the ambush has exposed the VIP car to fire from both sides, the trail car pulls up next to it so that the transfer of the VIP will take place with vehicles on each side for cover. Note that during an evacuation under fire, it is important that as many bodyguards as possible remain with the principal in case of a subsequent attack.

ESCAPE BY REVERSING

If an ambush is recognised early enough, it may be possible to reverse out of it. Indeed, if the road is impassable or blocked by a truck or bus, this may be the only option. Techniques for using the J- or Y-turn have already been discussed. However, it may also be necessary to reverse completely clear of the ambush before beginning to turn around. In this case, the trail car will act as a shield for the VIP car throughout the manoeuvre. If there is a lead car, it will also position itself as a cover car while this is taking place. Be aware, though, that when reversing at speed, it is much harder to control the vehicle and the likelihood of flipping is increased substantially.

COVERING FIRE

In some situations (*ie* when rocket launchers have been spotted with the ambushers), the lead car may stop and its occupants may debus to give covering fire (see figs. 8.9 and 8.10). If the area is very confined, as in an alley, the trail car may have to reverse all the way out to clear a path for the VIP car.

LEAD/TRAIL CAR TRAPPED

If either the lead or trail car is disabled or trapped in the ambush, its occupants will get out and engage the ambushers with heavy suppressive fire to cover

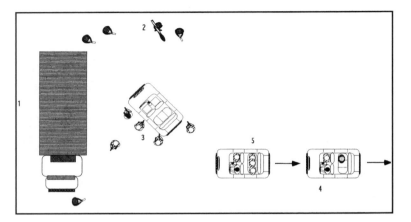

Left, fig. 8.10. *In this ambush, the trail car (5) pulls in front of the VIP car (4) to provide cover as both begin to reverse out of the killing zone.*

Facing page: *British bodyguard trainees practising counter-ambush skills.*

the evacuation of the VIP. If the VIP car becomes trapped or disabled, the evacuation-under-fire drill already discussed will be implemented.

NO VEHICLES ABLE TO MOVE

If all vehicles are trapped or disabled, there will be no choice but to stand and fight. In this case, the team leader must decide whether it is more advisable to keep the VIP in the hardened vehicle or to evacuate him or her to a point offering better cover. This judgment will be based upon the terrain and the threat posed by the attackers' weapons. It is quite common, however, for terrorist and guerrilla groups to have rocket launchers, which can take out even a hardened vehicle. If one vehicle of the VIP motorcade remains operable, however, generally it will be best to use it to evacuate the principal and as many bodyguards as possible.

MOTORCYCLE AMBUSHES

Particularly in Latin America, motorcycle ambushes are relatively common. A motorcycle with either one or two terrorists aboard can weave through traffic and pull up right next to a VIP vehicle before emptying a submachine-gun into the passenger compartment or into the driver. When training US Army general officer protective teams, we used a variation of this whereby a motorcycle roared up next to the 'general's' car to allow the motorcycle's passenger, a retired Secret Service agent acting the role of a terrorist, to place a magnetic mine on the vehicle.

COUNTERING WHEN MOVING

The best means of countering a motorcycle attack when moving is to weave the vehicle in front of the motorcycle to force its rider to concentrate on not hitting the vehicle broadside. Using this technique, it may even be possible to run the motorcycle off the road; if nothing else, the action should ruin the rider's aim.

COUNTERING WHEN STOPPED

If stopped in traffic and a suspicious motorcycle is getting closer, the team leader may have to ready his weapon to engage the motorcycle rider and/or passenger as soon as a weapon appears. This may be possible through a gun port or window (if it can be lowered) if the motorcycle is on the passenger side, but if on the driver's side, it may be necessary to open the door and engage the attacker over the top of the vehicle. Note that if the vehicle is

hardened enough that the team leader judges the weapon employed by the motorcycle assassination team will not penetrate, he may deem it advisable not to compromise the integrity of the vehicle by opening a window or gun port.

AMBUSH PRECEPTS

Some of the basic rules to bear in mind if ambushed are:

- Protect the VIP at all costs; provide body cover; get the VIP to the floor of the vehicle.
- Get the VIP away from the ambush site as soon as possible, but remember THERE IS ALWAYS ONE MORE AMBUSH COMING!
- Try to avoid having to stand and fight, but if you have no other option, hit the attackers hard; use fire and movement, and attempt to flank them if possible; use the radio to call for help so that time is on your side.
- Remember that any attack may be a ruse, and another attack may still be coming farther down the road; hence my warning – THERE IS ALWAYS ONE MORE AMBUSH COMING!

- Carry smoke grenades in the vehicles to cover a withdrawal.
- Surrender is usually not an option; bodyguards will probably be killed rather than taken prisoner.

Travel by vehicle is one of the most dangerous situations faced by protection teams. Terrorist assassins and kidnappers have many advantages when planning an attack against a VIP in a vehicle, including the choice of place and time. Well-trained VIP drivers, hardened vehicles and a skilled protection team can all help counter the threat of an attack while the principal is in the vehicle. It must be remembered, however, that for those in VIP protection, there is no such thing as a pleasant drive in the country. From the time the VIP leaves a residence, office or other venue to enter the vehicle until he or she is safely at the destination, every member of the protective team must be particularly vigilant. Even if the same journey has been completed thousands of times without incident, the VIP driver and the protective team must always undertake each journey prepared to 'switch on' if the ambush comes.

CHAPTER 9

TRAVEL ON PLANES, SHIPS AND TRAINS

When a principal travels far enough from home that it is not practical to use cars, additional specialised protective techniques are called for. Although vehicular travel is normally considered one of the most dangerous situations for a VIP who faces the threat of kidnap or assassination, it does have the advantage of giving the protective team a certain amount of control. When using public transport, much of that control is lost.

TRAVEL BY AIR

The form of transport that the VIP is most likely to employ will be aircraft. Because commercial aircraft journeys require the use of airports, and follow set routes and time schedules, the principal may be vulnerable. As a result, if available, private aircraft are preferable to commercial aircraft.

Corporate or private aircraft offer other advantages, too: members of the protective team will be able to carry their weapons on board more readily; the principal will not be seated among a group of strangers; and the protective team can work closely with the crew to ensure security of the aircraft on the ground. The main disadvantage of the private aircraft is that normally it will be serviced by contract personnel, and facilities for securing the aircraft may be limited.

PRIVATE AIRCRAFT SECURITY

Securing a private aircraft at its home base should be easier than when travelling. The best option is a private, secure hangar, which should be alarmed and/or staffed 24 hours per day. If this is not possible, storage in a shared hangar that is manned 24 hours a day, or at least alarmed, is the next best choice. If the aircraft must be parked in the open, it should be locked, and there should be good lighting around it and, perhaps, even a temporary fence with intrusion-detection systems. Shorrock Security Systems offers a portable microwave fence that can enclose an area of up to 120 square metres. Another option is a portable infra-red detection system known as Sentry, which is available from RDS Electronics Ltd. An additional advantage of the Sentry system is that if an intruder is detected, it will send a signal to a radio monitored by a member of the protective team.

PORTABLE SECURITY
The aircraft should be covered by CCTV cameras, preferably with a motion-detection capability so that a tape may be reviewed quickly. I understand that it is possible to mount small brackets at certain points on the aircraft, to which cameras may be affixed when it is on the ground. The advantage of this and other portable systems is that the same security devices may be used wherever the aircraft is parked.

ALARM SYSTEMS
There are also alarm systems that may be installed permanently in aircraft, much as they are in automobiles, although at much greater expense. Shepherd Intelligence Systems offers a system that will send an intrusion warning to a pager within ten miles of the aircraft. As long as the flight crew stays nearby, this can give a quick alert to an intrusion. Securaplane USA offers another highly respected alarm system for the private aircraft.

ANTI-TAMPER STICKERS

Many flight crews and security teams use a simple, but effective, system employing security stickers, which they affix across doors and access ports whenever the aircraft is left unattended. If a sticker is broken, it indicates that the aircraft has been tampered with.

LOCAL SECURITY

When travelling, it is usually advisable to have the company that performs local maintenance to contract security personnel to guard the aircraft on the ground. This company should also advise on a reliable caterer to supply food for the aircraft.

FUEL SUPPLY

Fuelling is a particularly critical function; therefore, a member of the flight crew should always supervise the operation. If there is no way to screen the fuel to ensure that there has been no tampering, it is best to select a fuelling vehicle at random. Unfortunately, however, at some small airports, there will be only one fuelling vehicle.

OVERNIGHT PROTECTION

The aircraft should always be kept locked when parked, and it is advisable not to have a corporate logo or a principal's name on the aircraft. At some destinations, it may be sensible to have a member of the crew sleep aboard the aircraft. Many companies that handle private aircraft actually have dormitory facilities for flight crew. Select one of these whenever possible.

If the principal travels to certain destinations frequently, it would be useful for the protective team to establish good relations with the airport police so that they will check on the aircraft during their patrols.

FLIGHT CREW

The crew members of a private aircraft are a critical element in security. Before being employed, they should have been vetted carefully, and the protective team should be alert for any indications of instability, drugs or alcohol. Members of the ground crew at the plane's home airport should also be vetted.

EXPLOSIVE DEVICES

Any searches of the aircraft for explosives should be carried out by the crew when they do a pre-flight inspection; however, a member of the protective team familiar with explosive devices should assist them.

Crew members should be briefed not to accept packages from strangers, not to answer questions about passengers or destinations, nor to allow any unauthorised access to the aircraft. Even though the number of crew and passengers will probably be relatively small, the crew should also match each piece of luggage to its owner to ensure that no potential explosive device has been added among the valid luggage.

CABIN STAFF

When choosing cabin personnel, such as stewards and stewardesses, those with language and/or nursing or emergency medical skills should be given preference.

MEDICAL ADVANTAGE

A private aircraft also offers a medical advantage in that its refrigeration facilities may be used to carry blood of the principal's type, which has already been screened for AIDs and hepatitis. If possible, blood may be carried for members of the protective team, too. On at least some protective teams, members build up a supply of their own blood, which they have drawn and stored for use in case of a serious injury.

CREW SECURITY

Although the primary concern of the protective team is the principal and family, at least some consideration should be given to crew security. In some countries, particularly if there are female crew members, their safety may be a concern.

Normal procedure is that aircrew stay near the airport, but if there are no acceptable hotels, compromises may have to be made. The team leader must be able to reach the command pilot at all times, no matter where the crew is staying. Mobile phones and pagers usually allow quick communications, although when travelling internationally, it may be necessary to make sure that your mobile phones can 'rove'.

CHOOSING AN AIRPORT

Selection of an airport can be important in limiting motorcade exposure time when entering a metropolitan area and allowing a quick departure when the VIP visit is complete. Consequently, if there is a choice of airport for a private aircraft, provided that the facilities are about equal, select whichever is nearest the part of the city that the principal will be visiting.

AUTHOR'S NOTE

I have information on file about various world airports and note, for example, that when flying on a private aircraft to Tokyo, Haneda is preferable to Narita, or to Buenos Aires, Jorge Newberry is more desirable than Exeiza. Each of these airports is a half-hour closer to the city centre and, thus, much better for getting a principal in and out with a minimum of exposure.

ARRIVAL AT THE DESTINATION

The advance team should work with local officials to arrange arrival at a secure stand, having customs clear the passengers and crew on the aircraft, and allowing the VIP vehicle to drive directly to it. Obviously, the more clout your principal has, the more readily such details may

be organised. If the principal is the CEO of a large corporation, usually someone from the local office can help with these arrangements.

When taxiing towards a private hangar area or the stand where the aircraft will be met, the flight crew should remain alert for any suspicious individuals or vehicles nearby.

SECURING THE CONCOURSE
A very important consideration during arrival and departure will be securing the concourse if the plane will be boarded from within a terminal. If not, guarding the perimeter around the boarding stand and aircraft will be important.

WEAPONS

Although good security should preclude the need for members of the protective team to use their weapons in flight, they should still be loaded with highly frangible ammunition while aboard the aircraft. Glaser Safety Slugs or MagSafe ammunition are good choices. The flight crew should also give the protective team a quick briefing on the location of critical hydraulic lines and electrical systems in case a shot in the cabin is ever necessary.

SECURE STORAGE
It is quite possible that some or all weapons will have to be kept aboard the aircraft when it is on the ground, in which case some type of locking storage compartment will be necessary. The protective team should also be prepared to keep unauthorised weapons off the plane when any guests are flying. A couple of hand-held metal detectors will prove useful for this and other tasks.

AIRPORT AND CITY FILE

Another real boon when travelling on private aircraft is a file on cities and airport facilities visited in the past, in case of a last-minute flight or even a diversion due to weather. Again, a laptop computer is invaluable for keeping such information literally at the fingertips.

CO-ORDINATION AND CLOSE CO-OPERATION

It is important to emphasise that close co-ordination with the aircrew is essential, as are good relations with airport police or security personnel. In countries where it is acceptable, always have gifts ready for the local security/police with whom you work. In many cases, these do not have to be very valuable, but instead can be items that show your respect and affection for them.

AUTHOR'S NOTE

I have a friend who is a US air marshal. On one flight, when the local police were checking his weapons, they were fascinated by his revolver speed-loaders. Upon departure, he made a point of presenting each of the ranking officers with one of them. I have also taken American gun, military and men's magazines; pistol holsters; special ammunition; alcohol; cigarettes; and other such small gifts to my police and security contacts on numerous occasions. In each case, they were presented in friendship, but they also bought me a great deal of co-operation.

COMMERCIAL FLIGHTS

Despite the advantages of flying on private aircraft, it is quite likely that, at some stage, most protective teams will travel with their principal on a commercial airliner.

When taking a commercial flight, the basic security concerns will normally break down into three main categories:

- the airport;
- the airline;
- the aircraft.

AIRPORT SECURITY

Within the airport, it is normally best to clear security check-points as early as possible. If you are travelling with a principal who has 'official' status and the team has a similar standing itself, normal security check-points may be bypassed to speed movement.

Once any check-points have been cleared, the principal should be taken to a VIP lounge to await boarding. Since almost certainly the principal will be flying first-class, he or she will have priority boarding. It may be, however, that not all of the bodyguards will be sitting in first-class. Those who are – usually at least the team leader – will board with the principal.

OBSERVE OTHER PASSENGERS

Even with priority boarding, you will probably have to spend a few minutes in the boarding area, so use that time to have a look at the other passengers. Watch for anyone on your own 'threat' list as well as anyone who looks or acts suspicious, or fits the aviation authority's profile of a potential hijacker. To gain access to this profile,

AUTHOR'S NOTE

Although, normally, I do not recommend socialising while on the job, on occasion I have let friends among the air marshals know that I was leaving from a certain airport, on the assumption that not only would they come by to say hello, but also would add additional well-trained eyes to our own pre-flight security.

it may be necessary to have contacts with the air marshals or airline security.

AIRPORT/AIRLINE REPUTATIONS
Try to avoid airports with particularly bad reputations for security – Athens for example. Also be aware of which airlines have a good reputation for security and which are likely targets for terrorist groups. El Al, for example, has excellent security, but also is a potential target. Beware of airlines with lax operating procedures as well. For example, a friend of mine was on an Olympia flight that started its take-off run with a door still open!

PASSPORTS

Consider the stamps that are in your passport and your principal's passport. An Israeli stamp when flying on some Middle Eastern airlines could lead to problems.

I have mentioned Athens' Hellinikon Airport and its problems. Be aware that an immigration stamp from that airport will be a flag to airline security personnel and may well delay your boarding. If

AUTHOR'S NOTE
You will find that if you travel a lot, you will notice some interesting characteristics of customs and immigration agents, which should be filed away mentally. For example, I have noticed that Russian immigration agents tend to stamp your passport on the page that corresponds with the date of entry. I don't know if this is an official policy, but I've seen it happen more than once. However, if your passport does not have thirty-one pages, I assume that this will not always be the case. I note this only because if an immigration agent did not follow this procedure in Russia, I would want to make sure that visas were in order in case another flagged this when leaving.

you've been anywhere 'odd' or anywhere with a reputation for terrorist activity, it might be wise to let airline security know in advance so that they can 'fast-track' you on boarding.

CARRYING ARMS

Official protective teams, particularly if flying with their country's flag airlines, will be allowed to be armed. On US airlines, personnel providing security for foreign dignitaries may be granted permission to be armed by the FAA, provided the correct paperwork has been filed by the principal's embassy in advance. My experience has been that if the dignitary is important enough, the request will be granted, assuming that the personnel to be armed pass FAA scrutiny.

AUTHOR'S NOTE
On at least some occasions when working in the Middle East, I was armed on flights, but was also expected to function as an air marshal. Since any hijacking attempt probably would have endangered my principal, there was a certain logic in the arrangement, and I had trained the air marshals for the country involved.

SECURITY SCREENING

Although most airports operate on the 'sterile' concourse system, whereby passengers have to clear security long before they reach the departure gate, this is not always the case. In at least a few airports, the security check is not made until passengers reach the gate. I have encountered this system at Schiphol Airport in Amsterdam.

Concourse screening is preferable, since it puts distance between the security check and the boarding area, making an attack at the gate much more difficult.

AIRPORT SECURITY EFFICIENCY

I like to know how efficient airport police are in responding to a threat. The American FAA has information available on response times at major airports. I would recommend determining police/security response time at any airport to be used. Note also that the FAA rates major US and foreign airports for overall security. For US airports, a Category X rating means that an airport is under substantial threat of terrorist incidents. If at all possible, obtain a current threat assessment for any airports to be visited.

MAKE YOUR OWN CHECKS

You can make some rule-of-thumb checks yourself to determine the efficiency of the security at airports. For example, notice how they deal with electronic devices at security check-points, since this will be a good indicator of alertness to explosive devices. Computers should be booted; radios, TVs, CD players and cameras should all be operated and examined carefully. In addition, watch to see if personnel are alert to anyone wandering outside the security areas. Observe patrolling security staff. Are they alert? Or, do they appear to be killing time until their coffee break?

If possible, I like to find out whether the airport has a Semtex detector and/or sufficient explosives sniffer dogs.

LARGE SUMS OF CASH

Another point to be aware of at security check-points is that if your principal is travelling with a large sum of cash, this can cause detention and questioning. With some principals for whom I've worked, carrying hundreds of thousands of dollars in cash is not at all uncommon. Plan on dealing with this issue in advance if it is likely to arise.

REDUCING POTENTIAL THREATS

Long before boarding a commercial airliner, various steps may be taken to reduce the potential threat. Choose a direct, non-stop flight to avoid the risk of dangerous passengers or luggage being added after the protective team has carried out its initial security screening. Whenever possible, obtain a passenger list in advance to allow a security check to be made. Usually, this will only be achievable if protecting a principal with official status. I also recommend choosing an airline that subjects all freight carried on passenger planes to a rigorous inspection for explosives and hazardous materials.

BOARDING

US air marshals, Israeli Mossad security agents and other specialists consider the period when an airliner is being boarded to be one of the most dangerous times, since passengers are bunched together, allowing an attack with grenades or submachine-guns to inflict horrific damage. Therefore, be particularly alert during this period.

If members of the protective team will be armed aboard the flight – difficult in most circumstances, but not impossible – position one or two armed personnel to interdict an assault during boarding. I even prefer to leave one team member or a member of the security team who will be remaining in the city from which we're leaving to secure the boarding area until the very last moment. Sometimes, even if protective personnel will not be allowed to carry their weapons during the flight, armed team members or local police officers will be allowed to stand by while the flight is boarding to provide security during this dangerous phase.

THE AIRCRAFT

Once aboard a commercial airliner, the basic threats include:

- explosives;
- crash landings;
- hijackings;
- assaults on the principal.

The protective team should take each threat into consideration.

IMPROVED DESIGNS

More recent aircraft designs have incorporated features to allow the plane to continue flying after an explosion in the cargo area. Therefore, it is advisable to determine which airlines have updated their fleets most recently when choosing a carrier.

Some types of airliner are more flame resistant than others and allow more time for evacuation during a fire. Airlines are not likely to offer this information, but some research in open sources should provide data on aircraft survivability in different situations. Again, if the client is 'official', this information will be available from the FAA in the USA and equivalent agencies in other countries.

SEATING

Normally, seating of the principal and protective team will be a trade-off between safety and security. First-class usually will be the best choice for ease of boarding and disembarking, as well as for limiting access to the principal. On the other hand, in most crash landings, it is safest to be in the back of an aircraft. I usually compromise and seat the principal in the last window seat in first-class, with members of his family, staff and protective team seated around him. I also put a couple of bodyguards at the front of coach- or business-class to intercept anyone approaching the principal's seat from the rear (see fig. 9.1).

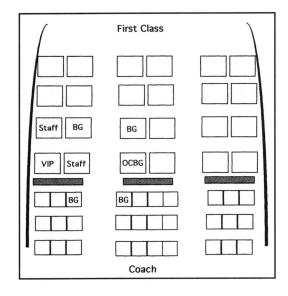

Fig. 9.1 *Although the exact seating arrangement in an aircraft can vary depending on the number of family and staff travelling with the VIP and the cabin layout, bodyguards should occupy aisle seats around the VIP to protect him or her from attack. Note that the team leader (OCBG) is across the aisle, allowing quick access to the VIP. If no staff or family were travelling with the VIP, the OCBG would occupy the aisle seat next to the VIP. Note also the two BGS at the front of coach-class to observe anyone approaching the area where the VIP is seated from the rear.*

If there are enough staff or family to fill the seats next to the principal and the row in front of him or her, protective personnel should be in the seat directly across the aisle and in the aisle seat directly in front of the principal's seat so that they have quick access to the VIP and ease of manoeuvring.

OTHER ARMED PASSENGERS

If you are authorised to be armed, the captain or head flight attendant will normally let you know if anyone else aboard the flight is armed. However, if air marshals are flying, this may not be the case, as their identity is usually kept secret. If there are law enforcement personnel escorting a dangerous prisoner, you will probably be informed. Make it a point to discover what the prisoner looks like.

Even if authorised to carry a firearm, you may want to have a good folding fighting knife as well, since in the close quarters of an aircraft cabin, this may be a more effective weapon.

THE CONCORDE

For international travel, many problems associated with standard commercial flights can be alleviated if one can travel on the Concorde, which, as I write, is coming back into service after a year's hiatus following the Air France crash. Of course, this aircraft only flies to certain locations and, thus, is only an option for certain junkets. Both Air France and British Airways have their own Concorde lounges, which one can enter soon after clearing security. Since one embarks directly on to the Concorde from these lounges, many of the security concerns that arise during normal embarkation are eliminated.

SELECT CLIENTELE
The cost of flying on the Concorde is such that many potential problems will be eliminated by the selectivity of the passengers. On the other hand, many principals will balk at paying the cost of flying a full protection team on the Concorde. In this case, some personnel may have to be sent ahead to await the principal's arrival.

SEATING ARRANGEMENT
The layout of the Concorde makes security easy, too. With only a hundred seats in twenty-five rows of four, two on each side of the aisle, the aircraft allows the principal to be separated from other passengers relatively easily if this is considered desirable.

Normally, I try to have a principal seated in the rear half of the aircraft when flying on the Concorde, since the entire cabin is first-class. I still like to seat security personnel and family or staff around the principal, with a member of the protective team in the aisle seat across from the principal and wherever else seems advisable. On most Concorde flights I've experienced, the aircraft was not full, so it was possible to request seats with empty rows in front or behind.

EXPRESS CLEARANCE
Yet another advantage of the Concorde is that express disembarkation is routine, and gets the principal off the plane and through customs more quickly. At Heathrow, in fact, the Concorde passengers benefit from express clearance through immigration control.

REDUCTION OF FATIGUE
A real bonus of the Concorde from the point of view of the protective team is that it cuts the fatigue factor considerably. After a transatlantic flight of only 3½ hours, it is much easier to stay alert while escorting the principal about his or her business than after an eight- or nine-hour flight. I have escorted a principal across the Atlantic on the Concorde, guarded him throughout an entire evening of entertainment and dining, yet still retained my energy level. After a normal flight, jet lag would have sapped my energy completely.

AUTHOR'S NOTE
One plus point I've noted on the Concorde is that the crew and passengers treat the presence of a protective team as almost routine. However, transporting firearms on the aircraft is only marginally easier than on other types of airliner. These days, it is very difficult to take handguns aboard British Airways flights unless one has high-level, official status. In the past, I have carried firearms relatively easily on Air France Concorde flights, but I was protecting a client who was a member of Middle Eastern royalty, which helped ease red tape considerably.

ADVANCE WORK IS THE KEY

When escorting a principal on a commercial flight, good advance preparation can lower the risks considerably. Work with airline security personnel to avoid crowds and situations where your principal will have to remain stationary. Determine if there are VIP drop-off and pick-up points that allow a vehicle to get close to the departure/arrival concourse. If there is some flexibility in the timing of the journey, make reservations that avoid the airline's busiest periods.

Normally, flights that attract business travellers are preferable to those that carry tourists. The more VIP treatment you can build in, the better. This includes first-class travel, the Concorde, express check-in, VIP lounges, etc.

As discussed in Chapter 4, a good airport file can be invaluable and save hours of time. It will be particularly useful to know the normal movement times between various key points within the airport.

AUTHOR'S NOTE

In my experience, when moving through an airport with a protective team, it is best to avoid very obvious protective formations. In simple terms, try not to look like bodyguards while still functioning as bodyguards.

As with many aspects of VIP protection, the more carefully the protective team pre-plans to avoid problems, as a rule, the more smoothly will be the escort operation on a flight.

9/11 CONSIDERATIONS

As a result of the attacks on the World Trade Center on 11 September 2001, those in the close-protection business have had to give some serious thought to airline travel. To be honest, most of the security people I know worry less about being hijacked today than about delays and hassles at airports. This is also true of the principals they protect.

CARRYING ARMS

Because members of protective teams will frequently be travelling armed or transporting weapons in luggage, tighter security, which in some airports causes long delays as a matter of course, presents even more problems.

There are some practical and easy solutions for dealing with the weapons issue while still flying commercial airlines. One is not to transport the team's weapons within the USA and simply to send them via UPS or FedEx for next-day delivery so that they are waiting for the team upon arrival. This isn't an optimum solution, but it is an answer. If members of a protective team hold a law enforcement commission, the FAA did offer a course that only took a few hours, the successful completion of which allowed personnel to fly armed on 'official business'.

GOING PRIVATE

The best answer, however, appears to be to use private or chartered aircraft. Flying privately has always appealed to principals and protective teams, but it has become even more attractive, not only because of the convenience, but also the cost. If the expense of paying a protective team as well as the value of the principal's time are weighed against the extra hours spent at airports today, a couple of thousand dollars extra for a charter flight may well prove a saving.

JET DEVELOPMENTS

I've been following developments in private jets for the last few years, and some are very interesting from the point of view of close protection in the near future. First, if one's principal is wealthy enough to afford a private jet, a supersonic aircraft with technology that will eliminate or shroud the sonic boom so that it can fly over land is probably only a decade away. Once airborne, such a jet will be expensive, but it will allow a principal and protective team to fly to a meeting on another continent and return on the same day. From a security point of view, that eliminates a lot of concerns about VIP overnights at unsecure or partially secure venues.

CHARTER FLIGHTS

Other developments in corporate and charter aviation are noteworthy for those in close protection. For one thing, more and more charter flights are available on what is essentially a regularly scheduled basis. By that, I mean that a charter flight leaves every day from one major city to another, often departing from and landing at a small airport that allows fast access to a city centre. When time is factored in, such flights may well be more cost effective.

CORPORATE JETS

If one works for a principal whose business operates a corporate jet, then he or she may well use that aircraft, but it is also possible to fly on other companies' jets. In many cases, a corporate jet will drop off its passengers, then return empty to its home base. However, there are services that allow individuals to buy space on those return flights. It might be worthwhile looking into this travel option.

SHARING COSTS

It is also possible to 'time share' private jets. By paying for a percentage of the aircraft, the principal would have access to it for a percentage of the time. The problem with this arrangement, of course, is that the jet might not be available on short notice if needed.

TIME/COST BENEFITS

I think it is very worthwhile following closely developments in private jets, charter flights and time-share jets. When one's principal travels, he or she wants it to be as hassle-free as possible. Time spent in lines – although first-class travel eliminates much of this – waiting for each member of the VIP party to have shoes checked, ID's matched, luggage searched, weapons documents examined, etc, is time not spent on business or on pleasure. There is hope that systems will come into effect for pre-screening frequent travellers by using retinal scans or palm scans to fast-track them through. Even so, the smart VIP protection professional will be working out alternative travel methods for his or her principal. Often, not only will there be time savings, but also cost savings if the down-time for the principal, his party and the protection team is factored against the cost of a charter flight or private jet.

HELICOPTERS

Many principals will have either a private helicopter or the use of a corporate machine. Since the helicopter can land in the grounds of an estate or on a building's roof, it is a very useful form of VIP transport. However, attention should be given to security at landing sites.

If the landing site is atop a building, access to the rooftop helipad should be restricted. If it is on an estate, its location should be selected with care so that it is not visible from a road.

SECURITY

Most of the comments concerning the security of a private aircraft apply to a helicopter in its hangar or at its landing pad. If the landing pad is located within the VIP's estate, however, it can easily be included within the estate's security plan, and covered by intrusion-detection devices and CCTV. The latter should also be provided at any rooftop landing sites.

THREAT FROM MISSILES

If the VIP is a political or military figure, there will always be at least some danger of the helicopter being targeted by a surface-to-air missile (SAM); however, military and other official helicopters may be equipped with countermeasures for use against hand-held

SAMs. Most VIP helicopters, though, will not have such sophisticated hardware.

Usually, the protective team will make a quick visual check with binoculars of potential launch sites, just before the helicopter lands or takes off, if SAMs are considered a threat. For most principals, however, SAMs are not looked upon as a high risk.

AVOIDING INJURIES

In fact, the greatest risks with a helicopter are either a crash or injury from the rotors. Consequently, the protective team should be sure of the competence level of the pilot, and check that both pilot and mechanic periodically run thorough safety and mechanical inspections on the machine.

To protect the principal during loading and unloading of the chopper, the team leader should place a hand on the principal's head or shoulder to ensure that he or she ducks under the rotor. Note that a surprising number of people run into the small tail rotor of helicopters, so it is important to be as wary of this as the main rotor.

SEATING CAPACITY

Most VIP helicopters will have space for a limited number of people, so quite often only the team leader will accompany the principal. As a result, the remainder of the protective team will have to make their own way to the destination or, if available, travel in a follow-up helicopter.

SECURING LANDING SITES

When training US Army general officer protective teams, I worked out a system for employing the protective team to secure the LZ (landing zone) during landing and take-off. The same method can be used if the principal is in an area where urban guerrillas are a problem or an insurgency is raging.

Using the drill, the protective team approaches the waiting helicopter in the usual box formation. Shortly before reaching the area covered by the rotor, the four bodyguards move to the corners of

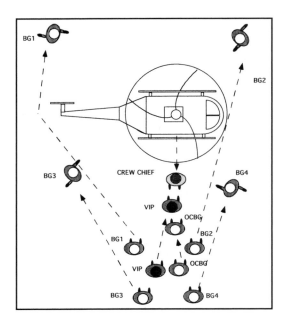

Fig. 9.2 When escorting a VIP aboard a helicopter at an unsecured landing zone, the bodyguards approach in a box formation. As they near the helicopter, BG1 and BG2 swing wide around the rotor and take up kneeling positions facing outward. BG3 and BG4 continue to cover the rear until the VIP and team leader (OCBG) are met by the crew chief. At this point, they move to positions to secure the other corners of the LZ. The

the LZ and adopt a kneeling position. With a military helicopter, usually the crew chief will come forward to meet the VIP and may make sure that he or she crouches to avoid the rotors. If so, the team leader gives body cover from the rear and follows the VIP to the chopper (see fig. 9.2). I would recommend, however, that the team leader also helps make sure that the principal crouches under the rotor.

Once the helicopter has taken off, the bodyguards at the corners of the LZ can board their own helicopter or proceed about their business.

OCBG makes sure the VIP avoids the rotor and covers his or her back while boarding the helicopter. If only one bodyguard can accompany the VIP, it is the OCBG. If additional bodyguards can board, BG3 and BG4 will be the first to board.

Above: *US Army general officer protection personnel practise placing a principal into a helicopter.*

Note that bodyguards accompanying the VIP around helicopters should wear eye protection because of the grit that will be kicked up by the rotors. The VIP should also be warned to wear eye protection.

'HOT' LANDING ZONE

For an arrival at a potentially 'hot' LZ, the bodyguards take up the same kneeling positions at the four corners to give cover. Once the helicopter has landed in their midst and the VIP has got out, they move to form their box around him or her.

PRIVATE YACHTS

When travelling at sea, the VIP is most likely to be aboard a yacht, whether his or her own, a friend's or a chartered vessel. The yacht offers a lot of advantages from the security standpoint, as it is a self-contained unit under the control of its crew.

Because of the importance of the crew, the protective team will want to check them for competence and security. If the yacht belongs to the principal, the team will probably know the captain quite well and will have established procedures with him or her.

SPECIALIST PERSONNEL

For yacht security, it is advisable that at least one or two members of the protective team have served as marines or combat swimmers so that they can carry out explosives inspections of the ship's hull and operate small boats to patrol around the vessel if thought advisable. In fact, if the principal owns the yacht, try to persuade the captain to hire crew members with such military backgrounds, as they can provide security for the vessel when it is not being used and augment the protective team when the principal is aboard.

Members of the protective detail with knowledge of boats and diving will also be be able to judge basic safety procedures aboard the yacht. For example, unless the yacht is owned by the principal and the team is sure of the captain's competence, security personnel should check that all communications gear is in good working order and that there are sufficient life jackets. It will be useful, too, if members of the protective team are competent with the vessel's tenders.

EXTRA MANPOWER
Crew members with a military special operations background can be invaluable, as, on all but the largest yachts, a full protective team may not be embarked. I have frequently worked yacht security assignments as the only bodyguard, or with only one or two associates.

THREAT OF PIRACY

At sea, one of the threats that must be considered is piracy, especially in the South China Sea, Malay Straits, Caribbean, Persian Gulf and even the Mediterranean. Most private yachts will not carry heavy armament, so the protective team must develop tactics for keeping attackers at a distance and repelling boarders. Counter-boarding drills can be run, using members of the protective team, applicable crew and passengers. If passengers come to view such drills as routine, much as with boat drills, in the event that security procedures have to be implemented, they will be more likely to clear the deck quickly.

DEFENSIVE ACTION
Care must be taken when moored in coves or otherwise near to shore. Any approaching boat that is not expected should be warned off, and the security team should be prepared to take defensive action.

Jamaica has a bad reputation for attacks from small boats, as do the Philippines and many other areas. Pirates or hijackers particularly like narrow channels or straits that limit the ability of a yacht's crew to manoeuvre, so be especially watchful in such areas. It is essential that whoever monitors the radar alerts security personnel of any approaching boats spotted on the screen.

WARNING SHOTS
The captain and/or yacht's owner can make the call on an approaching craft, based on their knowledge and experience. If they believe it to carry innocent fishermen, divers, etc, the security team should remain ready, but keep a low profile. If, however, a boat is approaching with armed occupants, and they are not obviously local coast-guard or naval personnel, the team should be ready to open fire if their warnings are not heeded. Warning shots can be fired at the boat's waterline prior to going after the occupants, but when facing heavily-armed pirates, I would normally advise that 'warning' shots be aimed at their centre of mass!

HEAVY WEAPONS
Depending on the political influence of the yacht's owner in his or her home country, it may be possible to have armament up to heavy, belt-fed machine-guns on board. A .50-, 12.7-, or 14.5-calibre heavy machine-gun should be able to keep just about any pirate vessel at a distance, or sink any small boat trying to approach the yacht.

If it is not possible to have a machine-gun aboard the vessel, a good alternative is one of the .50-calibre sniping rifles that are sold commercially in the USA. Very accurate at ranges of over 1000 yards, one of these weapons can be used to target the wheel-house, engine compartment or water-line of a hostile vessel. It can also blow a small craft out of the water.

ASSAULT RIFLES

Other weapons that are useful to repel boarders are select-fire and semi-automatic assault rifles and shotguns. For a machine-gun or assault rifle, I would recommend having armour-piercing/tracer ammunition available to increase the chances of knocking out an engine and/or starting a fire aboard an attacking boat. As an alternative to assault rifles, where 'battle rifles' are prohibited by law, large-calibre semi-automatic hunting rifles, such as the Browning .338, can be used quite effectively.

SHOTGUNS

Even when most other weapons cannot legally be carried aboard a yacht, shotguns usually will be allowed. Loaded with slugs, the shotgun can still disable any small boat that attempts to approach, and when loaded with buckshot, it can be very effective against boarders. Self-loading or slide-action combat shotguns are best, as they have large magazine capacities and shorter barrels for easy handling; however, even over-and-under trap or skeet guns, carried on board for 'sporting practice', can be loaded with slugs or buckshot.

HIGH-PRESSURE HOSES

Fire hoses may also be used to repel boarders in situations where lethal force is not deemed acceptable.

SECURITY IN PORT

Because a yacht offers so many potential hiding places for explosives, it is extremely important to restrict access at all times. Whenever the yacht is in port, a continuous watch must be posted at the gangplank. As long as they are reliable, crew members can carry out this function, although at night, if there are enough personnel, I'd prefer to have an armed member of the protective team on

deck. In fact, on large yachts, when I've had a full team available, I've normally had three members of the protective team on night duty – one on each side of the yacht and another in the passageway leading to the principal's cabin. If only one bodyguard is on deck duty, he should work with the crew member on watch to ensure that approaches from all directions are covered.

RESTRICT ACCESS

When all passengers and crew are on board, the gangplank should be raised. Any ladders should also be removed at night, while all exterior doors on the yacht should be locked so that an intruder who manages to elude detection still cannot easily gain access to the principal or other passengers.

In some ports, it is also advisable to move the yacht out into the harbour and anchor if possible. An exception is a marina that has a secure docking area, although specialists in yacht security still advise docking stern-on to limit boarding to one gangplank.

A secure marina will normally be gated and will have a 24-hour guard on the gate. Even so, I would keep my own security personnel on deck duty. When the yacht will be docked for more than one or two nights, I have found it useful to hire a dog and handler from a local security firm to patrol around the vessel at night. Many principals will consider such precautions over the top, but the threat level may indicate that extreme measures are advisable.

LIGHTING

The danger of a swimmer planting an explosive device remains ever present in port, so security lights that shine down into the water are an important addition to the yacht. Powerful searchlights should be available on deck to illuminate any boats that approach at sea or in port.

SHARED RESPONSIBILITY

The security team may end up short of personnel when passengers make excursions ashore – shopping, night clubbing, dining out, etc.

Frequently, the bodyguards will accompany the principal and family ashore, thus handing responsibility for the security of the vessel to the crew or local contract security personnel.

AUTHOR'S NOTE

In many dock areas, vigilance must be maintained to protect female passengers from rape. Once I cracked the trigger-guard of my Browning Hi-Power on the skull of an assailant who was attempting to rape a passenger on a yacht on which I was providing security. Highlighting the dangers in dock areas, this attempted rape took place within fifty yards of the yacht when the passenger was returning from a shop on the quay. Since we were operating with only two bodyguards on that cruise, she was lucky that I had decided to combine a patrol of the area near the yacht with walking to meet her and, thus, heard the struggle. The attacker was fortunate that I didn't want to face the legal complications of shooting him! Luckily, they managed to weld my trigger-guard at the dockyard.

LIFE ABOARD

One method used by some protective teams to cope with the limited accommodation aboard a yacht is to have a small team aboard the vessel when in transit, while another team travels from port to port by land and meets the yacht when it docks.

Often, because they will work long hours when the yacht is in port, a protective team will catch up on their sleep while at sea, with only one team member on security watch. However, reaction time at sea should be sufficient that they can still respond before a threat can get close to the yacht.

REMEMBER YOUR JOB

Protective personnel working aboard yachts must be careful that they do not lose their edge due to the nature of the environment. Lots of sun, sea breezes, beautiful women in bikinis – all can contribute to a relaxing of one's guard. It is also important to establish that although you recognise the captain as being in command of the vessel, you are not one of the crew. You do not scrape paint or wash decks. Your job is security.

Because of the close proximity of living accommodation aboard yachts, and the presence of people clad in skimpy attire, it must also be emphasised, as in all protective assignments, BODYGUARDS DO NOT BECOME SEXUALLY INVOLVED WITH CLIENTS' FAMILIES OR FRIENDS.

MEDICAL SUPPORT

Only on larger yachts with extremely wealthy or important clients will a doctor be aboard, unless as a passenger who is a friend of the family. Therefore, when selecting personnel to accompany a principal on a yacht, at least one team member should have good medical training.

STAY ALERT

Overall, yachts offer a relatively secure environment. However, the very isolation at sea, which grants substantial security, also means that help is probably far away. As a result, the protective team must remain alert and have developed tactics to deal with all types of possible assault on their principal's floating mansion.

THE QE2

Normally, those who are wealthy enough to have a protective team will not be embarking on the traditional cruise ship. However, there is one large vessel that does hold some appeal for many affluent individuals – the Queen Elizabeth 2. The last of the great ocean-going liners, the QE2 offers traditional Atlantic crossings in luxury.

The other type of 'cruising', as opposed to voyages on yachts, that might appeal to a wealthy

The author secures an area prior to the arrival of the VIP party aboard the Queen Elizabeth 2.

client is travel on one of the 'tramp steamers' that offer a few luxurious cabins and a first-class chef for those who have substantial leisure time. I have not carried out a protective effort on such a vessel, but I do know of a team that does it frequently, since they work for a shipping magnate who often travels on his own ships. I have, however, carried out protective assignments on the QE2, so I can comment on the special considerations needed for providing security on large ships.

THREAT LEVEL

One's first impression of mounting a protective assignment aboard the QE2 may be that it would be a nightmare. A team must guard its principal in a large, ocean-going luxury hotel with more than 2000 guests, plus another 1000 or so crew members, virtually unarmed, since only the highest-level official protective team is likely to be granted authority to carry weapons aboard the QE2. Another aspect of the QE2 that increases the threat level is its symbolic value as a terrorist target. To deal with potential terrorist threats,

there is usually a highly trained contingent of the Royal Navy's SBS (Special Boat Squadron) aboard the QE2. The ship also has its own security personnel.

COMBAT SKILLS

Working without firearms aboard the QE2 should not be as difficult as in many other environments, since the confined nature of the ship limits the distance at which an attacker can get off a shot. As a result, hand-to-hand combat skills and body cover offer a good possibility of stopping an attacker with a handgun. I would recommend, however, that members of the protective team wear their ballistic vests. Note that when boarding the QE2, passengers must pass through magnetometers, making it difficult to smuggle a weapon aboard.

BOARDING

In the golden age of transatlantic crossings, a passenger list was normally published, but this is no longer the case; therefore, it is easier to keep your principal's identity secret. Cunard's boarding procedures are relatively slow, so I would arrange for early or late boarding if possible, to keep your principal away from crowds. If this cannot be arranged, have a staff member or a member of the protective team wait in the check-in line and only bring the principal and family up for the actual check-in. Note the reference to the principal's family. It is quite likely that the family will be along for a crossing, so the protection team will have to plan accordingly. On one *QE2* assignment I worked, we had six family members and three bodyguards. It was not a relaxed crossing for the protective team!

DISEMBARKING

When disembarking, I recommend what Cunard terms 'self serve', which simply means that you take care off your own luggage. This avoids the luggage being taken off the ship and piled on the dock by Cunard employees, and also removes the need to mingle with the crowds waiting for their luggage. If the VIP party has so much luggage that this is not viable, escort them to their transport and detail a member of the protective team to supervise hired porters to deal with the luggage.

Another reason I prefer to avoid crowds upon arrival is that they may not have had to clear any security check-points.

VIP ACCOMMODATION

Probably the most important consideration for general security aboard the *QE2* is the location of the principal's cabin. In fact, there are only two decks that merit consideration for VIP accommodation – the Signal Deck and the Sun Deck. Both have only a limited number of cabins, which is a plus, but even more importantly, the passageways where these cabins are situated are not accessible from parts of the ship likely to be visited by passengers from other decks. This makes it easier for members of the protective team who are 'on the door' to quickly learn to identify who belongs in that passageway and who doesn't.

The most luxurious suites are located on the Signal Deck, the Queen Mary and Queen Elizabeth penthouse suites being the best Cunard has to offer. Among their other advantages, these two suites are separated by a doorway from the

rest of the suites on the Signal Deck. If the principal is willing to spend the money to reserve both suites – one for the family and the other for the protective team's command post/alert team sleeping quarters – the protective effort will be substantially easier. If both suites are needed for family members, the best place for the CP is either the Trafalgar suite or Queen Anne suite, which are located just aft of the penthouses, although on the other side of the aforementioned doorway. Since these suites are duplex suites, they allow the protective team to keep the CP manned, while providing sleeping quarters for other security personnel.

PERSONAL STAFF

If a VIP and family are making a crossing on the *QE2*, it is quite likely that the passage is intended for relaxation. As a result, most of the principal's staff will not be accompanying the party. Any servants will probably be accommodated on Four Deck or Five Deck, in the less-expensive cabins. If, however, the principal chooses to have servants and/or staff nearby, they should be booked into the suite across from the CP.

LARGE PARTIES

If the VIP party is particularly large (*ie* for a family reunion), the possibility of booking all of the accommodation on the Sun Deck should be explored, as there are only twelve suites. I should emphasise, however, that the penthouse suites are the easiest to secure and, by far, the best choice for the principal and family. Note, too, that neither the Signal Deck nor the Sun Deck allow passengers to stroll past the portholes of the cabins, another consideration in favour of this location for VIP accommodation.

DINING

A further advantage of the more upscale accommodations aboard the *QE2* is that dining arrangements are determined by cabin. The occupants of all cabins on the Signal Deck and Sun Deck dine in the Queen's Grill, which is the most exclusive of the three dining rooms and also the smallest, both factors that make providing security at mealtimes easier. This is another reason for having at least some of the protective team berthed on the more exclusive decks, since this will allow them to accompany the principal when dining.

The principal and family will probably prefer a view of the ocean while dining, which should be encouraged by the protective team, since tables near the large picture windows will limit the directions of approach to the principal's table. Members of the protective team should be seated at a table between the principal's party and the remainder of the dining room. If the principal is invited to dine at the captain's table and prefers to do so, the protective team can adjust their seating accordingly.

The duties of the protective team may preclude some members from dining at regular meal times. However, on the *QE2*, this is not as great a hardship as on many other assignments, since at least one of the ship's restaurants is open 24 hours per day, and room service is also available around the clock.

WAITERS AND STEWARDS

When dining along with the principal, I recommend letting the waiters know on the first day that an extra-large gratuity will be forthcoming in return for fast service, since the Queen's Grill is geared to very leisurely dining. In fact, I tip waiters and cabin stewards at the beginning and end of the crossing to ensure exceptional co-operation.

Cabin stewards make excellent sources of intelligence and should be cultivated. Always around the passageway, they can help keep an eye on the VIP suite.

The breakfast menu offers a variety of dishes, but stays the same throughout the crossing; thus, I recommend giving the waiter the protective team's breakfast order at dinner the evening before so that it can be served immediately. At breakfast, the waiter will have the lunch and dinner menus, allowing lunch to be ordered at breakfast, and dinner to be ordered at lunch, speeding the

process. In this manner, the protective team will always be prepared to depart as soon as the principal is ready while still having an opportunity to enjoy the fine cuisine on the *QE2*.

BOAT DRILL

The Queen's Grill is also the point where passengers on the Signal and Sun Decks will meet for boat drill. Anyone who has not made a previous crossing will be expected to attend the drill. Even if the VIP does not need to take part, as many members of the protective team as possible should go to learn the procedure. Security personnel should run through the evacuation route to the boats a few times, perhaps counting cross-passageways in case it is filled with smoke. As a precaution against smoke, I would recommend taking a few of the emergency smoke hoods mentioned in Chapter 5. The ship's personnel will know the evacuation procedures well, but in a real emergency there will be confusion, so the more the protective team knows about the drill, the better.

ON-BOARD ACTIVITIES

Entertainment and other activities aboard the *QE2* are varied, and the principal is likely to attend at least some of them. All members of the protective team should familiarise themselves with the ship as soon as possible so that visits to any venue can be carried out smoothly. Learn which lifts and stairways lead most directly to areas the principal is likely to visit – the Queen's Grill, purser's office, shopping concourse, entertainment areas, sauna, swimming pool, infirmary, etc.

Each night, the next day's itinerary is slipped under the door of each cabin. Arrange with the cabin steward to provide the team leader with copies as early as possible so that the next day's schedule can be co-ordinated with the principal and family, allowing members of the protective team to advance areas that will be visited during the evening.

Fortunately, the most likely areas of the ship to be visited are, for the most part, easy to secure. For example, the Royal Promenade, which contains the boutiques, receives a lot of traffic, but the shops are small enough that one or two bodyguards can readily secure the premises while the VIP and/or family are inside. The casino is often quite packed with people, but once again, its linear design makes it relatively easy to secure with two or three bodyguards. Because of the heavy traffic, if the principal is gambling, at least one team member should be positioned directly behind him or her.

The most likely lounge to be frequented by the VIP party is the Queen's Grill Lounge, which is also linear in design and quite easy to secure. If there are small children in the VIP party, the nursery, which is on the Sun Deck, is quite contained and can be watched by one member of the protective team. Kidnapping is not really a great threat on the QE2, since there is nowhere to take a child. On the other hand, molestation, followed by disposal of a small body overboard, must be guarded against, even if it is not considered likely.

OTHER PASSENGERS

Normally, the majority of the passengers on the QE2 tend to be British and American members of the upper middle class or above. Age tends to be in the fifties or above for most passengers, although some are younger. The demographics are not such, however, that normally the threat level will be considered high.

AREAS OF RISK

Two locations will require a higher degree of alertness on the part of the protective team. These are the open-deck areas of the Promenade and Sun Deck and the Grand Lounge. At night, even in summer, the North Atlantic can be very foggy and windy. In addition, the decks may be wet from condensation and precipitation. To give an idea of the strength of the winds on one August crossing, despite the fact that I weigh 200 pounds and have lifted weights for most of my life, I had great difficulty in climbing an outside stairway. Consequently, care must be taken if the

principal and/or family members decide to go for an evening stroll.

During the day, the weather can be quite rainy and foggy as well. The protective team must be alert not only for accidental falls, but also for anyone attempting to push the principal overboard. The portions of the deck used for jogging and strolling are narrow enough that such an attempt could readily succeed without instant action on the part of the security personnel. I would recommend, therefore, that whenever the principal is on deck, at least one and, preferably, two bodyguards are positioned between him and any potential attacker. Fortunately, those cabins likely to be chosen by the VIP party will have private balconies and deck space for sunning and walking; therefore, there may only be limited exposure on the public decks. Even so, the principal may want to jog, which will bring him into contact with many other passengers.

GRAND LOUNGE

The Grand Lounge is the site of most major shows aboard the QE2 and, therefore, may attract the VIP party at some point. Based on my experience of protecting clients in the Grand Lounge on two separate crossings, I would recommend that the principal be seated to one side of the stage. The view is still excellent, but this position allows fast departure and limits substantially the number of people around the VIP. It also guarantees that anyone approaching will be much more obvious.

If the threat level is deemed relatively high, or if there are enough team members to take extra precautions, one bodyguard can be positioned above, on the Grand Concourse balcony, opposite the VIP. This will preclude anyone from gaining access to the best position for shooting or throwing something at the VIP. Three team members can provide security in the Grand Lounge quite well.

DANCING

If the principal likes to dance, the Queen's

Room is where most of the ballroom dancing takes place. Younger members of the VIP party may choose to dance in the Yacht Club, where rock or pop bands normally perform. Two or three members of the team should be able to provide security in either of these dance venues. I must admit, however, that I have never developed 'dance escort drills', which entail members of the protective team dancing in formation around the principal!

SHIP'S SECURITY PERSONNEL

The *QE2* does have its own security personnel, and a meeting with the ship's master-at-arms is a must for any protective team, to co-ordinate security arrangements and let him know who you are. He should be particularly useful in helping to speed boarding and disembarking. Remember, though, that he works for Cunard, and his first responsibility is to the company and the passengers as a group. Consequently, assume that the ship's security personnel are competent, but still have your own plans for dealing with contingencies.

STUDY THE SHIP

Another very important piece of advice for anyone working a detail on the *QE2* is get to know the ship. There are ship's plans posted at various points around the vessel, and a detailed diagram will be included with your boarding materials. Study this plan! Familiarity with the ship will allow you to help your principal avoid crowds and to move him or her away from an area quickly. You must be aware, however, that some corridors have dead ends, and not all lifts serve all decks. Advance knowledge will prevent you from looking foolish or costing your team time in a crisis. Know the location of the infirmary and how to reach it quickly; also how to get to the ship's doctor in an emergency.

A LOW-PROFILE APPROACH

Bear in mind that the crew is used to dealing with wealthy, influential people, but they may not have experience of protective teams. Try to be as unobtrusive as possible. Keep the protective effort low-profile, which means dressing to blend in with other passengers as much as possible. This means formal attire for dinner. Enjoy the amenities of a great liner, but remember to stay alert. You are not on vacation!

SMALL BOATS

One other type of protective assignment involving boats should be mentioned. Some principals who have coastal or lakeside properties will own small pleasure craft, either motor or sail powered. As a rule, because these boats are so small, the presence of protective personnel aboard would be intrusive, although if the relationship is good, the principal may invite the team leader to ride along. Instead, the usual practice is to provide a fast boat so that the protective team can shadow the principal's craft and only approach if they are needed.

AUTHOR'S NOTE

A friend of mine relates an interesting story about a small-boat assignment. He was with George Bush Senior's Secret Service detail when Bush was vice president of the United States. At the family retreat in Maine, George Senior, who was always very competitive, liked to drive his high-powered motor boat. The Secret Service detail had a couple of boats of their own, which were particularly powerful to allow them to rapidly approach Bush's boat if needed. The only problem was that Bush Senior saw this as a challenge and kept having his own boat 'souped up' so that he could outrun the Secret Service boats. Although normally quite co-operative with his protective detail, Bush just couldn't resist the competition on the water. Most principals, however, will accept that the protective detail needs a very fast boat to respond to any threats.

RAILWAYS

In the past, railways were the primary mode of travel for the rich and powerful, many of whom owned their own private carriages. Bodyguards often accompanied their charges on their rail journeys, and on many of the legendary luxury trains – such as the Orient Express and the Trans-Siberian Express – they had to be prepared to deal with heavily-armed bandits. One of the more romantic tales from this golden age involves the arms merchant Sir Basil Zaharoff's bodyguard, who helped rescue a woman from her abusive husband aboard the Orient Express; the woman eventually became the love of Zaharoff's life.

Scotland Yard's Royal Protection Unit often guarded British monarchs on special royal trains, and the US Secret Service refined their railway procedures during President Harry Truman's 1948 'Whistle-Stop Campaign'.

The need to provide protection aboard trains has not vanished completely, either. At least a few powerful individuals retain private carriages or even complete trains. The King of Morocco, for example, had a private train until about a decade ago. Just as a crossing of the Atlantic on the *QE2* appeals to some principals, so does a trip on the current Orient Express or Eastern Orient Express. And many wealthy Americans now enjoy travelling the USA in rented private railway carriages.

TRAIN SECURITY TECHNIQUES

I do think at least a quick overview of basic techniques for providing protection during a railway journey is merited. To break down the possible situations a protection team might face, VIP railway journeys will probably fall into one of four categories:

1 Private train.

2 Private carriage.

3 Public carriage, but entirely booked by the principal's party.

4 Portion of a public carriage.

PRIVATE TRAIN

If the principal is important enough to have a private train, in most cases, additional assets may be drawn from the police or military to secure stations, bridges and other key points along the route. Extra security personnel can be embarked in special passenger carriages added to the train, and another train may even run just ahead of the VIP train to explode any mines or expose an ambush. A private train may also be routed to pick up or deposit passengers at points away from crowded terminals.

PRIVATE CARRIAGE

Obviously, there are many advantages to private trains, but organising one is an extremely expensive proposition and probably will only occur among the ruling classes in Third World countries. Far more likely is the attachment of a private carriage to a regular scheduled train. This still grants a great deal of control and privacy. A private carriage should be attached to the end of the train to limit possible access.

In the USA, I would recommend arranging with the train operator to have at least one member of the railway police assigned to the train at the principal's expense. This also applies to other countries with specialised railway police, This will augment the protection team with someone who not only has substantial authority aboard the train, but also a detailed knowledge of railway operations and procedures.

ACTION DURING STOPS

VIP train travel should be limited to express trains, which make the fewest stops, although with political travellers, stops at many small stations may be part of the agenda. The protective team should be aware of all scheduled stops the train will make and at what times. They should be ready to secure the platform outside the VIP compartment whenever the train stops. There are two basic philosophies for securing the platform. One stresses that members of the protective team should offer body cover to the VIP compartment whenever the train is stopped. Since this method identifies the compartment, I prefer, instead, for all the compartment's blinds to be drawn when in a station and for personnel securing the platform to move back and forth so that they do not focus attention on the VIP compartment (see fig. 9.3).

The team leader should be in contact with the train's conductor so that he or she knows about any unscheduled stops in advance. Tips to train personnel should help ease the flow of information.

BORDER CROSSINGS

On foreign trains, make sure you know when any borders will be crossed, and be prepared with the paperwork needed to cross those borders. If you have authority to be armed in one country, but not another, be ready to secure your weapons before crossing into the next country. Since many countries have railway police, arranging for at least one to be assigned in each country may be useful, but not always practical.

WEAPONS

Another point I should make in relation to weapons is choice of ammunition. Assuming the

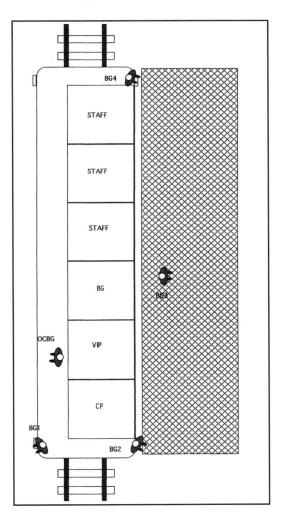

Fig. 9.3. *When a VIP railway carriage is stopped at a station, the team leader (OCBG) secures the door to the VIP compartment. BG1 covers the approach to the carriage on the side away from the platform. BG2 covers the entrance to the carriage nearest the VIP. BG3 moves around the platform outside the carriage. BG4 covers the entrance farthest from the VIP compartment.*

team aboard a train is armed, I would recommend carrying magazines loaded with two different types of ammunition. Since a train is a linear environment, over-penetraton can be a severe problem. Shooting a principal through a compartment wall while trying to stop an attacker is not good for job security. Consequently, highly-frangible ammunition, such as Glaser Safety Slugs or MagSafe, should be available.

On the other hand, if an attacker takes cover in a compartment or behind seats, it may be necessary to punch through obstructions to eliminate the threat. Therefore, highly-penetrative ammunition should be available in a spare magazine.

SELECTION OF WEAPONS
Certain protective rail assignments should only be carried out by armed personnel, and I would recommend that the head of security convince the principal not to undertake them if the protective team cannot be armed. In other circumstances, not only should the protective team be armed, but also it should have heavier weapons than handguns alone. If, for example, the principal is travelling on the Trans-Siberian Express, the situation in Russia would indicate that protective personnel should have AK-74s and/or AKSUs. For the Blue Train in South Africa, I would also recommend well-armed personnel. Any train operating in a country where there is guerrilla or terrorist activity requires an armed protective team.

PUBLIC CARRIAGES

Although I don't recommend placing the principal in a non-private carriage, on certain luxury trains, such as the Orient Express and Eastern Orient Express, it may be necessary. In this case, it is preferable to have members of the VIP party and protective team occupy all the compartments in the carriage. Security personnel should be stationed at each end of the train to restrict access, and one team member should be positioned at the door of the VIP compartment. If

on a train without private toilet facilities, such as the Orient Express, I would recommend choosing a VIP compartment relatively near the toilet. My own preference is to put the VIP and family one compartment away from the toilet, with members of the protective team occupying that compartment. Another bodyguard compartment on the other side of the VIP accommodation provides both privacy and security for the VIP.

One of the two compartments occupied by the protective team can serve as the command post, while the other can provide sleeping quarters. At least one team member in one of these compartments should watch the area alongside the tracks as the train is moving.

PARTIAL OCCUPATION OF CARRIAGE
Because the corridors in a train are so narrow, it will be easy for protective personnel to block access to the VIP compartment, but if the entire carriage has not been booked for the VIP party, it will be difficult to keep other occupants from passing through the corridor. Bodyguards on corridor duty must be very wary of anyone brushing past, as they will be vulnerable at that point to a close-quarters attack. In fact, the only time I had to take aggressive action on a train was to deal with a belligerent Bulgarian drunk who was lingering outside the compartment I was guarding aboard the Vien-Holland Express.

SPECIAL CONSIDERATIONS

Because of the elongated design of the railway carriage and the fact that potential threats can come through windows, walls or doors, the protective effort must be designed to cover each of these possible avenues of attack.

DON'T DRAW ATTENTION TO THE VIP
Since a VIP is relatively static aboard a train, whenever possible, his or her presence should be

kept low-profile. Again, this is an argument for having a private or fully booked carriage located at the rear of the train.

If the VIP has to go to the restaurant carriage, the possibility of him or her being identified or attracting attention increases substantially. Giving good gratuities to the conductor, chef and waiters will probably allow meals to be taken in the compartment; however, aboard such luxury trains as the Orient Express, the principal and family are likely to want to savour the dining experience. In this case, standard restaurant drills can be adapted as necessary.

In the main, the passengers on such a train as the Orient Express will be a relatively small, select group, but the protective team must still remain vigilant.

STATIONS

Embarking and debarking in crowded stations present potential danger, as do all situations involving crowds and distractions. If possible, arrange to join or leave the train at a small station just outside the city centre, where the VIP party can be met by trained drivers with vehicles. At some small stations, in fact, it is possible to park vehicles quite near the platform.

INHERENT DANGERS

Today, unlike air travel, rail journeys can almost always be avoided by those dignitaries who need a protective team. The fact that trains are slower and lack many amenities will often discourage many VIP travellers. Occasionally, however, ether a love of railways or the reputation of a specific luxury train will prompt a desire in one's principal to travel the rails.

My experience of escorting VIPs on trains has shown that the fatigue factor for the protective team is particularly high, since there is a need to be alert every time the train slows or stops during the night. Because a train's route is predetermined, the danger of encountering a pre-positioned explosive device must also be considered when guarding a high-profile political principal.

Given the dangers inherent in rail travel, if there is a high probability of the principal being a target for assassination, I would advise against this mode of transport. Otherwise, good planning and the application of the basic principles of close protection should allow the protective team to do their job while riding the rails.

There are, of course, other modes of transport that I have not covered. When protecting President Ronald Reagan, for example, Secret Service agents had to become proficient horsemen to be able to ride along with him. Other principals may enjoy bicycling, motorcycling (to be discouraged if at all possible because of the inherent dangers), snowmobiling, jet skiing, rollerblading, camel riding or various other forms of conveyance. Whatever the mode of travel, good bodyguards will always adapt their methods to provide the most effective protection for their principal.

CHAPTER 10

EXPLOSIVE ORDNANCE RECCE

VIP security professionals must be prepared to protect their principal from attacks with explosives as well as from direct assaults with firearms or other weapons. Experience has shown that the best way to carry out this defence is to secure vehicles and premises used by the principal to eliminate all opportunities of planting explosives. This may not always be possible, however, particularly since modern timing devices allow explosives to be placed months before they will detonate. Consequently, members of the protective team must operate on the assumption that a device may have been planted and must know how to carry out an explosive recce.

EXAMPLE

When an attempt was made to blow up Margaret Thatcher and other members of Britain's governing Conservative Party at a Brighton hotel, the explosive devices had been planted during renovations carried out three months before and employed long-term timers obtained from the Libyans.

BASIC REQUIREMENTS

Do not assume that those in VIP protection need to be trained as explosive ordnance disposal (EOD) experts; they do not. However, they do need to know how to spot explosive devices, to understand where a device is likely to be placed to create the most destruction, and to recognise the various types of trigger or initiation device that may be used. The bodyguard must also be aware of the difference between manufactured explosive

devices – such as military mines, grenades and satchel charges – and IEDs (improvised explosive devices), which may be constructed using triggering devices obtained at a local electrical or hardware store and plastic or home fabricated explosive.

To emphasise the ease with which the necessary materials can be obtained to create very destructive devices, the explosives expert who teaches that portion of my training course always waits until we arrive in the city where the course will be taught and purchases all of the materials for his triggers at local hardware and electronics stores.

CHARACTERISTICS OF EXPLOSIVES

Virtually all explosive devices share four characteristics:

1 An explosive charge.

2 An initiation device.

3 A power source.

4 A control process to determine when the device will be set off.

MECHANICAL TRIGGERS

Perhaps the most important concept that those in close protection must grasp is that an explosive device may be triggered in myriad ways. Among the possible mechanical triggers, for example, are:

- **Pressure Switch:** activated by the direct application of pressure (*ie* a switch placed beneath a board that sets off the explosive device when stepped on, or placed to set off a device when run over by a vehicle); many land mines employ pressure switches.
- **Pull Switch:** activated by tugging a string or lever, which initiates the device (*ie* a string affixed to a door could set off a device when the door is opened). A simple version of this was commonly used during the Vietnam War, when a grenade would be placed in a tin can with the pin pulled and a wire or string attached to the grenade. The latter would be stretched across a trail so that anyone hitting the wire would pull the grenade from the can, causing it to explode.
- **Tension Release:** activated by the sudden release of tension, often using a string or wire that prevents a trigger from completing its initiation sequence. One use of this type of trigger has been to detonate an explosive device attached to a vehicle. In this situation, the tension-release trigger is used in conjunction with a string, which is affixed so that it is wound tight as one of the vehicle's wheels turns. When, eventually, it breaks, the trigger is released.
- **Pressure Release:** normally spring-loaded, this type of switch is usually activated when a weight or other restraining mechanism is released. This type of switch is commonly used in booby-traps based on an object that is placed in such a manner as to encourage its removal.

IMPROVISED TRIGGERS

Various improvised triggers/switches, including the pressure-release type, may be constructed using a common clamp-style clothes peg.

AUTHOR'S NOTE

When carrying out VIP protection training, normally I schedule the lecture portion of the explosive recce session early in the morning. Then, while students practise explosive recce on a pre-prepared vehicle or examine switches, one of the instructors plants simulated explosive devices in some of their barracks, dormitories or hotel rooms. We make it a point not to leave devices in every room because, that way, trainees will never know whether their room has not been touched or if they have simply missed a device, thus simulating the uncertainty of a real explosive recce. Something we plant frequently is a pressure-release device, placed under a suitcase so that when the case is moved during a search, the device will sound a loud buzzer, indicating that the trainee has just been blown up.

As a variation, and to make the point that there may be more than one explosive device, with particularly sharp trainees, we may plant several simulated bombs.

On one of my courses there was a particularly competent member of the US Army Special Forces, and we knew that he would be expecting us to work hard at tricking him. We placed a pressure-release device under his suitcase and a photo-electric-initiated device (to be discussed later) that was designed to be set off as he entered his bathroom. He found both of them, then went to bed, basking in the fact that he had discovered our devices within fifteen minutes. However, at 3:15 am, our improvised 'mini-Claymore' – fabricated from a tiny digital alarm clock, modelling clay to simulate C-4 explosive and ball-bearings pushed into the clay – went off inside his pillow and jarred him awake.

ELECTRICAL INITIATION DEVICES

Various other switches or triggers employ some type of electrical initiation device, which may be triggered by various means:

- **Vibration Trigger:** activated by motion, this trigger may incorporate what is sometimes known as a 'mercury switch', which is sensitive to movement and will close an electrical circuit when subject to vibration. This type of switch is often used as an anti-tampering feature on explosive devices to counter any attempt to disarm them. It may also be incorporated in devices that are designed to explode when moved (*ie* something that appears to be a discarded can blocking a driveway).
- **Magnetic-influence Trigger:** more sophisticated magnetic-influence triggers work on the principle of disrupting a magnetic field and are often used in land mines. However, in IEDs, magnetic sensors of the type used in home burglar alarms can be affixed so that when one is moved away from the other, it sets off an explosive device.
- **Radio-frequency Trigger:** this type of trigger is frequently used for command detonation. Model aircraft radio control units have often been used to send the signal that initiates the explosive device.
- **Audio-frequency Trigger:** such a trigger may be used to detonate an explosive device in response to a sound nearby. Acoustic switches designed to turn on lights in a house when the owner enters have been used as triggers.
- **Timer:** this is one of the most common triggers for explosive devices. A timer can be fabricated from an inexpensive alarm clock, a candle (to burn through a string or wire) or acid (to eat through metal at a predetermined rate). Timer-initiated IEDs will normally be used when a target is expected to be at a certain place at a certain time; this is one reason why restricting access to schedules is important.

Among other types of electrical trigger are the following:

- **Light Sensitive:** employs a photo-electric cell connected to a micro-switch/battery/bomb circuit; when exposed to light, it will initiate an explosion.
- **X-ray:** employs an electrical device that is sensitive to X-rays connected to a bomb circuit; one possible use is a parcel bomb when it is known that X-ray screening equipment is used.
- **Infra-red Sensitive:** used in booby-traps to counter active infra-red night-vision devices; this type will rarely be encountered in VIP protection
- **Infra-red Beam:** uses the same technology as infra-red burglar-alarm sensors; when the beam is broken, the bomb is triggered. Both active and passive infra-red lenses can be employed; active infra-red can be detected by night-vision devices, but passive infra-red cannot. Note also that the infra-red-sensitive device could be used to provide an anti-tampering feature.
- **Microwave:** also uses technology found in intrusion-detection systems. Microwaves cannot be detected with night-vision devices.
- **Circuit Collapse:** uses the technology that indicates a low battery condition in an electrical appliance to trigger a device.
- **Heat Sensitive:** a household thermostat may be wired to an explosive device so that the change in temperature when air conditioning or heating is turned on will trigger the bomb. Heat-sensitive devices can also be wired into a vehicle's cooling or heating system.
- **Smoke Sensitive:** a smoke detector can be used to initiate a device when placed near a vehicle's exhaust or a barbecue.
- **Metal Detector:** a metal detector that employs magnetic sensors can be used as a trigger when metallic objects are near.

- **Hard Wire:** a simple system that allows the assassin to send a direct electrical signal along a wire to detonate the device on command. Its disadvantage is that it requires a line of sight to the target.
- **Altitude Trigger:** can be electrical or mechanical, but is designed to explode a device when an aircraft reaches a predetermined altitude.

MULTIPLE TRIGGERS

It should be borne in mind that many explosive devices will be equipped with more than one form of trigger (*ie* timer and infra-red) to ensure that they will go off and to deter anyone from attempting to disable them.

JOB OF THE PROTECTIVE TEAM

I would emphasise again that those in VIP protection normally are not expected to deal with explosive devices. They need to know the basic methods of searching for devices and recognising them, but once a bomb has been found, their job is to evacuate the area and call in specialists. Some close-protection teams will include former special forces soldiers or police officers with bomb-disposal training. Even so, they will not have the equipment to deal with explosive devices, and their primary job remains the protection of their principal, not disabling bombs.

OTHER TYPES OF DEVICE
When carrying out explosive recces, protective personnel must remember that they may encounter other types of booby-trap, including firearms with trip wires, pits containing *punji* stakes, hanging lines with fish hooks and even snakes placed in mail boxes! Team members

should also be aware that in place of explosive devices, acid, toxic chemicals or biological agents may be incorporated to create a lethal or harmful agent.

PURPOSE OF TRAINING

Although explosive ordnance recce training is designed to teach the VIP protection professional the basics of searching vehicles, buildings and other sites for dangerous devices, it is also intended to inculcate the need to keep vehicles, offices and residences secure so that a potential assassin is not given the opportunity to plant a device. In addition, the training provides members of the protective team with the knowledge they need to instruct the principal's staff in basic procedures to limit exposure to a device and to implement actions in case of a bomb threat. One of the most basic training assignments the protective team will usually carry out is familiarising office and household staff with precautions to be taken against letter and parcel bombs.

LETTER AND PARCEL BOMBS

When giving training in recognising suspicious letters and packages, normally samples that incorporate some of the characteristics of a possible letter/parcel bomb are used. Often, however, the indicators will be subtle. Nevertheless, many potential victims have been saved from letter and parcel bombs by recognising that there was something suspicious about the object.

The letter- and parcel-bomb characteristics listed overleaf should be learned by anyone working in VIP protection, and should be passed on to any staff who will deal with mail.

Letter and parcel bombs may display one or more of the following characteristics:

- at least a quarter of an inch thick;
- heavier than would be expected for its size;
- greasy marks caused by explosives;
- odd feeling of rigidity;
- unduly stiff or bends in an unusual manner, which might indicate stiffening to disguise the explosive;
- feels odd;
- unusual envelope;
- badly written address, perhaps containing misspelled words;
- over stamped;
- marked 'personal', 'private' or 'confidential';
- marked with a title rather than a name (ie 'To the company president') or addressed with a name, but the wrong title;
- no return address;

AUTHOR'S NOTE

Remember that bombers can be very creative. The explosive-devices instructor who works with me once purchased a birthday card that contained a tiny device that played 'Happy Birthday' when the card was opened. Having noticed that one of the trainees, a member of the security team for a corporate raider, would be celebrating his birthday during the course, he mailed the card to the trainee so that it would arrive during the course on or about his birthday. However, the instructor had also slightly altered the musical device so that on the final note of the tune it would send an initiating impulse, and he had inserted a thin piece of modelling clay to simulate a piece of C-4 explosive.

A genuine letter bomb, sent to Margaret Thatcher by a teenager, almost made it through the security screening process because it incorporated a very creative means of providing an electrical charge without using the normal type of battery.

- mailed from outside the country;
- small cuts or pinholes in the envelope (indicating that a pin safety has been withdrawn to arm the device after the letter/parcel was sealed);
- unusual smell;
- does not conform to mail usually received by addressee;
- hard and soft areas indicating battering;
- inner enclosures visible when the outer packaging is opened;
- protruding wires or foil;
- excessive use of tape, twine or other wrapping materials;
- specific opening instructions;
- in thick letters, the feel of an object that could be a small battery.

CONTENTS OTHER THAN EXPLOSIVES

Dangerous letters and packages may not necessarily contain an explosive device. Small packets containing HIV infected needles have been sent to public officials, as have packages of live rattlesnakes.

CHECKING SYSTEM

As electronics become increasingly sophisticated, potential triggering devices for use in letter and parcel bombs will become ever smaller, making them harder to detect. Nevertheless, members of the protective team must have an effective system for checking all mail and packages, and have a plan for dealing with any that appear suspicious.

Some type of secure holding area for letters and packages awaiting screening should be set aside. An area that is contained, but open at the top to channel a blast upwards, is best.

SUSPICIOUS PACKAGES

If a package is identified as a potential threat, it should not be handled further, although if a mail bomb pouch or bomb blanket is available, it can be enclosed or covered. Evacuation plans should have been developed and rehearsed so that the residence or business can be cleared quickly if a suspicious letter or package is identified.

To give some idea of the distance to which personnel might have to be evacuated, one table indicating the danger zones for explosive devices offers the following suggestions:

- 1–10 pounds of explosive will cause minor damage at a hundred feet, and the safe distance will be 900 feet;
- 50 pounds of explosive will cause minor damage at 340 feet, and the safe distance will be 2140 feet;
- 500 pounds of explosive will cause minor damage at 1120 feet, and the safe distance will be 3800 feet.

ACTION PLAN

Whether the device encountered is a letter or parcel bomb, or a device planted in the residence, office, private aircraft or other site, members of the protective team should have a plan in effect for dealing with the problem.

Steps to be taken in the event of discovering an explosive device may include the following:

1 Move everyone away from the device, and radio or call the mobile phones of other protective personnel to evacuate the principal, family and staff if they are nearby (see step 10).

2 Call the bomb-disposal squad or other applicable EOD (explosive ordnance disposal) personnel.

3 As a general rule, do not handle any suspicious item. In some cases, suspected package bombs that have been handled already may be moved to a safer area, but only when this may be necessary to save lives (ie in a hospital where patients cannot be evacuated quickly).

4 Do not place a suspected device in water.

5 Note the exact location of the device and write

down a description to aid EOD personnel. If a digital or Polaroid camera is available, take a photo, although bear in mind that the flash could set off a light-sensitive device.

6 If a suspected package or letter bomb or other explosive device is in the open, place a bomb blanket over it if available. Mattresses may also be placed around it, or it may be surrounded with sandbags, although they should not cover the top.

7 If a suspected device must be moved (see step 3), place it in the open, away from buildings. A contained courtyard, which will vent a blast upwards, may be acceptable.

8 If the suspected device is near gas pipes, shut off the gas; if near electrical cables, shut off the electricity.

9 Do not place a suspected device near flammable materials.

10 Do not use radios near the suspected device.

11 If an object is left inside a building, try to open windows and doors in the room where it is situated to dissipate the explosion somewhat.

A safe area for evacuation will be determined by the site and the location of the suspected device.

EFFORT REQUIRED

To get some idea of the time and effort required for a full explosive recce at the principal's home or office, look back over the list of triggers given earlier in this chapter, then glance around a room and consider all of the ways in which those triggers could be employed to detonate an explosive device in that room. Because it is so difficult to carry out a full explosive recce of a building, great effort is put into securing a principal's residence or office so that intruders cannot gain access to plant a device. Trained explosives sniffer dogs are also used in conjunction with a visual search to clear a site. Once that site has been cleared, it must be secured 24 hours a day to prevent a subsequent device from being planted.

Precautions against the planting of devices include 24-hour access control at the residence and office in addition to well-maintained intruder-detection systems.

PREPARATION FOR EXPLOSIVE RECCE

To make it easier to carry out an explosive recce/search, plans of the home, office and utilities should be on file with the protective team together with the results of previous security surveys; all places where explosive devices could be planted to best effect should be marked. As part of the overall security effort, as well as to facilitate searches, the protective team should have keys to open all doors, cupboards, etc, in the residence and office. In addition, the team leader should have access to a list of everyone with keys to each area and should be notified whenever a key is lost so that he or she can make sure the relevant lock is changed.

It is also very useful to take photographs of all electrical fixtures, fuse boxes, switch boxes and other areas where wires will be encountered so that comparisons can be made to identify extraneous wires. Similarly, it will be helpful to have photographs on file of furnaces, boilers, air conditioning systems and other such appliances for comparison purposes.

SEARCHING ROOMS

When searching a room for explosive devices, the following procedure has proved efficient:

1 Have a torch, screwdrivers, a thin piece of plastic to check for wires and an inspection mirror ready for use.

2 Standing in the centre of the floor, slowly look around the entire room to observe its layout and sense the general feeling. Listen for any mechanical/clockwork sounds.

3 Note all furniture, fixtures and other features, particularly those that will require detailed examination.

4 Start the search by inspecting the area between floor level and waist level, working around the room until everything in that zone has been examined. Repeat the process from waist level to head level, and then from head level to ceiling level. To make the head-to-ceiling search, probably a ladder will be required, although a chair may work in some rooms.

5 Inspect all furniture, cabinets, cupboards, lamps, switches, electrical appliances, electrical outlets, telephones and other items. Anything that uses electricity should be paid particular attention. Do not forget to check all locks for signs of tampering.

6 When checking around the walls, look behind pictures, remove electrical outlets and switch plates, examine fireplaces, including the flue, remove grates and look inside, look under rugs and behind wall hangings, and check within and behind curtains.

7 Bathrooms should be examined thoroughly, including toilet cisterns, basins, cabinets, waste bins, laundry baskets and toiletry bottles. Some bathrooms have removable panels to allow access to the plumbing; if so, check behind them.

8 If a hotel room is being searched, anything that has been delivered, such as ice buckets, complimentary champagne, etc, should be inspected particularly carefully.

This process should be repeated for every room in the site to be cleared.

SNIFFER DOGS

As a final check, some protective teams like to bring in an explosives sniffer dog after the building has been cleared visually. I have a lot of faith in well-trained sniffer dogs, so I prefer to bring one in first, then have the team make a follow-up search as the final check. That way, I have a better chance of the dog discovering an explosive device before I get too close to it!

ACCESS ALL AREAS

It is essential to check areas that may be inconvenient, cluttered or dirty, since an assassin may count on the protective team avoiding such places. I normally carry overalls on protective assignments, for use when checking attics, basements, vehicles or other areas where I might get dirty.

VEHICLE CHECKS

Most explosive recces will be carried out on vehicles. However, if proper precautions are taken and the vehicle is kept in a locked garage or under observation at all times when away from the garage, and it is fitted with a good alarm system, a bomber should have great difficulty in planting a device. That said, bear in mind that a device fitted with a magnetic clamp can be affixed beneath a vehicle in a matter of seconds.

POTENTIAL DANGERS

Explosive devices have been planted in vehicles in a variety of creative ways, and a search must attempt to counter all of them. Doors, bonnet and boot lid all open and can be affixed to devices with tension-release or pull triggers. Automobiles employ complex electrical systems, which allow

the attachment of various electronic triggers, including some that can be wired to the ignition. Pressure triggers can be placed under seats; heat triggers may be placed in the engine compartment; or a device can be attached to the odometer.

THE VALUE OF SECURITY

Vehicles offer the creative bomber myriad opportunities. However, sound security procedures, including the supervision of any maintenance by the driver or a mechanic working for the protective team, can restrict the potential bomber to devices that can be placed quickly. As a result, the full bomb search will not have to be performed on a vehicle that normally is kept secure, unless for some reason it has been left unattended, or something has caused the driver or members of the protective team to become suspicious.

FULL VEHICLE SEARCH

Although teams are reluctant to spend the time and effort to make a full explosives search each time a vehicle is used, all members of a protective team must know how to do it when necessary.

A full search prior to the VIP using the vehicle would entail:

1 Look around the garage to make sure that there has not been a forced entry. Security stickers of the type mentioned for use on private aircraft may be applied to windows and doors. The garage should also be fitted with an intrusion-detection system, as should the vehicle.

2 At this point, many teams leave the garage door open for ventilation and start the vehicle with a remote starter, letting it run for a few minutes so that any heat-sensitive device or a device wired to the ignition will detonate.

3 The next step is very important. Team members and/or the driver should walk around the vehicle, looking for anything out of the ordinary, including grease, footprints, hand prints on the vehicle (which should be kept spotlessly clean both for appearance and to indicate tampering), tell-tale wires, odd odours and any unexplained debris.

4 Using an inspection mirror, the undercarriage of the vehicle should be checked thoroughly. Usually, I divide the vehicle into four quadrants and examine each of them before moving on to the next. Using this method allows two members of the team to work on separate quadrants without getting in each other's way. However, each should be aware of all areas to be checked. Indicators that should arouse suspicion are unexplained wires, areas that have been cleaned of dirt or grease, and areas that are dirty when those around them are clean. Examine the wheels, brake lines, drive shaft and steering. Look particularly for devices around the fuel lines and tank. Again, photographs taken of the undercarriage when the vehicle is in for servicing can make a useful reference for comparison.

5 After checking the keyholes with a torch, the doors can be unlocked, but not opened yet. Each door should be opened only enough to allow a plastic strip to be run around slowly to check for trip wires. This procedure is repeated for each door, and for the bonnet and boot lid. Once a door, bonnet or boot lid has been cleared, it should be left open.

6 When the engine compartment has been opened, the battery should be disconnected to remove the power source for any device hooked into the electrical system. The engine compartment should be searched thoroughly, using a torch and mirror for inaccessible areas. Many bombers have attached devices in the area between the bulkhead and the engine block, so examine this carefully. When inspecting the boot, take a close look under the rear seat. Also check beneath the spare tyre and in any recessed luggage areas.

7 When searching the interior, look under the seats, inside the glove compartment, inside door side pockets and under the carpet or mats. Any other area where a device could be concealed should

also be inspected. For example, check that CD players or tape players have not had devices inserted. Also examine the air conditioning and heating vents to ensure that no gas or chemical dispensers, or explosive devices, have been placed in them.

8 Once satisfied that the vehicle has been cleared, take a final walk around it to make sure nothing 'rings any alarm bells'. Finally, the driver should carry out a full serviceability check of the vehicle, including tyre pressures, oil, coolant, wipers, lights, fuel level, radio, etc.

ACTION FOR SECURED VEHICLE
An inspection of the type described can be carried out in an hour or less by a trained driver and members of the protective team. If, however, the vehicle has been garaged securely and no alarms have been set off, most teams will not make such a comprehensive search. Instead, the driver will do a walk-around to look for any signs of tampering and may make a quick check of the undercarriage with a mirror. The threat level faced by the principal and the popularity of explosive devices with local terrorist groups will also influence the thoroughness and frequency of such explosive recces.

AUTHOR'S NOTE
IEDs intended for vehicles may not always be affixed to them. Russian organised-crime assassins, for example, use a device based on a beer can, which can be rolled beneath a vehicle or pitched through an open window.

OTHER TRANSPORT AND SITES

Explosive recces of private aircraft, yachts, railway carriages, etc, follow the same basic procedures as vehicle and site checks.

AIRCRAFT

As discussed in Chapter 9, it is extremely important to arrange secure hangaring for the aircraft or to have portable intrusion-detection systems that can be set up around the aircraft.

When it is necessary to carry out an explosive recce of a private aircraft, the first step will be to check those areas most susceptible to sabotage, including exterior wheel wells, inspection panels, service hatches, etc. Use of security stickers can help prevent tampering with the panels and hatches. Inside the aircraft, the cockpit should be examined first; then the searcher should move rearwards, checking storage areas, overhead luggage racks, under seats, inside the galley (including ovens and refrigeration units) and inside the toilet compartment.

BOATS AND TRAINS

A yacht search will be similar to an aircraft inspection, although divers will be necessary to check the hull beneath the water-line. A rail carriage will usually require assistance in checking the underside, since only someone familiar with railways will be able to determine what belongs under there!

CROSS SEARCH

When carrying out an explosive recce of a site, yacht, aircraft or railway carriage, many teams like to use the cross-search technique, whereby one team member starts from the front and one from the rear, each making a complete search of the entire site, etc. This system provides a double check on each searcher without adding undue time to the process.

ENSURE VIGILANCE

The main precept that should be grasped from this chapter is that it is far easier to provide good security for a site or conveyance to prevent tampering than to make frequent searches of the site or conveyance. Any driver or bodyguard under my command who has left a vehicle unsupervised, thus necessitating a comprehensive explosive recce, has been chastised severely. Members of the protective team must make a real effort to ensure that those on area security assignments take their job seriously and remain vigilant. Surprise inspections at unusual times are one way to instill alertness.

TECHNICAL ASSISTANCE

A variety of devices can be employed to assist in carrying out explosive recces. X-ray machines and metal detectors, for example, are often used for inspecting parcels and letters. Hand-held metal detectors designed for body searches can also serve to check letters and parcels for metallic objects, which might indicate the presence of a battery. There are also very expensive explosive 'sniffers', which can detect fumes. Even the best of these mechanical devices, however, cannot match a good explosives dog. I would recommend having a security firm with trained explosives dogs on a retainer so that the bomb dogs can be called upon if needed.

In conclusion, try to use a combination of intrusion-detection systems and security personnel to keep the VIP's vehicles, aircraft, yacht, residence and office secure from intruders who may plant explosives. When travelling, it will also be necessary to keep hotel rooms, or venues where the principal will appear, secure once they have been checked for explosives and declared clear. And, when it is necessary to make an explosive recce, take it very seriously, stay alert, be methodical and patient, and DO NOT TAKE SHORTCUTS!

CHAPTER 11

WEAPONS AND TACTICS

Although the basics of combat shooting remain consistent for those serving on VIP protection teams, some adjustments must be made to standard combat engagement techniques when training bodyguards to use their weapons. For example, when instructing police officers or others in the use of deadly force, attention is normally given to the use of available cover when a shooting situation is anticipated. In close protection, on the other hand, the bodyguard is trained to remain in position and give body cover to the principal. As a result, the bodyguard practises shooting while standing upright and placing his or her body between a threat and the principal.

ENGAGEMENT FROM FOOT ESCORT

One shooting drill that members of protective teams practise assiduously is engagement from a foot escort formation. This technique is best learned if pop-up targets are available. In fact, the US Secret Service has streets constructed at their training facility, which allow various 'friendly' and 'unfriendly' targets to appear in windows and doors, around corners and from various other points of concealment.

IMMEDIATE ACTION

In practising engagement from the foot escort formation, the protective team will normally walk along with a member of the team acting as the principal. Upon the appearance of a 'threat', the bodyguard nearest the threat will interpose his or her body and engage the target, while the rest of the team practise their evacuation drills. In some

scenarios, if several 'attackers' are encountered, the two bodyguards nearest may engage, while the remainder of the team evacuates the principal.

COVERING FIRE

Only after the principal is clear of the 'kill zone' will those bodyguards who stood and engaged the attackers break for cover. Because it may take a number of seconds to get the principal clear, those engaging the attackers should be trained to give rhythmic covering fire at the rate of about one round per second so that they do not run out of ammunition too soon. When the US Secret Service started practising AOP (attack on principal) drills, they found that this was a very common problem, as there was a tendency to fire as many rounds as possible, as fast as possible, at the attackers.

USEFUL DRILL

One drill I usually incorporate in training for bodyguards is the engagement from the escort formation by two team members, followed by a break for cover, then a continuation of engagement. This drill will vary depending upon the team and its armament. However, it is most effective when each team member carries at least one high-magazine-capacity automatic pistol, but preferably two.

Once the initial engagement of the attackers has neutralised the threat through scoring incapacitating hits on the targets, or the principal is clear, the two bodyguards break for the nearest cover, reloading on the move or after having drawn their second handgun. Once behind cover, they engage any additional attackers.

To determine at what point the initial attackers have been neutralised, targets constructed of rubber and/or balloons clad in clothing and masks, which are designed to deflate and collapse when a chest or head hit occurs, are

VIP protection trainees practise two-man engagement and evacuation drills.

Trainees practise shooting while moving the principal behind the bodyguard for cover.

often used. This drill teaches initial engagement from the escort formation, rhythmic covering fire, accurate shot placement, teamwork when breaking for cover and continuation of fire from cover. For very well-trained protection teams, this drill may also include engagement of targets while moving towards cover.

ONE-HANDED SHOOTING

Although most bodyguards are taught the Weaver stance, which utilises two hands for shooting, bodyguards must also learn to shoot with one hand, since the other hand may be engaged in moving the principal behind the bodyguard, pushing him or her behind cover or propelling the VIP into a vehicle. One-handed engagement will often be combined with the draw so that the bodyguard becomes used to drawing and

engaging while remaining aware of the principal's position *vis-à-vis* the attacker.

USE OF 'WEAK' HAND

One-handed shooting practice will also include shooting with the 'weak' (or non-dominant) hand. Situations requiring the bodyguard to shoot with a 'weak' hand might occur if the other arm, hand or shoulder is injured; or the 'strong' hand is needed to move the principal to safety; or the only way to properly use available cover requires a 'weak-hand' shot. Normally, the second handgun will be carried so that it may be drawn easily by either hand.

CLOSE-RANGE DRILLS

Yet other handgun shooting techniques will be employed in conjunction with hand-to-hand combat skills. At very close range, normally there will not be time or room to draw a weapon quickly enough to stop an armed assassin. Instead,

martial-arts disarming techniques will usually be more expedient. However, there will be times when the trained bodyguard can use martial-arts skills to gain time to bring a weapon into play.

PUNCH-AND-DRAW TECHNIQUE

In some cases, the punch-and-draw technique may be employed. In this manoeuvre, the bodyguard makes a hard, open-hand strike against the chest of the attacker to drive the individual back and off

The author demonstrates a one-hand shooting technique while placing a principal in a vehicle.

British bodyguard trainees practise draw and engagement techniques.

balance, while drawing his or her own weapon and firing from the hip at close range. A variation of this technique might be termed 'immobilise-and-draw'. Using this tactic, the bodyguard grabs the attacker's gun hand and forces it up or down, while driving the attacker off balance and drawing and firing with the other hand. Generally, however, both hands will be needed to control an attacker's gun hand, so a draw may be difficult.

SPEED ROCK

Yet another technique practised by bodyguards is what is usually termed 'the speed rock'. This is a technique of drawing the weapon at very close range by 'rocking' it out of the holster and bringing the muzzle to bear on the attacker while the handgun is still at waist level, then firing.

BREAKING AMBUSHES

Members of protective teams must also learn shooting techniques for breaking an ambush.

During five-man AOP (attack on principal) drills, two bodyguards engage while three cover and evacuate.

When on foot, this may entail engaging several targets rapidly.

DOUBLE TAP

Although many combat shooting instructors train their pupils to use the 'double tap', whereby two quick shots are fired at the opponent's centre of mass (*ie* chest cavity) to increase the likelihood of stopping hostile action, this technique may not be the best for the bodyguard facing several attackers. Instead, the bodyguard should practise taking a quick centre-of-mass shot at each attacker, then quickly re-engaging any still standing.

BODY-ARMOUR DRILL

A variation of the double tap may be known as the 'body-armour drill'. It is based on the assumption that an attacker who is shot with a powerful handgun in the chest and does not go down may be wearing body armour; the second shot is directed at the head. Bodyguards must practise taking head shots, since in many assassination attempts, a face and a hand holding a gun will be all that will be visible.

WEAPON MALFUNCTIONS

In addition to tactical engagement drills that simulate situations likely to be encountered by the bodyguard, the trainer of VIP protection personnel must also organise scenarios that duplicate common malfunctions that occur with the automatic pistol and submachine-gun. These include failures to feed or extract, which render the weapon *hors de combat*.

IMPORTANCE OF DRILLS

Provided malfunction drills are practised often enough, however, if a feed/extraction problem does occur during actual close combat, it can be cleared quickly with an instinctive wipe of the palm or a quick tilt of the weapon and rack of the slide. Special 'red-handled' guns can be employed for initial training in malfunction clearance drills, then the bodyguard can move on to live-fire clearance drills on the range, where the occasional dummy round can be loaded into the pistol or submachine-gun magazine.

MEETING AN ATTACK

Part of the teamwork required of members of a protective team who have to engage attackers – and remember that normally this will not be more than two, as the remainder will be rushing the principal to safety – is deciding who will engage which attackers. As a rule, if the attack is launched from the right, the two bodyguards on that side of the formation will turn to engage the threat. Each will take the attacker closest to them, then pivot in the direction away from the other bodyguard to engage other attackers.

However, members of the protective team should be trained to make rapid judgements about which threat to engage. For example, although the normal rule of thumb is to eliminate the closest threat first, if that attacker has a small handgun and one a few

The submachine-gun, in this case an H&K, allows the bodyguard to break an ambush or mass attack.

feet farther away has an assault rifle, it might be better to deal with the attacker with the heavier weapon first. Drills duplicating situations involving several attackers with varying types of weapon can help speed team members' reaction times in dealing with such threats effectively.

REALISTIC TRAINING
The use of Simunition adaptors for the H&K MP-5, or the Blue Glock, which is designed for Simunitions cartridges, provides very realistic training in counter-ambush techniques, since it allows trainees actually to engage each other during simulations. Laser vests and special laser pistols have also been used for such training. Video systems, such as the FATS (Firearms Training System) among others, can also produce realistic scenarios geared to specific situations likely to be faced by a protective team.

VALUE OF THE SUBMACHINE-GUN

If used correctly, the submachine-gun is a very effective weapon for breaking an ambush. Unlike film heroes, who hold a submachine-gun in one hand and empty it on full auto fire at the enemy, the skilled 'sub-gunner' will control the trigger to fire short bursts, usually two or three rounds at a time. In fact, many current submachine-guns incorporate a two- or three-round burst setting.

FIRE DISCIPLINE
When engaging several attackers and breaking an assault or ambush, bodyguards armed with SMGs must display excellent fire discipline so that they can quickly deliver a burst on each attacker.

ADVANTAGES
The great advantages of the submachine-gun for the protective team are that it produces a high volume of fire and offers greater range than the handgun, yet it uses pistol-calibre ammunition,

which is less likely to over-penetrate in an urban environment.

ESSENTIAL PRACTICE
Just as the bodyguard must practise bringing a handgun into action from the draw, the bodyguard armed with an SMG must practise rapid deployment and engagement drills. These may be further complicated if it is necessary to extend or unfold the stock, or if the weapon is concealed in a briefcase, in a golf bag or beneath a jacket.

DEPLOYMENT OF SUBMACHINE-GUNNERS
The placement of submachine-gunners will vary between protective teams. Many will have at least one SMG in the VIP car, usually placed so that it can be reached by the team leader and/or driver. Another SMG, possibly more, will also be in the chase or trail car. When the team is moving in formation, at least one member will be armed with a compact SMG slung beneath a jacket. This bodyguard's job will be to break a mass attack with devastating firepower.

Other teams employ a 'tail-gunner', who is separate from the actual escort formation, but follows closely behind the protective box and is armed with an SMG. In the US Secret Service, the 'tail-gunner' will often carry an Uzi SMG in a briefcase that allows the weapon to be fired without removing it. Such briefcases are also available for the MP-5K.

LONG-RANGE ENGAGEMENT

Another specialised shooting skill, which is useful for those in VIP protection, is long-range engagement with the handgun or submachine-gun. Many terrorists and assassins may be armed with that most popular of 'people's liberation' weapons, the AK-47. A substantial percentage, however, will have little skill in using this or any

other weapon. As a result, even though 'outgunned' by the attacker with the assault rifle at fifty or even a hundred yards, the bodyguard armed with a submachine-gun, or even a handgun, who has practised long-range shooting skills may still have the advantage. I'll discuss this factor in more detail later in this chapter, when I cover handguns that are specifically useful for long-range use.

ENGAGEMENT FROM VEHICLES

Because they may have to debus from a vehicle under fire when ambushed, or leave their vehicle under fire to help evacuate the principal from a disabled vehicle, members of the protective team must have drilled in shooting from inside the vehicle and immediately upon exit. I should point out that it is very difficult to shoot from a moving vehicle and takes substantial practise.

Generally, a submachine-gun is the most effective weapon for shooting from within a moving vehicle. Because of the noise level generated inside the vehicle when firing a weapon, a suppressed SMG, such as the H&K MP-5SD, is a good choice. The MP-5SD is also more controllable.

OVERWHELMING FIREPOWER
More likely will be the need to engage attackers after leaving the vehicle. I have already discussed debussing under fire in Chapter 8, but I want to emphasise again that if members of a protective team do have to leave their vehicle, it is important to engage the attackers with overwhelming firepower, yet to conserve ammunition in case reinforcements take a long time to arrive or more attackers surface.

WEAPONS SAFETY
It is important to be aware of weapons safety when getting out of the vehicle. I teach teams that

US Army general officer protective personnel practise evacuation-under-fire drills while under attack from two directions.

they should not draw their weapons until after they have left the vehicle. As the first two team members to leave take up positions behind the front and rear wheel wells, they should draw their weapons and give covering fire for the others as they get out.

If one or more bodyguards in a vehicle is carrying an SMG, it should have a loaded magazine in place, but a round should not be chambered. Whether the weapon is an open-bolt or closed-bolt design, the bolt should be down on an empty chamber. As soon as the 'sub-gunner' has left the vehicle and taken up position, the bolt can be racked and the weapon brought into action.

If the situation is critical enough that attackers are rushing the disabled vehicle, the two bodyguards on the side facing the assault may have to fight from within the vehicle until the others have got out. In this case, when they are ready to debus, they should place their weapons on safe and keep them pointed upward as they leave the vehicle and take up cover positions.

FLANK AND REAR ATTACKS
It should also be borne in mind that attackers may attempt to flank the team or attack it from the rear. Consequently, I teach that the last bodyguard to leave the back seat of the car takes up a prone position with the best cover possible

from the rear wheel well and faces the rear. The two outer defenders at the front and rear wheel wells watch their respective flanks as well as giving fire to the front.

AMMUNITION

I mentioned the need to deliver as much firepower as possible when under heavy attack. As a result, the members of a protective team must carry as much spare ammunition as possible within the bounds of practicality. I will discuss extension magazines and other methods for accomplishing this later.

ONLY FIRE WHEN NECESSARY

The bodyguard must also learn fire discipline. If it is not necessary to fire at attackers to keep them at bay, then don't fire at them. Assuming that someone in the protective team has been on the radio or mobile phone to call for help, time is on the side of the team, not the attackers.

COUNTERING SNIPERS

It is desirable to have some type of counter-sniper capability within the protective team. A skilled marksman can employ a pistol-calibre SMG out to a hundred yards quite effectively, but a better method of dealing with attackers at long range is to use compact rifle-calibre carbines or submachine-guns. Although chambered for a more powerful rifle cartridge, these weapons are often as compact as many pistol-calibre SMGs. They can be made even more effective in the counter-sniper role through the addition of optical sights, such as the Trijicon ACOG, which allows a compact M-16 to be used quite effectively to 500 yards or more.

USES OF ASSAULT RIFLES

Full-sized assault rifles will be employed by protective teams in a variety of situations – when an insurgency is raging and it may be necessary to face heavily-armed urban guerrillas; to protect a high-ranking military officer in combat; in estate security; and in certain other special cases. Although .223-calibre assault rifles are very popular with protective teams, there is an argument to be made for the use of .308 weapons loaded with armour-piercing ammunition, since these will be much more effective at stopping a vehicle attempting to crash the security gate of an estate or to break through a security cordon.

LEGAL ALTERNATIVE
For estate security in countries where the protective team cannot legally use assault rifles, a .375 H&H big-game rifle loaded with 'solids' can stop a vehicle with a few well-placed shots. Some estate security teams opt for even heavier armament and employ belt-fed machine-guns.

However, the .50-calibre sniping rifle can work quite well, too, if sited to engage any vehicles attempting to break through intrusion barriers.

COUNTER-SNIPER TEAM

Large protective teams may employ specialist trained counter-snipers. Unlike the sniper who is trained to move into a desirable shooting position and wait for the opportunity of a shot, the counter-sniper serves as an intelligence source for the protective team and as a means of guarding against the assassin armed with a long-range weapon.

BEST POSITION
The counter-sniper team will occupy the optimum site to neutralise sniping locations. In fact, prior to selecting their positions, counter-snipers will stand where the principal will stand and move where he or she will move to determine the most likely places a sniper would choose. Once in position, they will watch for anyone in windows, in wooded areas, on rooftops or anywhere else from which a sniper could operate.

COVERT DEPLOYMENT
There are many arguments in favour of deploying a counter-sniper team covertly so that they can observe and meet a threat without detection. For example, their ability to provide intelligence and early warning will be much greater. However, in certain circumstances, the overt deployment of counter-snipers on rooftops and in other very visible positions will be preferable as a deterrent. Occasionally, too, the counter-sniper team assigned to an official protective effort will take up its position covertly, while local SWAT snipers will offer a very visible presence on particular roofs, usually those that the counter-snipers specifically want to deny to potential snipers.

RAPID REACTION
Counter-snipers are trained to acquire a target and take their shot very quickly, since normally

they will not know the location of a sniper until a shot is fired. Members of US Secret Service counter-sniper teams, for example, are trained to identify a target, get into shooting position, determine the range, adjust the optics for that distance and take the shot within fifteen seconds.

SOUND JUDGEMENT
The judgement of the counter-sniper must be very sound, as normally such individuals will have a 'green light' to take a shot without checking with a supervisor. At a site where the principal will be speaking or appearing, the counter-sniper team will normally determine distances to various possible sniper locations to speed adjustment of optics for elevation. Often, they will prepare a counter-sniping plan, which will be, in effect, a map of the area marked with ranges and arcs of fire. If there are known individuals in an area who present a particular threat, counter-sniper teams may be provided with photographs of the subjects to aid identification.

RESPONSE TEAM
Frequently, when a counter-sniper team is deployed, a response team will also be organised, in case the counter-snipers spot suspicious activities in the locale prior to the arrival of the principal. The response team can quickly check the potential threat before bringing in the principal for the appearance. US Secret Service counter-sniper teams have even marked large numbers on buildings so that radio communications about the location of a potential sniper are very clear, thus speeding the arrival of a response team, or alerting protective personnel or other counter-snipers.

COVERING FIRE
It should not be forgotten either that a counter-sniper team can give precision covering fire during an evacuation by targeting attackers.

GENERAL RULE
Having discussed the use of counter-sniper teams, I should point out a rule of thumb

employed by those in VIP protection. The rule is that if a site dictates the need for a counter-sniper team, try to find another site!

COMBAT SHOTGUNS

Another weapon that sees limited use with protective teams is the combat shotgun. Normally, a shotgun would not be carried by the close-protection team because it is viewed as an area weapon. That said, a good shotgun can certainly clear an assault as well as a submachine-gun.

SPECIFIC USES
Tactically, the combat shotgun is most useful in two specific situations that arise in security operations. When a protective team must face a hostile crowd, the shotgun is not only a very effective weapon at sweeping away attackers, but also a very intimidating weapon, which can encourage a crowd to keep its distance. The shotgun is very useful in area security situations as well, such as patrolling an estate or defending the entrance to an urban property where there really isn't much opportunity to create a defence in depth. In this case, the ability of a shotgun to stop a group of attackers cold is quite desirable. When loaded with slugs, the shotgun makes an effective anti-vehicle weapon for use at barriers to prevent access to an estate or other site.

LEGAL ALTERNATIVE
Finally, it should be mentioned that sometimes the shotgun will be chosen because other weapons are not available legally in certain areas. As a result, an estate may be protected by a group of 'gamekeepers' roaming its environs.

SAFETY TRAINING

Because members of close-protection teams are often former soldiers or police officers, it is easy to overlook the importance of safety training with weapons.

Bodyguards will be carrying their firearms around a residence, which may be filled with children, staff and servants, so they must take great care in handling the weapons and in keeping them secure at all times. The command post should be provided with a vault or armoury for locking up any weapons that are not in use. Members of the protective team must also make sure that they do not leave their weapons unattended.

SHARED WEAPONS

In some cases, a protective team will be restricted in the number of weapons that can be imported to a country, resulting in the bodyguards of one shift having to hand over their weapons to those of the next as they come on duty. Consequently, great care must be taken in clearing the weapons and loading them safely.

IMPORTANCE OF DRILLS

Because members of protective teams practise drills that require them to draw and fire their weapons very close to other members of the team, safety drills must be enforced rigorously on the range so that, in an actual incident, safe gun handling will be instinctive. Bear in mind that a principal shot accidentally by a member of the protective team is just as dead as one shot by an assassin!

CHOICE OF WEAPONS

Although small protective teams may allow personnel to carry their weapons of choice, there are many arguments for a large team having standardised armament. These include consistency in training, ease of maintenance and availability of spare parts, interchangeability of ammunition and spare magazines among the team, and familiarity of each team member with other members' weapons in case of the need to use them in an emergency.

Some bodyguards carry a pair of the same pistol; in this case, two Gunsite Service Pistols in .45 acp.

STICK WITH SAME WEAPONS FAMILY

Since many bodyguards carry several handguns, choosing from a family of weapons offers many advantages. Two such families, Glock and Para-Ordnance, are particularly appealing for those in VIP protection.

GLOCK

The Glock offers excellent durability – there are Glocks at training facilities that have fired hundreds of thousands of rounds and are still functioning. The Glock is also easy to repair; a fully qualified armourer can be trained on the weapon in a day. Yet another advantage for members of protective teams who may operate all over the world is the wide availability of Glock parts. Alternatively, the protective team's armourer

Some protection personnel like machine pistols such as this full-auto Glock 18.

can easily carry spare parts to deal with virtually any malfunction.

INTERCHANGEABLE MAGAZINE

The family of Glock pistols makes it possible to carry several weapons to meet a variety of needs, yet only need one type of spare magazine. For example, the Glock 17 (the full-size service model), the Glock 19 (the medium-size concealment weapon) and the Glock 26 (the compact version) can all utilise Glock 17 magazines, although they will protrude from the magazine well of the smaller pistols. This allows the ten-round Glock 26 to be reloaded with a seventeen- or nineteen-round Glock 17 magazine to give greater sustained gunfighting capability. Even better, the thirty-three-round 9x19 mm magazine for the select-fire Glock 18 may also be used in any of these pistols. Those wanting a longer-range capability can choose the very accurate Glock 17L or the Glock 34, which offers a compromise between greater accuracy and portability.

TAILORED ARMAMENT

The individual bodyguard or the team choosing the Glock family can tailor the armament to the assignment. For example, I like the Glock 19 and its .40-S&W-calibre equivalent, the Glock 23. As a result, I usually carry a pair of these pistols for close-protection assignments; however, I take spare magazines for the larger Glock 22 to give me more rounds.

I also own a Glock 27, which is the compact .40-S&W-calibre Glock. I have a holster designed to carry this weapon affixed to my ballistic vest beneath my shirt. Consequently, I can carry it as a deep-concealment back-up gun, which will still accept magazines from my larger Glocks. I have another holster designed for this compact Glock that allows me to carry it in a jacket or trousers pocket. For longer-range capability, I can choose a Glock 34 in 9 mm or Glock 35 in .40 S&W. These pistols use the same magazines as the Glock 17 and Glock 22 respectively. As mentioned previously, the 9 mm Glocks have the advantage of taking the thirty-three-round Glock 18 magazine.

Thus, a protective team preferring the 9x19 mm round could issue each bodyguard with a pair of Glock 17s or Glock 19s, as well as two thirty-three-round Glock 18 magazines to be carried for reloads. Or the team could issue a combination of models, such as a Glock 34 and a Glock 17, or a Glock 19 and a Glock 26.

I would recommend that each bodyguard be given some choice within the family of weapons as long as all carried the same spare magazines. I would also want at least some members of the team to have a Glock 17L or Glock 34 to give better long-range engagement potential.

IDEAL CHOICE

If I were arming a protective team with 9 mm Glocks today, I think I would try to talk my principal into paying for three weapons for each bodyguard. Each would be issued a Glock 26 for deep concealment, and would have their choice of a pair of Glock 17s or Glock 19s as primary weapons. The reason for offering the choice is that some find the grip on the compact Glock far more comfortable. On the other hand, I find the medium-size Glock more comfortable and can shoot more accurately with it. The best shooters on the team would be asked to carry one Glock 17L or Glock 34 in lieu of one of their other weapons.

MORE POWER

For those wanting more powerful pistols, there is the Glock 20 in 10 mm and the compact Glock 29 in the same calibre, or the Glock 21 in .45 acp and the compact Glock 30 in the same calibre. However, my recommendation for protective personnel wanting a larger-calibre weapon is to choose from the Para-Ordnance family.

PARA-ORDNANCE

Para-Ordnance offers its .45 acp pistols in four different sizes: the fourteen-round P-14, thirteen-round P-13, twelve-round P-12 and ten-round P-10. Again, a combination of Para-Ordnance pistols

Para-Ordnance offers the potential for a battery of up to four pistols in different sizes, which will take the P-14 magazine for reloads. Shown here are the P-14, P-13 and P-12.

may be carried in various sizes. I like the P-13 and P-12, but carry spare P-14 magazines for their larger capacity. The P-10 is small enough to be carried on the ballistic vest or in a jacket pocket, while the P-14 offers a full-size combat pistol.

VARIANTS

I like the alloy-framed Para-Ordnance models because they are light and easy to carry, but versions in steel and stainless steel are available. To give the longer-range capability I find desirable, there are also versions of the P-14 with various accuracy features and adjustable sights.

ALTERNATIVE HANDGUNS

Although I like the versatility that the Glock and Para-Ordnance pistols offer in size and magazine capacity, there are many other good handguns for VIP protection personnel. For decades, the two most popular automatic pistols for bodyguards were the Browning Hi-Power and the Colt Government Model. Both offered the rapid reload capability that makes the self-loading pistol the weapon of choice.

Those who wanted large magazine capacity normally chose the Hi-Power, while others who liked the stopping power of the .45 acp cartridge opted for the Government Model. Actually, many of those who preferred the Government Model favoured the lightweight and slightly more compact version, the Colt Commander. Both pistols remain popular in close-protection circles, although the Para-Ordnance offers both high capacity and .45 acp chambering, which has gained it some converts. The availability of many other automatic pistols with high cartridge capacity has also eaten into the Hi-Power's popularity somewhat.

Some clients will present the bodyguard with a fancy pistol as a sign of appreciation, in this case an engraved, gold-plated Browning Hi-Power.

One of the most popular weapons among bodyguards world-wide is the SIG P-226.

DOUBLE ACTION

Many bodyguards who liked the Browning Hi-Power, but wanted a double-action pistol for the first round have opted for the Czech CZ-75. Because the weapon has been available all over the world, it has proved particularly popular with bodyguards who work in African and Middle Eastern countries.

SIG PISTOLS

SIG pistols have also seen substantial use among VIP protection personnel. The US Secret Service have used the 9 mm SIG in the past and recently adopted the SIG SP2340 in .357 SIG calibre as their standard-issue sidearm. I have carried the SIG P-226 for protective assignments and found that its combination of high magazine capacity and excellent accuracy makes it a good pistol for the bodyguard. For long-range use, I have carried the SIG P-210, arguably the finest automatic pistol in the world. In situations where I considered that a shot over fifty yards was a possibility, I normally carried my P-210 as a second gun.

HECKLER & KOCH

At one time, the Heckler & Koch P-7 was popular with those in close protection, since it is compact, accurate and ambidextrous. However, it is also

Above and above right: *To provide a concealable, long-range-engagement capability, some bodyguards carry the SIG P-210. To make it even more effective at long range, Vector illuminated-trajectory loads may be used.*

Right: *Using the SIG P-210 and firing prone, the author practises giving suppressive fire at ranges of 50–100 yards.*

heavy for its size and does not have a large magazine capacity.

WALTHER

More recently, the Walther P-99 has achieved some popularity with bodyguards, particularly in Europe and the Middle East. Accurate, reliable and possessing a large cartridge capacity, the P-99 is one of the best of the latest generation of pistols for close protection. As with many other self-loading designs, it is available in both 9 mm and .40 S&W. Other choices include the Beretta 92 and the Smith & Wesson third-generation auto-loaders.

STECHKIN MACHINE PISTOL

One other self-loading pistol should be mentioned, since it was widely used by bodyguards within the former Soviet sphere of influence. The Stechkin machine pistol is a select-fire weapon with a twenty-round magazine capacity and chambering for the 9x18 mm Makarov round. KGB bodyguards liked the Stechkin because of its large magazine capacity and its ability to fire full auto if necessary to break an ambush. Because it accepts the Makarov round, which has less recoil than the 9x19 mm round, the Stechkin can be controlled relatively well in full auto fire, even without its shoulder stock/holster. Some Soviet bodyguards did not even take the holster stock with them, but instead carried the Stechkin in a shoulder holster along with two spare twenty-round magazines.

REVOLVERS

Although the self-loading, or automatic, pistol has superseded the revolver with most protective

AUTHOR'S NOTE

Once, when I had to escort a principal on a visit to a ranch that raised fighting bulls, I added a four-inch Smith & Wesson Model 29 .44 Magnum to my armament on the slight possibility that a bull would get loose. To be honest, this was probably due as much to my city boy's distrust of large animals with horns as to practical prevention, but I felt better knowing that it was slung under my arm. I have also known of bodyguards on hunting trips with their principal who have carried a heavy revolver as insurance against bears in the USA and large cats in other countries.

teams, because of its greater cartridge capacity, the revolver does still see use. The US Secret Service carried Smith & Wesson Model 19 .357 Magnum revolvers until the 1980s, and members of France's GSPR protective teams were armed with the excellent Manurhin .357 Magnum revolver.

Revolvers also continue to have special uses with protective teams. For example, Smith &

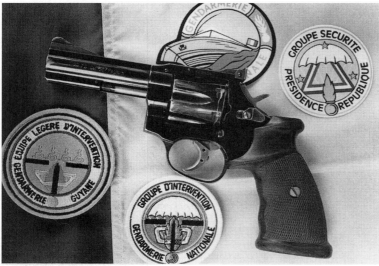

Above left: *The select-fire Stechkin was widely used by Soviet and some Third World bodyguards.*

Left: *Although most protective teams today use automatic pistols, some French bodyguards still prefer the Manurhin .357 Magnum revolver.*

The Russian PSM pistol is small, but is designed for use against attackers wearing ballistic vests.

Wesson offers hammerless .38 Special and .357 Magnum revolvers that are very light due to titanium construction. These revolvers may be carried in a coat pocket and fired from concealment in an emergency.

RUSSIAN WEAPONS

Russian bodyguards today often rely on heavier weapons, usually the Krinkov SMG, which I will discuss later in this chapter, but normally they carry the Makarov 9x18 mm pistol as their sidearm. Reliable and compact, the Makarov is a good pistol, but it lacks magazine capacity and stopping power for a bodyguard's primary weapon. Various new Russian automatic pistol designs offer more power and greater magazine capacity, and will, no doubt, see substantial use in

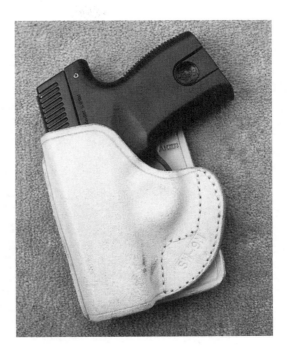

One of the best concealment arms for the bodyguard is this Smith & Wesson SW9M, shown in an Aker pocket holster. Note that this weapon can use Federal 9 mm +P+ loads.

that country, where VIP protection is definitely a growth industry!

PISTOL-CALIBRE SUBMACHINE-GUNS

Although the Stechkin and Glock 18 machine pistols have found limited favour among VIP protection units, the submachine-gun is normally chosen as the select-fire weapon for most close-protection teams. Offering greater firepower and range than the pistol, yet still using a pistol

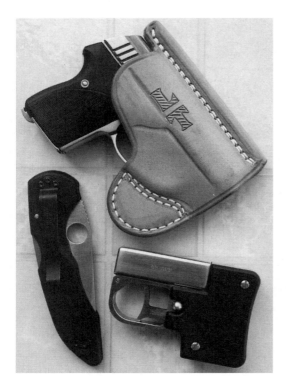

Often the bodyguard will carry a small secondary weapon. Shown are the Seecamp .32 auto in a Thad Rybka pocket holster, the Downsizer WSP single-shot .45 derringer and a folding knife.

cartridge, and, with a folding or collapsible stock, quite portable, the SMG is extremely effective in the hands of WELL-TRAINED close-protection personnel.

HECKLER & KOCH

As it has in other police and military missions, the Heckler & Koch MP-5 has become the most popular submachine-gun for VIP protection

teams. The compact version, the MP5K, features a front pistol grip for control, but the weapon is still very difficult to use well. If fitted with a stock, it is more controllable, but it is really not that much more concealable than the H&K MP5A3. With the telescoping stock collapsed, this version of the MP-5 may be hidden beneath a top coat or carried easily in a vehicle, yet it can be used quite effectively.

SHOULDER RIG
Swedish VIP protection teams have been equipped with a very clever shoulder rig for the MP5A3, which allows it to be slung beneath a coat with the stock collapsed, but when it is brought into firing position, the shoulder strap deploys the stock. This is a very fast, efficient way to carry the weapon.

MAGAZINE SIZE
The MP-5 offers magazine capacities of fifteen or thirty rounds. Although the latter magazine is most effective for breaking an assault, the shorter fifteen-round version is often chosen when the weapon is being carried concealed.

VARIANTS
The MP-5 may also be obtained with various modes of fire, including a two- or three-round burst capability as well as full auto fire. Many protective teams choose the two- or three-round burst model, which allows a choice of four settings: safe, single-shot, two-round (or three-round) burst and full auto.

THE UMP
The recently introduced H&K UMP SMG offers a polymer-framed .40- or .45-calibre weapon that is light, yet very accurate and reliable. My only real objection to the UMP for close-protection teams is that its magazine – thirty-round .40 S&W or twenty-five-round .45 acp – is rather long to allow the weapon to be carried easily under a coat. For teams armed with .40- or .45-calibre handguns, however, the UMP is an excellent SMG for carrying in a vehicle.

SUPPRESSED WEAPONS

Note that at least some teams have carried H&K MP5SD suppressed submachine-guns in vehicles, since these weapons are not only quieter, but also more controllable.

THE UZI

After the Heckler & Koch, probably the most popular submachine-gun with protective teams is the Uzi, its use by the US Secret Service helping to promote its acceptance in VIP protection. This is at least partially because Secret Service agents receive extensive training and are very skilled in its use. Some protective teams prefer the more compact Mini-Uzi because it can be concealed more easily beneath a jacket. I like the Mini-Uzi's folding stock, which may be deployed more quickly than the full-size Uzi's bi-folding stock.

One reason the H&K MP-5 has achieved such popularity is that it fires from a closed bolt, normally providing greater accuracy. Although originally an open-bolt design, the Uzi submachine-gun is offered now in closed-bolt versions as well.

OTHER PISTOL-CALIBRE SUBMACHINE-GUNS

Among other pistol-calibre submachine-guns, the Beretta M-12 has seen some use by protective teams. Its front pistol grip is a real aid in controlling the weapon and one reason I've always favoured this SMG. I also like its grip safety.

Walther's MPL has been employed, as have the Star Z-62 and Z-70. Although an older design, France's MAT-49 has also seen substantial use by protective teams. Its folding magazine housing is one of its appealing features, since this allows it to be concealed relatively well.

Many countries that have an indigenous SMG design will issue it to protective teams, but ethnocentricity aside, today the MP-5 and Uzi dominate the market, with the Beretta M-12 and Star Z-62/70 seeing use in Africa, Latin America, Italy and Spain.

The author has used the Beretta M-12 on various protective assignments.

ASSAULT CARBINES

One of the most useful weapons for the protective team is the rifle-calibre submachine-gun, designated by some the 'assault carbine'. This compact weapon is easily carried, yet gives members of a protective team an effective tool for use against guerrillas armed with assault weapons, vehicles or attackers behind cover.

THE KRINKOV
Because so many protective teams are operating in the former Soviet Union, probably the most popular assault carbine is the AKSU 'Krinkov', the SMG version of the AK-74. Chambered for the 5.45 mm round, this weapon is quite compact – only 16.5 inches overall with the stock folded – yet it takes the standard AK-74 thirty-round magazine. Whether operating in Russia, former Soviet Republics, Africa or anywhere else it is available, this is an excellent compact assault weapon for the protective team.

HECKLER & KOCH G36K
The most favoured compact assault carbine for Western protective teams used to be the Heckler

& Koch 53, and this is still very popular, but the H&K G36K, which is also chambered for the 5.56 mm NATO round, is achieving wide acceptance as well. With stock folded, the G36K is about twenty-four inches in overall length, but it has the advantage of accepting a ten-round magazine, making it easy to conceal. The standard high-capacity magazine takes thirty rounds, but for real counter-assault firepower, the G36K can be fitted with a hundred-round drum. With a very comfortable stock and a Picatinny rail to allow the use of the latest optical sighting devices, the G36K is an excellent compact assault weapon.

COMPACT M-16
Compact versions of the M-16 rifle, including the M-4 carbine or even shorter versions, are also popular with protective teams. The M-16 has the advantage of accepting a hundred-round drum, providing substantial sustained firepower.

SIG 552
Perhaps the best of all the compact assault carbines, however, is the SIG 552. This compact version of the Swiss military rifle is outstandingly accurate and has excellent ergonomics, exactly what one would expect of an assault weapon designed for a nation of riflemen. If a protective

Russian AKSU 'Krinkov' is an excellent weapon for close-protection teams.

The French-made FAMAS bullpup assault rifle has been used by French and African protective teams.

team particularly wants a compact weapon that allows effective engagement of an attacker at 300 yards or more, I would recommend the SIG 552.

The French FAMAS also is a compact bullpup design that has been used by protective teams, but I find that I cannot use its sights very well.

BULLPUP ASSAULT RIFLES

Another solution to the need for an assault weapon that is compact enough for a close-protection team to carry easily is the bullpup assault rifle. The bullpup offers the advantage of a full-size fixed stock with a compact overall length. My own preference for protective assignments is the Steyr AUG, which is only twenty-seven inches overall in the sixteen-inch barrel configuration. The AUG has the additional advantage of an optical sight that aids accurate shooting. Nevertheless, I consider the AUG a 200–300-yard weapon.

The British SA80 is another bullpup design, but it is rather heavy for ease of use in close protection. Its SUSAT sight, however, does, allow it to be used quite effectively to 500 yards or more.

FULL-SIZE ASSAULT RIFLES

When heavier weapons may be carried more openly – as in rural areas when an insurgency is raging or on estate security assignments – or concealed in the VIP and trail vehicles, full-size assault rifles can be invaluable to the protective team. The M-16, SIG 550, Galil and FNC are favourites of mine in 5.56 mm NATO calibre. In some areas, the AK-74 or AK-47 will be most readily available and can serve quite well. For estate security, particularly, the .308 assault rifle offers the ability to stop a vehicle more easily. My own preference is for the FN FAL, which is widely distributed around the world and is, therefore, often available. The H&K 91 or G3 is also widely distributed. The US Springfield M1A is another .308 weapon that can be quite effective.

The Steyr AUG is one of the more popular assault rifles with protective teams.

OPTICAL SIGHTS

To enhance the effectiveness of the assault rifle, I would recommend the addition of optical sights to allow the rifle to be used accurately at greater ranges. Among the best examples of these sights, which have proved durable enough for combat conditions, are the ACOG, SUSAT and ELCAN.

COUNTER-SNIPING RIFLES

Particularly for protective teams that deploy counter-snipers, but for others as well, the precision sniping/counter-sniping rifle grants the best choice for long-range engagement of snipers and suppressive fire. Since the counter-sniper may have to engage an attacker quickly, some of the heavier sniping rifles are not as desirable as they are for the sniper, although the same rifles may be used. Even small teams can pack one or more precision rifles in the boot of the trail car, or have one or two available at a country estate for security use. In fact, to keep the protective effort low-profile, some patrols on large estates or

ranches are carried out by 'hunters' armed with scoped rifles.

CHOICES FOR SMALL TEAMS

Highly trained, dedicated counter-sniper teams, such as those deployed by the US Secret Service and other national protective teams will often have purpose-built precision rifles or will employ military rifles. For the small protective team that still wants a counter-sniper capability, perhaps supplied by only two team members in special circumstances, I have three rifles that I particularly like.

The first is Remington's Light Tactical Rifle, which, with its twenty-inch fluted barrel, is easily transported, yet offers the ability to shoot sub-MOA (Minute of Angle – basically under an inch for every hundred yards). I use a Light Tactical Rifle personally and have found it outstanding.

Another favourite is the custom ROBAR QR2-F. Based on the same Remington action as the Light Tactical Rifle, the QR2-F is designed as a high-precision rifle with a folding stock for compactness. My own QR2-F has a 16.5-inch barrel and is only about twenty-six inches overall with the stock folded, allowing it to be transported in a large briefcase or gym bag. The QR2-F is designed to take M-14 magazines, which gives it a twenty-round capacity for when suppressive fire is called for.

Finally, Steyr's Tactical Scout Rifle is light and compact, yet quite accurate. With its ten-round detachable box magazine, it also grants the ability for suppressive fire.

ANTI-MATERIAL RIFLES

One other specialised type of sniping rifle should be mentioned for estate and yacht security. Long-range rifles, sometimes designated 'anti-material' rifles and chambered for the .50 Browning Machine Gun round or alternatively the Russian 12.7 mm Machine Gun round, may be deployed in positions to command approaches to an estate to stop any vehicle that attempts to crash intrusion barriers. Among the rifles that are particularly accurate and effective are those from Barrett, Harris and Stoner.

SHOTGUNS

The situations in which the shotgun may be useful for protective teams have been discussed already, but it should be mentioned that some shotguns are more useful than others. Pump- or slide-action shotguns have the advantage of allowing the use of special-purpose crowd-control munitions when it is necessary to disperse a group of people without using lethal force. Rubber batons, rubber buckshot, tear gas and flexible ('bean-bag') batons may be fired readily from the slide-action shotgun, whereas they will not operate the action of a self-loading shotgun.

PUMP-ACTION WEAPONS

Remington's 870 and Mossberg's 590 are probably the most widely used pump-action combat shotguns and are available with magazines that take seven or eight rounds of twelve-gauge buckshot as well as less lethal munitions. Remington 870s modified by Scattergun Technologies may offer the ultimate in slide-action fighting shotguns.

If used for estate patrol or deployed on security around a town house, standard eighteen-inch-barrel versions of these shotguns may be employed. However, if they are actually issued to the protective team, special versions with fourteen-inch barrels and folding stocks are preferable, since they may be concealed beneath a coat. Note that short-barrelled shotguns with pistol grips are very hard to control, except at point-blank range, and are not recommended. Other good slide-action shotguns include FN's Police Model and the FABARM FP-6 distributed by Heckler & Koch.

SELF-LOADERS

Among self-loading shotguns, which have the advantage of being very fast for engaging several attackers, the best are the Benelli M1 Super 90, FABARM Fast-20 and Remington 11-87 Police. Again, if to be deployed with the close-protection team, the version with a fourteen-inch barrel should be chosen. Scattergun Technologies also offers a combat customising job on the Remington 11-87 Police model, which makes it even more effective.

OTHER TYPES OF WEAPON

Other specialised weapons may be available to the protective team, including gas guns and, for a few yacht and estate security situations, belt-fed medium or heavy machine-guns. Many bodyguards carry other weapons as well.

The ASP baton, a collapsible impact weapon, is widely used by close-protection personnel, including the US Secret Service. I like the lightweight version, which may be carried in a suit jacket without causing undue sag. Useful in close combat against human attackers and dogs, the ASP may also be employed in situations where a window has to be broken.

Some bodyguards like to carry a chemical

spray, such as Mace, again for use against humans and dogs. Most also arm themselves with some type of knife, primarily for cutting seat belts and other non-aggressive tasks, although some also want a blade that can be used at very close range to quickly eliminate an attacker.

AUTHOR'S NOTE

On at least one assignment at the gaming tables in San Remo, I carried a folding knife in my hand, since the crush was such that I felt I would not be able to bring my handgun into play quickly enough. On another occasion in Amsterdam, where I was not allowed to carry a handgun, I chose a folding fighting knife as my primary armament.

In some circumstances, a bodyguard may not be able to carry a firearm. In such situations, folding fighting knives or the ASP baton can still function quite effectively in close combat.

Weapons are an important asset in the bodyguard's task of keeping a threat at a distance or eliminating a threat when it approaches the principal. Consequently, the good bodyguard must be skilled at bringing those weapons into action and using them effectively once they have been deployed. However, the close-protection professional will realise that when it is necessary to start shooting, attempts at threat avoidance and prevention have failed, and things are looking grim! A problem avoided is much better than a problem solved; thus, the good bodyguard prefers to steer clear of situations where weapons must come into play. Once, when I was being interviewed about working on close-protection details, I was asked to name the best handgun for the bodyguard. My answer was, 'The one I have in my hand when the attack comes!' I would probably revise that answer today and say, 'The one that I can avoid using through my training and my brain, but which I have utter confidence in should I have to use it.'

There is a tendency to romanticise the work of the bodyguard, since he or she will often have the opportunity to travel around the world, mingle with the rich and powerful, and observe important events at close quarters. What those who may take a romantic view of the bodyguard's job do not see is the bone crushing weariness of working twelve-hour shifts, seven days a week, much of it on one's feet. They do not see the necessity to urinate in a potted plant or out of a window in a hotel corridor because the bodyguard cannot leave his post at the principal's door, and the team is so overstretched that there is no one to relieve him so that he can 'relieve' himself. The romantic image of the bodyguard does not take into consideration the bruises from armoured limo doors, swinging doors, elbows in crowds and myriad other protrusions that he or she may encounter while moving with the principal. The romantic portrayal does not include the large bottle of antacids in the suitcase to counter hastily eaten meals and the anxiety generated by being constantly alert for danger from all quarters.

Nevertheless, I'll admit that there is a certain amount of pride and perhaps romanticism to be gained from doing a good job in executive protection. You can be on a 'high' knowing that leaders of government and industry respect your skills enough to place their lives in your hands. Each time a VIP visit passes without a hitch, you have the sense of accomplishment, of knowing your advance work and planning helped make that visit a success.

APPRECIATION

The bodyguard can't count on outsiders much for appreciation. They will see the one minute in tens of thousands of hours of protection when a threat arises. Principals who realise that it is intelligent to show appreciation to those who guard their lives may give the occasional Rolex wrist-watch or envelope containing hundred-dollar bills as a thank you. Usually, however, the only people who really appreciate the job a professional bodyguard performs are other bodyguards, who can recognise escort formations that move their principal smoothly from place to place, or understand the choreographed operation of a team that manages to remain unobtrusive, but gives the principal 360-degree coverage.

Actually, there may be one other group that appreciates a good protective effort. Perhaps the greatest compliment a protective team can receive is from the terrorist group or assassin who decides that the principal presents too much of a 'hard target' and looks elsewhere for a victim. Only rarely will the bodyguard realise that this ultimate compliment has been paid, but bodyguards know that their appearance, demeanour, training and professionalism can contribute to potential threats looking for a 'softer' target.

AUTHOR'S NOTE

I always thought a friend of mine was paid the ultimate compliment as a bodyguard. Those planning to assassinate the Middle Eastern ruler he protected waited until he had gone on leave to carry out their attempt. Obviously, the ruler only became a soft target when this British bodyguard was away!

WHAT MAKES A GOOD BODYGUARD?

I am often asked what characteristics are desirable for a good bodyguard. In some ways, the answer is easy, and in others, difficult. The best bodyguards possess myriad skills that allow them to handle very diverse situations. The good bodyguard does not have to be as large as a heavyweight boxer, but reasonable size and strength are helpful in dealing with physical threats. My own experience has been that very large bodyguards do have a deterrent effect, but they also attract attention. Physical fitness is often more important than sheer size.

The good bodyguard must possess strong marksmanship skills, but these must be honed with practice in the specialised situations that may be encountered on the job. The bodyguard must be a diplomat in dealing with people, yet must be able to project controlled menace if necessary. For example, I have often cleared a path through a crowd by politely, but firmly, invading the space of those blocking the way, saying, 'Excuse me,' as I prodded their feet with steel-toed shoes and placed my chest or elbow against them to move them back. Many were still irate, but certainly not as many as there would have been had I given them a push with a muttered, 'Clear the way.'

APPEARANCE

Appearance is important for those in VIP protection. Neatness, cleanliness, and an aura of health and physical fitness are certainly necessary. My wife claims that any time she has met friends of mine who are in the Secret Service, they look like they were sent over by Central Casting to play Secret Service agents. This is not by accident. Those around the president of the United States reflect upon him and the country he represents. As a result, Secret Service agents on protective details are selected, at least in part, for appearance. The same is true of those who protect members of the British Royal Family or other world leaders. Executives who are immaculate themselves do not want to be surrounded by thugs in cheap suits.

Speaking of 'cheap suits', the bodyguard should have a wardrobe that allows him or her to operate in the surroundings the principal will

frequent. I have found that at least three well-tailored business suits and one tuxedo are a minimum wardrobe, particularly since close protection can be hard on clothing. In fact, I order two pairs of trousers with each suit. Also find a tailor who will cut clothing to fit properly when carrying weapons. If a side-pocket holster is used for a back-up weapon, the pocket should be reinforced. A 'gun guard' should be sewn into the lining of jackets so that the butt of a pistol does not wear through the lining. Remember, too, that ballistic vests should be worn when being fitted for a suit.

Fortunately, today, women bodyguards do not have as much trouble in finding conservative suits that are well cut as they once did. Many tailors are also used to catering for women agents and police officers, and now know how to cut women's clothing for weapons just as they cut it for men.

ESSENTIAL SKILLS

Two skills I have only mentioned in passing are important for the bodyguard: a knowledge of martial arts and basic training in emergency medicine. I chose not to include specific chapters on these, as I feel both are much better taught during hands-on courses. However, I will make a few comments that I feel are relevant.

No one martial art is necessarily better for those in close protection than any other, although one that incorporates blocks, strikes, throws, arm bars, kicks, disarming techniques, offence and defence with impact weapons and blades, and situational awareness is most desirable. It is important that skills are practised regularly to keep them sharp. This may be difficult, as may be exercising, but both are necessary to keep fit, especially when travelling.

As far as medical training goes, every member of a protective team should have received a minimum of CPR and first-aid training, and should qualify in each regularly. The US Secret Service and many other protective teams practise what is called 'ten minute medicine', based on the assumption that the job of the protective team is to keep their principal alive for ten minutes until reaching a hospital, or until emergency medical technicians can attend. Normally, this will include training in emergency measures relating to breathing and airways, heartbeat, bleeding, burns, trauma, poisoning and shock. Whenever possible, at least some members of a protective team should be former emergency medical technicians or military medics.

Among the characteristics desirable in the bodyguard are:

- decisiveness;
- calmness;
- patience;
- an analytical nature;
- physical fitness;
- quick reflexes;
- dependability;
- promptness;
- adaptability;
- loyalty;
- logic;
- thoroughness.

Among the skills in which the bodyguard should be trained are:

- weapons;
- unarmed combat;
- emergency medicine;
- explosive recce;
- protective functions and techniques;
- VIP driving;
- intelligence and threat analysis;
- communications;
- area security.

Other useful assets include:

- training as a pilot;
- foreign languages;
- extensive foreign travel and familiarity with other cultures;
- training in psychology;

- computer expertise;
- the ability to handle small boats;
- skiing;
- horsemanship;
- training in electronic countermeasures.

A MATTER OF TRUST

The good bodyguard must earn the principal's trust and not betray it. Bodyguards do not talk to the Press, nor give inside business information to competitors. They do not tell wives about mistresses. The principal must trust them sufficiently to let them stay close enough to do their job. On the other hand, bodyguards should make sure that the principal does not ask them to perform illegal acts. I know of bodyguards who have been asked to beat up journalists, obtain drugs or prostitutes, cover up vehicle accidents for intoxicated members of the VIP family, even assassinate a political rival. The answer to any of these or other illegal requests must be, 'No.' No matter how good the pay, bodyguards must be willing to walk away from a principal who expects them to break the law.

BE PREPARED

Perhaps the best final comment on what it's like to work as a bodyguard can be gleaned from the check-list of items I carry about my person on a typical protective assignment:

- primary handgun;
- secondary handgun;
- spare magazines;
- ballistic vest;
- ASP baton;
- folding knife, normally with serrated blade for cutting seat belts;
- at least £66 ($100) worth of currency for the country in which I'm working, including the correct coins for local pay phones;
- mobile phone;
- small torch;
- small notebook with phone numbers and other necessary information, and a pen;
- radio;

- spare vehicle keys;
- mini tape recorder;
- spare glasses;
- sunglasses, both glare and eye protection;
- ear plugs for use around helicopters or other noisy areas;
- Leatherman or SOG combination tool incorporating compact pliers, screwdrivers and so on;
- wallet, passport, pistol permits and other necessary documents.

My stuffed pockets and sagging belt, I guess, say something about the myriad tasks the bodyguard might have to perform in his daily routine. And, for the most part, routine is what it is. Nevertheless, the professional bodyguard must be ready for that one minute out of thousands of days when it stops being routine and he or she must focus all of the training and skills on keeping a principal alive. That very routine can be as great an enemy as any assassin or terrorist!

THREAT ASSESSMENT PROTECTEE QUESTIONNAIRE

Client's personal life:

Name _____ Place of birth (Nationality) _____

Places lived within the past 20 years _____

Places frequently visited on business or pleasure _____

Current profession or government position _____

Past profession or government position _____

Military or diplomatic service _____

Any military combat experience _____

Known medical problems _____

Spouse – name and nationality _____

Pertinent info about spouse (*ie* profession, government service, etc) _____

_____

Children – names, ages, place of residence _____

_____

Noteworthy relatives, business associates or friends _____

_____

Religious affiliation _____ Political affiliation _____

Social/fraternal affiliations _____

Employees – at residence _____

_____

Personal employees (*ie* admin asst, secretary) _____

_____

Lifestyle – private/low profile or outgoing/high profile _____

How often photographed – society page, business page, sports section, entertainment
section, scandal sheets _____

Vices – gambling, drinking, lovers _____

Is there a driver? For the principal _____ For spouse _____

    For children _____ Are the drivers trained? _____

Known enemies _____

Have there been threatening phone calls, letters, etc? _____

Have there been threats or attacks in the past? _____

What is the nature of any threats – Assassination? Kidnapping? Against the family?

_____

What security precautions are already in effect? _____

_____

Client's professional life:

In what type of business is the client engaged? _____

Who provides the primary competition? _____

Are there any pending lawsuits, particularly over injuries? _____

Is the client a corporate raider or engaged in hostile take-over actions? _____

_____

How are employee relations? _____

Any particularly disgruntled employees? _____

Any who have been fired or have left with substantial bitterness? _____

Any strikes or other labour unrest? _____

What type of security is in effect at the place of business? _____

_____

Is there a secure parking facility? _____

What type of screening is in effect for visitors, mail and phone calls? _____

_____

If in government service, do the client's decisions affect:

   Military affairs or operations _____

   Law enforcement _____

   Relations with other countries _____

   Financial or trade matters _____

Where does the principal travel on business? _____

Is there a private aircraft and/or yacht? _____

Who does the travel planning? _____

Who normally knows the itinerary? _____

Where does the principal usually stay when travelling? _____

_____

How often and where does the principal make public appearances? _____

_____

CITY FILE

(Items marked with * have a related security survey on file)
(Maps and diagrams to be attached)

City _____ Country _____
Principal language spoken _____ Time difference from Greenwich _____
Last visited _____ Currency and current exchange rate _____
Airport _____ Airport code _____
Distance from airport to city centre _____
Police contacts: Local _____ National _____
Private security contacts _____
Electronic security specialists _____
Bomb dog handler _____
Limo services and trained drivers _____
Linguists/translators _____
Acceptable medical facilities _____
Medical evacuation air service _____
English speaking/US or European trained doctors _____
_____

Favourite hotels:
_____ Manager/Reservations and number _____
_____ Manager/Reservations and number _____
_____ Manager/Reservations and number _____
Favourite restaurants:
_____ Manager and number _____
_____ Manager and number _____
_____ Manager and number _____
Special threats or dangers:
Criminal _____
Terrorist _____
Ethnic/religious _____
Medical _____
Weapons restrictions and licences _____
Gun shop/armourer/gunsmith _____

Embassies:
  US _____
  UK _____
  Other applicable _____
Information regarding use of radios (frequencies, regulations, etc) _____
_____
Information regarding use of mobile phones _____
Local customs regarding gratuities (and bribes) _____
Important local taboos _____
Principal religions _____
Location of:
  All-night pharmacies _____
  Dry cleaners & laundries _____
Other transportation:
  Yacht basin/harbour _____
  Rail station _____
  Heliport _____
Other useful information:

AIRLINE CHECK-LIST

Name of airline _____ Flight number _____ Gate number _____
Contact person and number _____
Airline security contact and number _____
Departure time _____ Arrival time _____
Type of aircraft (attach cabin diagram) _____
Special notes on aircraft type _____
_____
Origin of flight _____ Any stops? _____
Preferred seating for principal and party _____
Preferred seating for protection team _____
Are there any other known VIPs on the flight? _____
Do they have a protection team? _____
Is this an airline that flies with armed security personnel? _____
Express check-in procedures _____
Location of airline VIP lounge _____
Special VIP disembarkation arrangements _____
Special baggage procedures _____
Procedures for transporting weapons _____
Alternate flight in case of cancellation _____
Flight reconfirmed on? _____
Other information:

AIRPORT CHECK-LIST

Airport _____ City _____

Airport code _____ Time +/- Greenwich _____ Distance to city centre _____

Hub for which airlines _____

Other major airlines providing service _____

Number of concourses (attach airline map) _____

Is there a separate international terminal? _____ Transfer time? _____

Passenger volume _____ Approx. flights per 24 hours _____

Flights announced in which languages? _____

Location of, and numbers for:

  Airport police _____

  Airport emergency medical services _____

  Lost luggage _____

  VIP lounges _____

  VIP drop-off points _____

  VIP pick-up points _____

  Car rental agencies _____

  Limo services _____

  Taxi stands _____

  Restaurants _____

  Express baggage claim _____

Normal waiting time for luggage? _____

Customs and Immigration _____

Time from representative gates to limo pick-up area _____

_____

Normal time to clear Customs? _____

Bureau de Change _____

Other information:

ROUTE CHECK-LIST

(NOTE: A route check-list is most effective if it is prepared in conjunction with a map upon which features may be marked. Computer programs now allow the generation of maps, to which comments, alternate routes and potential problem areas may be added.)

Date and time route will be travelled.

Distance to be covered.

Driving time based on advance team travelling the route.

Mark factories, offices, schools and other buildings that increase traffic at certain times during the day.

Locations of police stations.

Locations of hospitals with emergency centres.

Locations of overpasses.

Locations of bridges.

Locations of tunnels.

Points where road construction may cause slow-downs.

Other traffic choke points.

If an official motorcade, note whether police can control traffic lights to speed progress.

Note any parades or other events scheduled that will affect traffic.

One-way streets and the direction of their flow.

Wooded areas including parks.

Buildings that offer particularly good shooting positions for snipers.

Mark particularly dangerous sites for a command detonated explosive device.

Pedestrian areas, especially where crowds are likely.

Communication dead zones.

Areas where loud noises may occur, especially if they could be mistaken for gunfire or explosions.

Note potential alternate routes at critical points.

Note speed limits.

Will a local police officer or officers be assigned to a motorcade?

How many cars will comprise the VIP motorcade?

Are several cars of the same type available?

Mark entrance to be used at destination.

(If a map generation program is used or an overlay added to a standard street map, it may be useful to colour-code the route, alternate routes and other key features.)

HOTEL CHECK-LIST

City _____ Date of visit _____

Hotel _____ Address _____

Phone _____ Fax _____

Web site/e-mail _____

General manager/manager _____ Phone _____

Head of security _____ Phone _____

Rooms needed for members of the party as follows: Principal _____

 Family _____ Staff _____ Protective team _____

Reservations made: Date _____ Under what name? _____

 Confirmed _____ Rooms reserved _____

Command post location _____

Check-in/check-out procedures _____
_____

Restaurants (including hours of service and acceptable attire):
_____
_____

Hours of room service _____

Special facilities:

 Computer/business centre _____

 Gym and spa _____

 Swimming pool _____

 Shops _____

 Medical _____

 Valet/dry cleaning/laundry _____

 Translators _____

 Security vault/safe deposit _____

Hotel security:

 How many guards on duty each shift? _____

 How are they dispatched? _____ Are they armed? _____

Nearest police station _____

Fire safety:

 Check smoke detectors _____

 Check electrical wiring _____

Check fire extinguishers _____

Check fire hoses _____

Nearest fire station _____

Evacuation procedure _____

Nearest hospital with an emergency centre _____

Number of hotel entrances _____ Exits _____

How many allow a limo to pull up nearby? _____

Lifts _____

Are any lifts express? _____

Can it be arranged to lock out one as an express?_____

Are lifts limited access by key card? _____

Staircases _____

Parking facilities _____

Can secure parking be arranged? _____

Other personnel and phone numbers:

Assistant manager _____

Concierge _____

Restaurant managers _____

_____

Head waiters _____

_____

Head porter _____

Doorman _____

Other useful information:

(Attach floor and room plans, restaurant and room-service menus, photos of key staff.)

RESTAURANT SURVEY

Name of restaurant _____ Date of visit _____

City _____ Address _____

Phone _____ Serving hours _____

Manager _____ Head waiter _____

Secure parking _____

Number of entrances/exits _____

Acceptable attire _____

Normal seating capacity _____ Bar/lounge _____

Number of private dining rooms _____ Private seating capacity _____

Average time for a four-course meal _____

Average cost for a four-course meal with wine _____

Are any receptions, banquets, etc, scheduled on day of visit? _____

If so, what type? _____

Does restaurant attract persons of any specific ethnic/national background? _____

_____

Do employees tend to be of a specific ethnic/national background? _____

_____

Best points to locate members of the protective detail _____

_____

Nearest police station _____

Normal police response time _____

Nearest hospital with emergency centre _____

Do restaurant and kitchen appear clean? _____

Are emergency exits easily accessible? _____

Are any portions of the restaurant particularly vulnerable to attack from the street?

_____

How well lit is the restaurant? _____

Other information:

(Attach diagram of restaurant, menu, wine list, etc.)

VIP APPEARANCE SITE SURVEY

Site _____ Type of site _____

City _____ Date of appearance _____

Site manager/event organiser _____ Phone _____

Time of event _____ Approximate duration _____

Will principal speak? _____ When? _____ Approximate duration? _____

Will principal dine? _____ Will there be a receiving line? _____

Preferred receiving line set-up _____

Entrances to site _____ Exits from site _____

Preferred entrance _____

Preferred exit _____

Alternate entrances _____

Alternate exits _____

Command post location _____

Additional security: Local law enforcement _____ Private security _____

Other protective teams? _____

Number of fixed security posts (mark on diagram) _____

Liaison with local police _____ Phone _____

Liaison with private security _____ Phone _____

Number of radio channels needed _____

ID badges needed: Protective team _____ Local law enforcement _____

   Armed private security _____ Unarmed private security _____

   Other personnel _____

How much publicity has the VIP visit received? _____

Number of employees at site: Permanent _____ Temporary _____

Special security precautions in effect _____

_____

Will a search be carried out by bomb-detection canines? _____

When will it be carried out and will the site be sealed afterwards? _____

Nearest police station _____ Phone _____

Normal response time _____

Nearest hospital with emergency centre _____

If a sporting event, is there a rivalry with a history of violence? _____

_____

For sporting events, where is the most secure seating (boxes, private clubroom, etc)?
_____

For theatre, opera, etc, where are the most secure boxes? _____
_____

Counter-sniper team deployed? _____

Where? _____

If the principal is speaking outside, can podium/platform be positioned to limit exposure to snipers? _____

Other information:

(Attach plans, diagrams, schedules, etc.)

DAILY OPERATIONS ORDER

Principal:
Name _____
Family members and staff accompanying _____
_____

Special considerations:
   Health problems _____
   Religious idiosyncrasies _____
   Political affiliation _____ Member of royalty? _____
(Attach photos of all relevant members of VIP party if not known to all team members.)
Date _____ **City** _____
Predicted weather _____
Intelligence:
Local situation:
   Government _____
   Police _____
   Military _____
   Economic _____
   Other _____
(Attach photos of local persons of importance whom team members should be able to
recognise.)
Potential threats:
   Political _____
   Religious _____
   Personal _____
   Criminal _____
   Terrorist _____
   Other _____
(Attach photos, descriptions, *modus operandi* of identified threats; also attach summary of
overall threat assessment.)
Itinerary:
0000–0200:
0200–0400:
0400–0600:

0600–0800:
0800–1000:
1000–1200:
1200–1400:
1400–1600:
1600–1800:
1800–2000:
2000–2200:
2200–2400:
Meetings and appointments (relevant information) _____
_____
(Attach blueprints, floor plans, advance surveys, photos, etc.)
Routes between venues and estimated travel times:
(Attach maps, surveys, etc.)
Meals (for principal and team members): Times _____
_____
  Locations _____
_____
(Attach surveys, menus, etc.)
Local security assistance at venues:
  Venue _____
  Private _____
  Local _____
  State _____
  National _____
(Include names of supervisors and/or liaison officers; include ID procedures.)
Protection team:
Team leader _____
Asst team leader _____
Security advance party _____
Drivers _____
Medic _____
Others and assignments:

_____   _____

_____   _____

_____   _____
_____   _____
_____   _____

Attire _____

Equipment:

Weapons to be carried _____

Medical kit _____

Communications equipment (include frequencies) _____
_____

Other _____

Vehicles:

_____
_____
_____

(Include types, licence numbers, driver assigned to each, location of spare keys, garaging or parking arrangements, etc.)

Co-ordination:

(If working with several teams, with teams for other VIPs, etc, include special co-ordination instructions, ID procedures, etc.)

_____
_____
_____

Fixed-post security:

Office _____

Residence/hotel _____

Other venues _____

(Include all relevant information including ID procedures.)

Phone numbers:

Police _____   Fire _____

Ambulance _____   Doctor _____

Hospital _____   Embassy _____

Residence/hotel _____   Other _____

RECOMMENDED READING

Advanced General Officer Protection. (Manchester, MO: CQB Training, 1990)

Consterdine, Peter, *The Modern Bodyguard* (Chichester: Summerdale, 1995)

Geraghty, Tony, *The Bullet Catchers: Bodyguards and the World of Close Protection* (London: Grafton Books, 1988)

Hampton, Steven, *Security Systems Simplified* (Boulder, CO: Paladin Press, 1992)

King, James A., *Providing Protective Services* (San Diego, CA: EPS International, 1990)

Kobletz, Richard W., ed., *Providing Executive Protection* (Berrywille, VA: Executive Protection Institute, 1991)

Kobletz, Richard W., ed., *Providing Executive Protection*, Vol. II (Berryville, VA: Executive Protection Institute, 1994)

Kozlow, Christopher, *Jane's Counterterrorism* (Alexandria, VA: Jane's Information Group, 2000)

Lonsdale, Mark, *Bodyguard: A Practical Guide to VIP Protection* (Los Angeles: Specialized Tactical Training Unit, 1995)

Moore, Kenneth C., *Airport, Aircraft, and Airline Security* (Boston: Butterworth-Heinemann, 1991)

San Luis, Ed., et al, *Office and Office Building Security* (Boston: Butterworth-Heinemann, 1994)

Scotti, Anthony J., *Executive Safety and International Terrorism: A Guide for Travelers* (Englewood Cliffs, NJ: Prentice-Hall, Inc., 1986)

Scotti, Anthony, *Police Driving Techniques* (Englewood Cliffs, NJ: Prentice-Hall, 1988)

Shannon, M.L., *Bug Book: Everything You Ever Wanted to Know About Electronic Eavesdropping But Were Afraid to Ask* (Boulder, CO: Paladin Press, 2000)

Shannon, M.L., *The Phone Book: The Latest High-Tech Techniques and Equipment for Preventing Electronic Eavesdropping* (Boulder, CO: Paladin Press, 1998)

Thompson, Leroy, *Dead Clients Don't Pay* (Boulder, CO: Paladin Press, 1984)

Members of corporate, government or military protective teams who have questions about techniques discussed in this work, or other issues relating to close protection, may contact the author at the following address:

Leroy Thompson
P.O. Box 1739
Manchester, MO 63011
USA

Please write on letterhead and include an e-mail address for a reply.

INDEX

A

Access controls 25
Advance team 27, 30, 66
    work 27–35, 122
Air marshals, U.S. 119, 121
Airport/airline security 29, 117, 179, 180
Air travel, security considerations 114–125
Ambush/counter-ambush 96–97, 107–113,
    150–151
American Society for Industrial Security (ASIS)
    38
Area security 36–56
Armoured limousine 11
Assault carbines 166–167
    rifles 167–168
Attack on Principal (AOP) Drills 76–77, 88

B

Ballistic vest 14
'Bullet catchers' 82, 85–86

C

Casinos, security at 62–63, 170
Central Intelligence Agency (CIA) 11
Chartered aircraft 29, 122
Children, protection of 49–51
City and country files 28, 116, 177–178
Closed-circuit television (CCTV) 25, 36, 37,
    39, 41, 44, 47, 48, 49, 52, 53, 54, 55,
    62, 114
Combat shotguns 156, 169
Command posts 46, 48, 50, 53, 54
Communications security 23, 41–43
Concorde 32, 121
Counter-assault team (CAT) 21, 105
Counter-sniper rifles 168–169
    tactics 77–78, 155
    team 34, 155–156
Crash barriers 39
Crowds 74–77

D

Defence in depth 36
Department of State, U.S. 28
Dogs, security 40, 147
Drivers, VIP 94–97, 101–102
Duress code 26

E

El Al 118
Electronic countermeasures 42–43, 47
    security 54, 55, 114
Embus/debus drills 97–100
Escalators, security when riding 84
Explosives recce 34, 51–52, 138–147

F

Federal Aviation Administration (FAA), U.S. 29,
    118, 119
Federal Security Service (FSB), Russian 11
Fence-line situations 78–79
Fire security and prevention 43, 54, 55
Foot escort techniques 71–88, 148–149

G

General officer protection teams, U.S. Army 78
gratuities 33

H

Haneda Airport 116
Health risks 17
Heathrow Airport 104
Helicopters, security considerations 123–125
Hospital security 48–49
Hotel security 30–32, 44–48, 182–183

I

ID procedures 34, 52, 64
Information security 55
Intelligence 28
Intrusion-detection systems 37–38, 44

J
John F. Kennedy Airport 32
Jorge Newberry Airport 116

K
KGB 6, 7, 104

L
Letter and parcel bombs 141–143
Lift security 45, 82–84
Lighting, security 39–40

M
Magnetometers 65
Mail security 52
Maxim Detection Device 93
Metropolitan Police, London 21, 91
Morocco 11
Mossad, Israeli 119
Motorcades 104–107

O
Office security 23, 51–56
OPEC (Organization of Petroleum Exporting
   Countries) 51
Operations order 187–189
Overseas travel 18

P
Panic button 50
Paparazzi 32
Perimeter defences 36
Protection, level of 18–19

Q
Queen Elizabeth 2 (*QE2*), security aboard
   128–133

R
Railways, security aboard 134–137
Receiving line 34, 68
Residence security 23, 40–41
Restaurant security 32–33, 57–59, 184

Reykjavik 33
Route planning and security 24, 29, 30, 34,
   102–104, 181

S
Safe room 26, 41
St Petersburg, Russia 33, 74
Schiphol Airport 118
Scotti Driving School 13, 95
Secret Service, U.S. 6, 17, 19, 21, 34, 49, 105,
   133, 134, 137, 169
Security advance party 27, 35, 58, 59, 82
   lighting 25, 39–40
   survey 18
Shopping, security while 85
Site surveys 185–186
Speaking engagements, security at 63–68
Special Air Service (SAS) 21, 69
Special Boat Squadron (SBS) 129
Special Forces, U. S. Army 139
Sporting events, security at 61–62
Submachine-guns 152–153, 163–165
Surveillance/counter-surveillance 24

T
Theatre security 59–61
Threat assessment 15–22, 27–28, 175–176

V
Vehicles,
   engagement from 153–154
   explosive recce 145–146
   VIP 24–25, 89–94
Vienna 61
VIP driver 20, 25

W
Weapons,
   choice and tactical use of 148–170
   malfunction drills 151

Y
Yachts, security aboard 125–128